Charles Dickens

LONGMAN CRITICAL READERS

General Editor:

STAN SMITH, Professor of English, University of Dundee

Published titles:

K. M. NEWTON, *George Eliot*

MARY EAGLETON, *Feminist Literary Criticism*

GARY WALLER, *Shakespeare's Comedies*

JOHN DRAKAKIS, *Shakespearean Tragedy*

RICHARD WILSON AND RICHARD DUTTON, *New Historicism and Renaissance Drama*

PETER WIDDOWSON, *D. H. Lawrence*

PETER BROOKER, *Modernism/Postmodernism*

RACHEL BOWLBY, *Virginia Woolf*

FRANCIS MULHERN, *Contemporary Marxist Literary Criticism*

ANNABEL PATTERSON, *John Milton*

CYNTHIA CHASE, *Romanticism*

MICHAEL O'NEILL, *Shelley*

STEPHANIE TRIGG, *Medieval English Poetry*

ANTONY EASTHOPE, *Contemporary Film Theory*

TERRY EAGLETON, *Ideology*

MAUD ELLMANN, *Psychoanalytic Literary Criticism*

ANDREW BENNETT, *Readers and Reading*

MARK CURRIE, *Metafiction*

STEVEN CONNOR, *Charles Dickens*

CHARLES DICKENS

Edited and Introduced by

STEVEN CONNOR

LONGMAN
LONDON AND NEW YORK

Addison Wesley Longman Limited
Edinburgh Gate
Harlow, Essex CM20 2JE, England
and Associated Companies throughout the world.

*Published in the United States of America
by Addison Wesley Longman Inc., New York*

© Addison Wesley Longman Limited 1996

First published 1996

ISBN 0 582 21016 X CSD
ISBN 0 582 21015 1 PPR

British Library Cataloguing in Publication Data

A catalogue record for this book is
available from the British Library

Library of Congress Cataloging-in-Publication Data

Also available

Set by 20 in 9/11½pt Palatino.
Produced by Longman Singapore Publishers (Pte) Ltd.
Printed in Singapore

Contents

Contents

General Editors' Preface

The outlines of contemporary critical theory are now often taught as a standard feature of a degree in literary studies. The development of particular theories has seen a thorough transformation of literary criticism. For example, Marxist and Foucauldian theories have revolutionised Shakespeare studies, and 'deconstruction' has led to a complete reassessment of Romantic poetry. Feminist criticism has left scarcely any period of literature unaffected by its searching critiques. Teachers of literary studies can no longer fall back on a standardised, received, methodology.

Lecturers and teachers are now urgently looking for guidance in a rapidly changing critical environment. They need help in understanding the latest revisions in literary theory, and especially in grasping the practical effects of the new theories in the form of theoretically sensitised new readings. A number of volumes in the series anthologise important essays on particular theories. However, in order to grasp the full implications and possible uses of particular theories it is essential to see them put to work. This series provides substantial volumes of new readings, presented in an accessible form and with a significant amount of editorial guidance.

Each volume includes a substantial introduction which explores the theoretical issues and conflicts embodied in the essays selected and locates areas of disagreement between positions. The pluralism of theories has to be put on the agenda of literary studies. We can no longer pretend that we all tacitly accept the same practices in literary studies. Neither is a *laissez-faire* attitude any longer tenable. Literature departments need to go beyond the mere toleration of theoretical differences: it is not enough merely to agree to differ; they need actually to 'stage' the differences openly. The volumes in this series all attempt to dramatise the differences, not necessarily with a view to resolving them but in order to foreground the choices presented by different theories or to argue for a particular route through the impasses the differences present.

The theory 'revolution' has had real effects. It has loosened the grip of traditional empiricist and romantic assumptions about language and literature. It is not always clear what is being proposed as the new agenda for literary studies, and indeed the very notion of 'literature' is questioned by the post-structuralist strain in theory. However, the uncertainties and obscurities of contemporary theories appear much less worrying when we see what the best critics have been able to do with them in practice. This series aims to disseminate the best of recent criticism and to show that it is possible to re-read the canonical texts of literature in new and challenging ways.

RAMAN SELDEN AND STAN SMITH

The Publishers and fellow Series Editor regret to record that Raman Selden died after a short illness in May 1991 at the age of fifty-three. Ray Selden was a fine scholar and a lovely man. All those he has worked with will remember him with much affection and respect.

Acknowledgements

We are grateful to the following for permission to reproduce copyright material;

AMS Press, Inc for the article 'Writing as a Woman: Dickens, *Hard Times*, and Feminine Discourses' by Jean Ferguson Carr from *Dickens Studies Annual*, 18 (1989); Columbia University Press for the article 'Homophobia, Misogyny, and Capital: *Our Mutual Friend'* from *Between Men: English Literature and Male Homosocial Desire* by Eve Sedgwick (1985), copyright © Columbia University Press; the Editors of the journal *Essays in Criticism* and the author Jeremy Tambling for the article 'Prison-Bound: Dickens and Foucault' from *Essays in Criticism*, 36 (1986); Johns Hopkins University Press for the article 'The Bad Faith of Pip's Bad Faith: Deconstructing *Great Expectations'* by Christopher D Morris from the journal *English Literary History*, 54 (1987); Alfred A Knopf, Inc, for the chapter 'Repetition, Repression, and Return: The Plotting of *Great Expectations'* from *Reading for the Plot: Design and Intention in Narrative* by Peter Brooks, copyright © 1984 by Peter Brooks; Penguin Books Ltd for extracts from the 'Introduction' by J Hillis Miller from *Bleak House* by Charles Dickens (1971), 'Introduction' copyright © Penguin Books, 1971; University of California Press for extracts from the article 'Discipline in Different Voices: Bureaucracy, Police, Family and *Bleak House'* from *The Novel and the Police* by D A Miller (1988), copyright © 1988 The Regents of the University of California; University of California Press Journals and the author John Kucich for the article 'Repression and Representation: Dicken's General Economy' from the journal *Nineteenth-Century Fiction*, 38 (1984), © 1984 The Regents of the University of California; University of Texas Press for the extract 'Discourse in the Novel' from *The Dialogic Imagination* by M M Bakhtin, edited by Michael Holquist, translated by Caryl Emerson and Michael Holquist, copyright © 1981; Verso Ltd for extracts from *Criticism and Ideology: A Study in Marxist Literary Theory* by Terry Eagleton (1976); Vision Press Ltd for the essay 'Polyphony and Problematic in *Hard Times'* by Roger Fowler from *The Changing World of Charles Dickens* edited by Robert Giddings (1983).

1 Introduction

Dead or Alive

If Dickens is a difficult writer, then it is in an unusual, and really rather a *difficult* sense. The difficulty of Dickens is not that of identifying some enigmatic and fugitive essence, of piecing together a dispersed but everywhere impending truth about him. For, where another writer may seem to deliver too little of their essence, Dickens gives us too much, too indefatigably, in too many versions. His is a writing of raw and excessive self-evidence, of a visibility pushed to a certain painful, perplexing limit. The essential reality of Dickens's writing is not masked by its appearance, for it is writing that functions in the mode of *apparition*, or of appearance heightened into hallucination. The Dickens world is lit with the lurid glare of melodrama or pantomime, rather than the discreet chiaroscuro of chamber realism. If there is mystery and strangeness in Dickens's work, then they come, not from its sly dissimulation of latent truth, but from the worrying exorbitance of its manifestness. As many have in praise or blame observed, Dickens's characters do not give the sense of psychological depth, nor hint at that secret, dark interiority which has been the guarantee of the plausible in realist writing for the last couple of centuries; in Dickens's art of crass and flagrant caricature, the superficiality goes, so to speak, all the way down. One must add to this all the other kinds of excessiveness that seem to characterise Dickens's writing; the swaggering extravagance of his language, or the Babelian cacophony of his languages; the celebration of the physical body, both in the splendour of its appetite and in the grotesqueness of its ruin; the unabashed excess of the emotional investment in character and situation; and in the sheer associative overload, the 'opulence and great, careless prodigality', in Kafka's phrase, of his plots and narrative structures.[1]

All of these characteristics have proved a recurrent source of trouble for criticism from the nineteenth century onwards, not least because this is the period in which the dignity and cultural centrality of the novel, the form with which Dickens is so famously associated, has been under patient, painful construction. If the gratuity of Dickens's writing is a worry for literary critics, it is as part of the wider problem of the novel as a form, the problem of how to spruce up into respectability this most unruly, polymorphous and, as we might say, *polygeneous* of genres. As such, Dickens's work presents a miniature version of the general problem of distinguishing authentic culture from the degraded or parasitic forms of popular culture, a problem which came to focus on the novel as a borderline or test-case, since, for all of its aesthetic and cultural aspiration as a literary form, the novel consorted so stubbornly with the threatening energies of mass and popular culture. Nearly all of the nineteenth-century readers of Dickens acknowledge the qualities of energy, excess and invention in his work; but from mid-century onwards, the problem comes to be seen as the absence of a sense of the general forms, aesthetic, moral and social, which might convincingly curb and contain its delinquent particularity. As early as 1865, Henry James, who was to be the chief upholder of the aesthetic dignity of the novel over the next 50 years, was intricately appalled by the lack of a common standard of humanity in *Our Mutual Friend*, in which the characters 'have nothing in common with humanity at large'.[2] By 1913, Swinburne was criticising in a similar way – and in a sentence which seems unconsciously to mimic the Dickensian dilapidation it laments – 'the incomparable incoherence of the parts which pretend in vain to compose the incomposite story' in *Little Dorrit*.[3]

For the mid-nineteenth century onwards, the problem of Dickens seems to have been laid out, if not yet laid to rest, in the following way; how is the urgent but dissociative *force* of his writing to be reconciled with the constraining demands of *form*? For the nineteenth century, the question of form became bound up in a complicated way with the idea of biological life. Central to the work of many mid-century social critics, such as Ruskin, Arnold and Carlyle, was the concept of 'organic form', an ideal of self-creating and self-sustaining natural forms of order. Organicist social criticism very rapidly became a form of social critique, a form of resistance to what were increasingly perceived as the blind, inhuman and mechanical energies associated with industrial and urban expansion. The question of Dickens's relation to the ideal of organic life is a difficult one for critics to resolve. Assuredly, everyone agrees, there is an abundance of 'life' to be found in Dickens, but it is a heaving, surging, uncontrollable kind of life, that vandalises the organic ideals of spontaneous, self-creating unity, the orderly unfolding of natural and immanent design and the alloying of inner essence and outward appearance.

Walter Bagehot gives voice to this anxiety in 1858 when he runs together Dickens's particular capacity to register the unnatural fragmentation of city life ('Everything is there, and everything is disconnected . . . each scene, to his mind, is a separate scene, – each street a separate street') with what he calls his faculty of *'vivification'*, by which he means the intensification of external characteristics to the point where they assume the whole life of the characters. In such a world, he says, characters do not have attributes, they *are* their attributes, enlarged, multiplied, and grotesquely animated:

> [Dickens] sees people in the street, doing certain things, talking in a certain way, and his fancy petrifies them in the act. He goes on fancying hundreds of reduplications of that act and that speech; he frames an existence in which there is nothing else but that aspect which attracted his attention.[4]

What is striking here is the way in which vivification and petrification, death and life, natural and unnatural production, cross and cooperate. For Bagehot, Dickens's vivification is in reality founded upon a lethal reductiveness, propagating life out of an *a priori* of petrifaction. The metaphor which silently animates Bagehot's evocation of distorted growth is surely that of industrial mass production; with its 'hundreds of reduplications', and its uncanny blending of multiplicity and repetition, of difference and similitude, mass production seemed to the tradition of critique that grew through the nineteenth century to be most threatening not because it was merely deathly, but because of its disturbing deployment of death and life as cooperative principles. The problem seems to be that, while Dickens's work can obviously be recruited to the tradition of organic critique, and represented as standing on the side of life against the mechanism of materialist ideology, the very form of his writing draws deeply on the dangerous energies of modern capitalist production and the dissociated kinds of life it requires and procures.

Henry James's criticism of *Our Mutual Friend* is corrugated by a similar kind of anxiety about the life-in-death of Dickens's later writing. The book, he seems to claim, is grotesquely both dead and alive:

> In all Mr Dickens's works the fantastic has been his great resource; and while his fancy was lively and vigorous it accomplished great things. But the fantastic, when the fancy is dead, is a very poor business. The movement of Mr Dickens's fancy in Mrs Wilfer and Mr Boffin and Lady Tippins, and the Lammles and Miss Wren, and even in Eugene Wrayburn, is, to our mind, a movement lifeless, forced, mechanical.[5]

A moment earlier, James has said that he can bring himself only to congratulate Dickens 'on his success in what we should call the *manufacture* of fiction [my emphasis] . . . Seldom, we reflected, had we read a book so intensely *written*, so little seen, known, or felt.'[6] Like the worlds of commerce, industry and the steadily growing State institutions that accompanied and shadowed them, Dickens's writing is at once excessive and deficient; the thinness and lack of real, recognisable 'life' that James laments in *Our Mutual Friend* is contradicted by the continuing sense of extravagance and abundance. There is both too much and too little 'life' in this writing that is at once intensely alive and disturbingly drained of vigour. Margaret Oliphant had struck a similar note in 1862 in complaining of the falling away of 'fertile fullness' in Dickens's later writing. The 'forcible and abundant' art of Dickens's early novels is imaged as a kind of handicraft, which has given way to something like abstract mass production:

> He now carves his furniture grotesquely and makes quaint marks upon his friezes; but he has no longer patience to keep up the strain so long as it is necessary for the perfection of a character . . . The book [*Great Expectations*] reminds us of a painter's rapid memoranda of some picture, in which he uses his pencil to help his memory. After he has dashed in the outline and composition, he scribbles a hasty 'carmine' or 'ultramarine' where those colours come. So the reds and blues of Mr Dickens's picture are only written in. He means us to fill in the glow of the natural hue from the feeble symbol of the word which represents it, or perhaps to go back in our own memory to those forcible and abundant days when he wrought out his own odd conceptions minutely as if he loved them.[7]

From Force to Form

Nearly a century later, Dorothy Van Ghent's famous essay on *Great Expectations* from *The English Novel: Form and Function* (1953) evidences an abiding concern with the problem of the spurious forms of life in Dickens's writing, and with the relation between the animate and the inanimate. Like Bagehot, she observes the strange process of interchange in which objects in the material world accrue a malicious and unnatural vitality, while human beings are reduced to the condition of inert objects or endlessly repeated mechanical processes. But, in contrast to Bagehot's baffled intuitiveness, Van Ghent is quite clear and explicit about the connection between formal principles and the processes of industrial production.

Dickens's art, she suggests, is a direct response to the processes of nineteenth-century reification, or the reduction of processes to things:

> People were becoming things, and things (the things that money can buy or that are the means for making money or for exalting prestige in the abstract) were becoming more important than people. People were being de-animated, robbed of their souls, and things were usurping the prerogatives of animate creatures.[8]

The most striking difference between Bagehot and the many other writers of the nineteenth and early twentieth centuries who were concerned by the bizarre life-in-death of Dickens's writing lies in the question of literary form. For Bagehot, as we have seen, it seems to be the unconscious congruence between Dickens's own narrative modes and the dissociating world of urban capitalism that is perturbing. For Van Ghent, by contrast, it is necessary to make a distinction between the force of Dickens's writing and its form, between the thwarted and distorted patterns of life that are the subject of Dickens's writing and the patterning effect of that writing itself. This marks a very important transition in the critical reception and constitution of Dickens. According to the account that had become customary by the middle of our century, the life of Dickens's writing is to be found in its moral form rather than in the spasmodic and adventitious energies of its content. Thus, if the inner life of what Van Ghent calls the 'fungoid' Miss Havisham is unimaginable, nevertheless, 'in the *art* of Dickens (distinguishing that moral dialectic that arises not solely from the 'characters' in a novel but from all the elements in the aesthetic structure) there is a great deal of "inner life" '.[9] Here, the intricate responsiveness of novelistic form, balancing and contrasting different attitudes, rounding into a whole the disaggregated gratuity of human difference, serves to compensate for the lack of obvious or exemplary value or moral sensibility within the individual characters, or in the person of the narrator.

Obscure and difficult though this notion of 'moral form' is, it has a very successful career in different versions of Dickens criticism throughout the twentieth century. One may say that, where earlier criticism tended to exclude Dickens's work from the kind of organic critique that the form of the novel came to represent, the maturing of that cultural critique into its literary-aesthetic form in the twentieth century was accompanied by a growing sense of the necessity of recruiting Dickens. Dickens's exceptional status was what made it more than ever necessary to present his work as exemplary. The history of twentieth-century attempts to read Dickens is the history of attempts to accommodate his unruly vitality to the odd, but powerful, blend of vitalism and formalism which dominated literary and cultural theory up to about the 1960s.

One can begin to find some early signs of this process of accommodation in the work of the Jamesian critic Percy Lubbock. In his remarks on *Bleak House* in *The Craft of Fiction* (1921), Lubbock suggests that Dickens's writing, for all its effect of spreading and ungoverned accretion, is in fact highly structured. Following in his customarily formulaic way the Jamesian recommendations of dramatisation over summary, direct 'showing' rather than second-hand 'telling', and looking for the characteristic Jamesian coordination of immediacy and elaborate structural artifice, Lubbock discovers a principle of unity in *Bleak House* which had escaped many earlier commentators. Unlike Balzac's, writes Lubbock, Dickens's imagination 'is not . . . divided against itself. The world which he peopled with Skimpole and Guppy and the Bayham Badgers was a world that could easily include Lady Dedlock.'[10] The principle of unity is to be found not in any particular encompassing theory or vision, but in a more abstract principle of structural isomorphism, in the fact that 'They and she alike are at the same angle to literal fact, they diverging one way, she another.'[11] Oddly, the very feature which for most critics hitherto had militated against that wholeness of vision required of the novel, Dickens's tendency to abstract and enlarge incidental characteristics in place of rounded characters, becomes for Lubbock a mark of Dickens's *structural* attentiveness, his determination to frame and organise his work in the most dramatically immediate ways. In Dickens, the incidental character may be dissociated from the world she inhabits at the level of plot, but she is profoundly integrated into it in terms of scenic organisation; such a figure 'is always a little human being who figures upon a scene, in a group, a visible creature acting her small part; she is always dramatic'.[12] Dickens's metonymic identification of characters with isolated characteristics is thus no longer seen as a shrinking down of human diversity, but is an intensifying act of 'crystallization' and 'formulation'.

Percy Lubbock's hints were to be developed through a number of writers influenced by the American New Criticism from the 1940s onwards, who sought to transform the critical understanding of novels in the light of the huge enlargement of attention to the devices and techniques of poetry. Here the emphasis was to be not on the uncontrollable fecundity of Dickens's imagination, or the haunting indefiniteness of his atmosphere, the themes of an earlier brand of criticism, but rather on the careful and intricate development of structure and increasing techniques of control in his novels. Typical of one form of such Dickens criticism from this period is Lionel Trilling's analysis of *Little Dorrit* of 1953. Trilling's essay focuses influentially on the novel's images of prisons and imprisonment, showing how imprisonment is not merely a conspicuous and recurring feature of the plot, but a symbol which serves to organise the complex social vision of the novel as a whole. Trilling sets this view of Dickens the aesthetic technician against the established preference for his more spontaneous, more densely populous novels. Dickens's later works are characterized, he says, not purely by fatigue, or the lessening of vitality, for 'if we are aware that Dickens is here expending less of one kind of creative energy, we must at the same time be aware that he is expending more than ever before of another kind'.[13] This net gain is achieved by the movement of force into form, for 'The imagination of *Little Dorrit* is marked not so much by its powers of particularization as by its powers of generalization and abstraction. It is an imagination under the dominion of a great articulated idea.'[14] Interestingly, Trilling is also drawn to the idea of industrial production in characterising this designing intention; Dickens, he says, identifies his Dantean pride in the artistic design of the novel with the figure of Daniel Doyce 'who, although an engineer, stands for the creative mind in general and for its appropriate virtue'.[15] Here, Trilling accurately senses the ways in which Dickens in his own writing sought to solve the contradiction between production and creation, manufacture and art, which had governed much of the contemporary criticism of his work. Another example of the growing sense of Dickens the artificer might be W. J. Harvey's discussion of *Bleak House* in his book *Character and the Novel* of 1965. Harvey begins by suggesting that James's prescription of the absolute cooperation of part and whole in organic synthesis is inappropriate to a novelist like Dickens, in which the molecular intensification of the singular and the episodic is so important. But he nevertheless reinstates almost immediately the ideal of a constraint of intensity by form, of a balance between energy and design: the greatness of *Bleak House* is therefore said to derive from 'a tension between the impulse to intensify each local detail or particular episode and the impulse to subordinate, arrange and discipline'.[16]

In Britain, it is the work of F. R. Leavis, in his essay on *Hard Times* of 1947, and the book *Dickens the Novelist* (1970), coauthored with Q. D. Leavis, of which the essay forms a kind of centrepiece, which brings together in the most significant and culturally prosperous manner the emphasis on form, symbolism and patterning to be found in New Criticism and the tradition of the vitalist critique of modernity represented in the tradition of Ruskin, Arnold and Morris. The Leavises aimed to rescue Dickens from the variously genial or hostile construction of Dickens as a histrionic *ingenu*, the fecundity of whose work consists precisely in the way it overflows the limits of form. More particularly, they are arguing against G. K. Chesterton's view of 'the primary inexhaustible creative energy, the enormous prodigality' of Dickens's genius and his belief that the 'colossal cataract' of his work has little to do with the 'strict form of fiction' such that it is, indeed, 'not to be reckoned in novels at all'.[17] Given this,

> You cannot discuss whether *Nicholas Nickleby* is a good novel, or whether *Our Mutual Friend* is a bad novel. Strictly, there is no such novel as *Nicholas Nickleby*. There is no such novel as *Our Mutual Friend*. They are simply lengths cut from the flowing and mixed substance called Dickens – a substance of which any given length will be certain to contain a given proportion of brilliant and of bad stuff.[18]

To reclaim Dickens from this spontaneist account meant reclaiming the novel itself as a form. Against Chesterton's view of Dickens's novels as the product of an unsupervised textile mill ('lengths cut from the flowing and mixed substance called Dickens'), the Leavises set the Jamesian ideal of the 'figure in the carpet', the absent, but critically apprehensible ordering of the disparate relations within the individual work: indeed, they cite as one of the epigraphs to their book a passage from James's *The Figure in the Carpet*, in which the central character, a writer, is promising that ' "The order, the form, the texture of my books will perhaps one day constitute for the initiated a complete representation of it." '[19] The novel must be reclaimed for art from its condition of merely 'popular' profuseness, and Dickens must be seen, not just as passively responsive to the pleasures and energies of nineteenth-century urban life, but as actively organising them. Thus, the Leavises insist that 'if we are to say that he saw himself as a popular entertainer, it must not be with any suggestion that he did not think of himself, and with justice, as having, *qua* artist, a penetrating insight into contemporary civilization, its ethos, its realities and its drives, that it concerned him to impart' (p. 30).

This is to say that the necessity of claiming Dickens as conscious and controlling artist is associated, for the Leavises, with the necessity of recruiting Dickens to the particular form of cultural critique which they held so dear and so tirelessly practised: which is to say, the promotion of the self-directing energies of 'life' against the 'technologico-Benthamism' that seemed to the Leavises to reduce and abstract the natural and spontaneous forms of social living. At the centre of this lies their influential reading of *Hard Times*, with its warm approval of Dickens's openness to 'generous, impulsive life, finding fulfilment in self-forgetfulness – all that is the antithesis of calculating self-interest . . . that is lived freely and richly from the deep instinctive and emotional springs' (p. 191). However, as we have seen, the alleged vitality of Dickens's writing is rather slippery in its nature and effects, since it can just as easily be associated with or borrow from the energies of industrial capitalism as it can oppose them. It is necessary for the Leavises repeatedly to stress that Dickens's vitality is organised rather than disorganised life, 'packed richness' (p. 206) rather than mere expenditure, fullness rather than excess, form rather than force. Against the sprawling, indefinite and pathologically 'female' energies of mass culture and its popular forms like the sentimental novel and the melodrama, the Leavises characterise Dickens's writing in terms of a phantasmatic male anatomy, whose strength lies in the way it bends and bounds the formlessly kinetic into a tautly muscular torque:

> the Dickensian vitality is there in its varied characteristic modes, which . . . are free of anything that might be seen as redundance: the creative exuberance is controlled by a profound inspiration that informs, directs and limits . . . Dickens's art, while remaining that of the great popular entertainer, has in *Hard Times*, as he renders his full critical vision, a stamina, a flexibility combined with consistency (pp. 188, 189)

The image of this in *Hard Times* is the horse-riding, which is neither indulgence on Dickens's part in the vulgar delights of the popular, nor mere abstract or conventional symbolism, but rather 'evokes for us spontaneous and daring vitality disciplined into skill and grace' (p. 210). There is an interestingly managed glide here between what the Leavises say the metaphor of the horse-riding *means* and the way in which they are claiming that it *works*; here it is Dickens's art itself that has become the ideal fusion of energy and controlling will.

The problem for the Leavises is how to maintain this required balance between force and form. Allow the idea of Dickens as the practitioner of 'a richly poetic art of the word' to go too far, and the emphasis on structure and technique may end up parching the passion of felt life; give the 'astonishing and irresistible richness of life . . . [the] extraordinary energy of perception and registration' too much slack and it may be hard to rein it back into form. The problem that the Leavises repeatedly seek to dispel without, however, quite being able to acknowledge it *as* a problem, is another version of the problem that we have seen haunting commentary on Dickens since the nineteenth century; it is that Dickens's writing in *Hard Times* so resembles what it seems to oppose, its dynamism seeming to draw too deeply on the appalling blind energies of industrial production, the diagrammatic flatness of its moral solutions reproducing the abstraction of Utilitarianism at whose door it lays so much blame.[20] 'There is no need to insist', say the Leavises, 'on the force . . . with which the moral and spiritual differences are rendered here in terms of sensation, so that the symbolic intention emerges out of metaphor and the vivid evocation of the concrete' (p. 191). Given that such a compounding of the sensual and the abstract is an imaginary solution to an only partially grasped contradiction in *Hard Times*, one might think, on the contrary, that there is every need for the Leavises to insist, indeed no other way for them to argue, *but* to insist.

Authorship and Authority

One of the most important areas of debate regarding Dickens's writing has been the question of the degree and quality of his authorship. From the beginning, the controversy about the dignity and degree of achievement of fictional form in Dickens was closely related to the question of how far Dickens can be said to be in control of his art. Dickens criticism is radically unsure whether to characterise that work as the product of an unnatural excess of controlling will, or an undisciplined paucity of it. As early as 1856, Hippolyte Taine was suggesting that Dickens's imagination was that of the monomaniac:

> To plunge oneself into an idea, to be absorbed by it, to see nothing else, to repeat it under a hundred forms, to enlarge it, to carry it thus enlarged to the eye of the spectator, to dazzle and overwhelm him with it, to stamp it upon him so tenacious and impressive that he can never again tear it from his memory – these are the great features of this imagination and style.[21]

Here, egotism cooperates strangely with possession (the monomaniac both unnaturally imposes his obsessions upon everything he sees, and yet also loses his self in those obsessions) and monomania with a troubling tendency towards multiplication, repetition, enlargement. The scene that Taine here projects involves agency and passivity at once, for it has Dickens first of all being involuntarily absorbed in his material, and then imperiously transmitting that passivity to the reader. For many other writers, the power of Dickens's work comes precisely from the suspension of control, or a certain hyperassertiveness which goes paradoxically beyond the forms of rational control or designing intelligence. Writing in 1925, Virginia Woolf has a more benign view of this process than Taine:

> This is the power that cannot fade or fail in its effect – the power not to analyse or to interpret, but to produce, apparently without thought or effort or calculation of the effect upon the story, characters who exist, not in detail, not accurately or exactly, but abundantly in a cluster of wild and yet extraordinarily revealing remarks, bubble climbing on the top of bubble as the breath of the creator fills them.[22]

For Woolf as for Taine, the 'fecundity and apparent irreflectiveness' of Dickens's writing affects and disturbs the customary commerce between writer and reader, since 'they make creators of us, and not merely readers and spectators. As we listen to Micawber pouring himself forth and venturing perpetually upon some flight of astonishing imagination, we see, unknown to Mr Micawber, into the depths of his soul.'[23] Against this tendency to see Dickens as the inspired but unconscious creator, later twentieth-century criticism tended to construe Dickens as a craftsman, following the Leavises' affirmation that 'with the intelligence inherent in creative genius, he developed a fully conscious devotion to his art, becoming as a popular and fecund, but yet profound, serious and wonderfully resourceful practising novelist, a master of it'.[24] Lionel Trilling also articulates this changing view of Dickens when he stresses the movement in *Little Dorrit* from the autonomous and involuntary life of Dickens's early novels to the carefully and intentionally controlled structures of the later novels: 'We do not have the great population of characters from whom shines the freshness of their autonomous life. Mr Pancks and Mrs Plornish and Flora Finching and Flintwinch are interesting and amusing, but they seem to be the fruit of conscious intention rather than of free creation.'[25]

However, a few years before Trilling's essay, a contrary argument had been influentially framed in Edmund Wilson's essay 'Dickens: The Two Scrooges', namely, that Dickens's power comes, not from artistic control of what is excessive in his temperament, but from a powerful failure to temper that excess. The essay argues that the energising principle of Dickens's work is to be discovered neither in the lavishness and poetic extravagance to be found in the early novels, nor in the earnest anatomy of social ills to be found in the later works, but in a recurrent, barely controlled alternation in Dickens between identification with the social insider and with the social

outsider; between the bright pieties of official domestic ideology and
the dark obsessions of the criminal, the murderer and the anarchist.
Dickens, Wilson suggests, is at the mercy of an unstable dualism, in
which the wholesomenesss of Dingley Dell, of Litle Nell, and Esther
Summerson is always threatened by the diabolic, self-creating energy
of a Fagin, a Quilp or a Magwitch. For Wilson, the concern with
social conflict in Dickens is really the vehicle for a more private but
equally insoluble moral problem. For this reason, he finds the most
representative text in Dickens's oeuvre to be the one in which this
particular moral problem is neither resolved nor evaded, namely
the unfinished *Edwin Drood*. He argues that the novel shows clearly
that Dickens was intending to dramatize in the person of John Jasper
a *doppelgänger* theme similar to that found in Poe's *William Wilson*
and Stevenson's *Dr Jekyll and Mr Hyde*, a dramatization that would
be at once social and profoundly psychological in its exploration of
the relation between respectable middle-class society and those who
variously secede from it and haunt it as nightmare. Here, finally, and
in a sense triumphantly, 'the protest against the age has turned into
a protest against self'.[26] Wilson's theory – borrowed and elaborated
from a couple of earlier solutions to the mystery – is that Jasper was
to be revealed as a member of a Hindu Thuggee cult operating in
England and that the climax of the novel is to be the confrontation of
his criminal and respectable selves in the condemned cell.
Significantly, for Wilson, it was not possible for Dickens to engineer
this confrontation, since, he believes, 'Dickens in his moral confusion
was never to dramatize himself completely, was never in the last phase
of his art to succeed in coming quite clear' (p. 103).

The unresolved question of identity in Dickens's characters reenacts
the irresolution of Dickens's own identity, and is thus bound up for
Wilson with the question of Dickens's sense of his own power. Wilson
dwells on the interest in mesmerism which Dickens had cultivated
since the 1840s and sees it as related to the question of the power
which Dickens attempted to exercise over his audiences, both in writing
and in the series of arduous public readings which he undertook in
the last years of his life and which perhaps contributed to making
them the last. The extraordinary power that Dickens attempts to exert
over his audience, and his exultation in the hysterical responses he
was able to bring about (once, after a reading of *Sikes and Nancy* at
Clifton, he estimated with satisfaction that 'we had from a dozen to
twenty ladies taken out stiff and rigid, at various times'[27]), is the mark
of a certain sort of possession *by* his material as well as of his
possessiveness towards it and its audiences. Wilson recalls the episode
recounted by his daughter Kate Perugini in which Dickens actually
gave mesmeric treatment during the 1840s to an Englishwoman

suffering from obsessive delusions. This bears out Wilson's claim that
Dickens both enjoyed the exercise of control and was himself subject
to the hallucinations he controlled: 'one gets the impression that
these bloody visions were as real to him as they were to her', writes
Wilson (p. 96). It suggests that mesmerism in Dickens's last,
unresolved novel is not merely part of its 'machinery of mystification',
as Wilson describes it (p. 99), but that it has to do with the constantly
renewed struggle on Dickens's part to control or even to stage the
dualism of his nature. This is a struggle that, as Wilson's account
begins to show, is paradoxical; power is required to present and
organize the dualism – the novel's 'most powerful artistic effect is
procured by an installation into the greenery, the cathedral, the winter
sun, the sober and tranquil old town, of the suggestion of moral
uncertainty and evil' (p. 101) – even as it is the unrestrained and
spasmodic exercise of power that makes the very dualism of power
and order unsteady, since it is a power that is always liable to burst
out of the form of the very contrast between the natural and the
unnatural, between form and force, that defines it. While it lends
impetus to that growing tendency to read Dickens's work as
complex and concentrated symbolic structures rather than as a series
of spontaneous and brilliant eruptions, the importance of Wilson's
work lies in its stress on the ways in which Dickens's work resists
the enclosing and organizing aesthetics which other critics had either
lamented the absence of or attempted to supply. It is significant that
the Leavises felt called to define their position not only against the
Chestertonian tradition of reading Dickens (what Wilson himself calls
'pseudo-poetic booziness', p. 3) but also against that tendency to see
Dickens's work as 'the volcanic explosions of a manic-depressive'
which they believe Wilson inaugurated and encouraged (*Dickens the
Novelist*, p. xiii). At issue here is precisely the question of the authority
of the artist, in devising and controlling his work. As we shall soon
see, contemporary criticism has attempted to go beyond the duality
in which Dickens is either to be admired as the deific controller of
his fictional world, or to be compensated for his failure to control
that world.

The Leavises' purpose in rescuing Dickens from diagnostic or
psychological criticism is to restore the idea that Dickens's work is
centred and controlled and therefore *whole*, without excess or
superfluity. However, there are other psychological readings which
do not, like Wilson's, threaten the idea of Dickens as controlling
maker, or represent Dickens's work as the turbulent overflow of
pathology. One such example is J. Hillis Miller's important
phenomenological account of Dickens's writing in *Charles Dickens: The
World of His Novels* (1958). Miller follows other psychological critics

in representing Dickens's works primarily not as the reflection of an age, nor as intricately devised Dantean artifice, but as the expression of consciousness. However, this process is not merely passive and the works therefore not reliably to be explicated as the unwilled expression of a given or preexisting authorial pathology or set of psychological factors. Rather, the work itself is to be seen as a process of psychological self-making: in writing his works, Dickens can be seen constructing himself in his psychological relation to the world. Miller's technique is to cluster together elements and motifs – the description of actions, the forms of interior monologue, the evocation of particular scenes – which testify to the distinctive relations between mind and world set up in Dickens.

In this, Miller's work draws heavily on the phenomenological approach to literary texts exemplified in the work of his mentor, Georges Poulet, an approach that describes texts as forms and activities of consciousness, which simultaneously bear the impress of the author's originating mind and are the concrete means of that author's intentional engagement with the world. As Miller puts it: 'A poem or novel is indeed the world fashioned into conformity with the inner structure of the writer's spirit, but at the same time it is that spirit given, through words, a form and substance taken from the shared solidity of the exterior world'.[28] Typically, phenomenological readings focus upon the sensations and struggles of identity, the forming and maintenance of patterns or order, and the experience of time and of the material world.

In Miller's account, the problem of aesthetic form is displaced into the question of the formation and sustaining of identity, which therefore becomes something allied and analogous to the devising of a work of art. Miller takes as his focus in Dickens's work the theme of 'the search for a true and viable identity', and, in following through the forms of this search, aims to bring to light the 'impalpable organizing form, constantly presiding over the choice of words' which lies behind that work.[29] As we will see, Miller has subsequently moved rather a long way away from this view of Dickens's novels.

Miller's idea that Dickens's work is unified not so much by conscious and creative intention as by a certain kind of acting out of the self and its relations to the world is taken up and developed in a book that appeared a few years later, Robert Garis's *The Dickens Theatre* (1965). Garis starts from a sense of the residual maladjustment of Dickens's novels to the post-Jamesian ideal of the novel as complex but coherent organic structure. For Garis, 'the Dickens problem' springs from the fact that the novels belong so much, in their language and forms, to a set of conventions and traditions which are not easily to be transmuted into high art. These conventions are principally popular and dramatic, Garis suggests, and his powerful reading of Dickens suggests that his work is best seen, not as social analysis, nor as realism, social or psychological, nor yet as complex poetic symbolism, but as a certain style of *performance*. No matter how remorselessly they are subjected to critical processes which emphasize the modernist impersonality and devising detachment of the author, the novels refuse to let us forget the presence and effect of the act of narration and the propinquity of the narrator, who is continuously, urgently 'present before us, not as a personality, with particular personal feelings, attitudes, and habits, but as a performer, as a maker and doer'.[30]

For Garis, the warm palpability of the sense of performance in the novels is betrayed by their critical calcification into symbolic or poetic artefacts. At the heart of his argument is the chapter in which he argues against what he sees as Leavis's overestimation of such qualities in *Hard Times*. The intelligence and organisation of this novel are functions, Garis suggests, not of its 'moral form', but of a virtuoso theatricality. The vitality of the novel is therefore not the tautly coordinated vitality of a dynamic structure, but 'the impudent vitality of the performing voice, enjoying its indignation and confident of its power to denounce and banish what makes it so angry' (p. 161). Garis suggests that this performative mode is characterized by exteriority rather than interiority, the focus on singular and distinct elements rather than their structural coordination, linearity rather than spatiality, rhetoric rather than symbolism and intensity rather than form. Garis comes close to suggesting that these alternative modes belong to cultural forms – the melodrama, the farce, the detective novel – which are betrayed by institutional criticism when they are read according to the values of high art. But at the same time, it must be said that Garis in some sense colludes with or reinforces those values simply in the way in which he identifies the performative voice in Dickens's work as itself a sort of centring aesthetic principle, turning egotism into a kind of impersonality and, in the end, effecting the transmutation of the popular into the high that he nevertheless so effectively suggests Dickens's work resists or confounds. In other words, in Garis's book, the very notion of the novel as a performance again effects the transition from free or ungoverned force to the containments of form.

Garis is a little unusual in taking the problem of Dickens's seemingly constitutional maladjustment to the formal requirements and values of contemporary literary criticism so openly as his point of departure. But, by the mid-1960s, the models of high art and literary value that Garis believes are challenged by Dickens's work were beginning to feel those early tremors of self-doubt which were to

develop into the massive theoretical upheavals and reconstitution of
the cultural landscape during the 1970s and 1980s. The essays
represented in this collection bear the traces of some of these
upheavals and bear witness to the changed landscape in which
Dickens's texts currently feature.

Meaning, Identity and Language

We can begin to understand the general shift in the criticism of
Dickens that has been wrought by the arrival of various forms
of Continental theory during the 1970s and 1980s in terms of the
antagonism I have identified between *force* and *form* in the work of
Dickens. I have so far been suggesting that, in most nineteenth- and
twentieth-century criticism of Dickens, criticism occurs in and as the
transition from force to form; in which the indefinite and excessive
energies of Dickens's writing, spilling beyond generic and cultural
categories of all kinds, are transmuted, contained and disciplined by
being organised around certain culturally prestigious forms or
principles; the controlling author; the notion of the novel as exposé
or social criticism; the novel as organically functioning artifice, the
'figure in the carpet'. Criticism is the name of the process whereby
the purely energetic is turned into the economic, which is to say,
made subject to measurement, distribution and calculative appraisal.
If it were possible to generalize across all the examples of more
contemporary critical reading of Dickens that this collection gathers
together, one might say that all of them try not only to undertake that
process of translation, but also to reflect on the particular ways in
which Dickens's novels may resist as well as incite that process.
They are all concerned not to efface or interpret into invisibility those
forms of resistance to coherence and intelligibility which characterize
Dickens's work, but to try to preserve and understand them. In part,
this involves a complication of the simple model in which the
intensely charged but unreflective mass of Dickens's work is given
sense and intelligibility by the act of criticism which supervenes on
it from the outside to inform it of its own meanings and significances.
The kinds of criticism that are currently being developed to read
Dickens's novels suggest that those novels are always already
concerned with the question of how intensity is to be ordered into
intelligibility, force channelled into moral, aesthetic and political form.

The opening essay of the collection, Peter Brooks's essay on *Great
Expectations*, exemplifies this reflexiveness very well, for it examines
the ways in which the novel's own plot develops out of the search of

its central character, Pip, for a 'plot' that will plausibly organize his own life. Brooks's essay is a distinguished example of a style of psychoanalytic reading that has flourished in recent years, in which texts are not read simply as the literary embodiments or dissimulations of psychological truths or conditions. Assuming that the functions and devices we call 'literary' or 'rhetorical' or 'narrative' are in fact fundamental to the ways in which human subjects imagine and constitute themselves in the first place, such criticism does not expect to be able to dig out the hidden truths behind such literary forms. The psychoanalytic 'truth' revealed by literature is that the self is intimately bound up with, if not actually made up of, certain kinds of literariness, here most notably in the desire for the meaningful coherence conferred by narrative.

The relation of force and form that we have identified as a particular concern in Dickens's novels and in the criticism that interprets them, here undergoes a distinctive mutation. The reader's slow grasp of the narrative of Pip's life is an effect of binding, a concentration of force into form; but since the emergence of significance and truth also depend upon the revelation that plot itself, and the patterns of connection it promises, is a kind of error, or deviance, this binding is simultaneously an unbinding, a relaxation of the stabilizing authority of form. The force and the value of form are thus both asserted and discredited in this novel, in which coherence and incoherence, truth and mystery, plot and contingency, identity and its negation are not simple opposites, but propagate and prosper upon each other. The forms of interpretation or (psycho)analysis that criticism carries out upon the novel are consequently not entirely distinct from the forms of binding and emplotment that preoccupy and constitute the novel itself, and not wholly immune either from the energetic loosening of the authority of such forms that takes place in the novel.

For Brooks, the question of identity which is so much at issue in *Great Expectations* is closely implicated with the question of the power and effects of language. Unlike earlier criticism of Dickens, which attempted to distinguish what was idiosyncratic or essential in Dickens's own use of language, many contemporary theoretical critics are interested in the ways in which Dickens's novels explore the forms, effects and authority of language itself. Nowhere is this more than the case than in those styles of critical interpretation that derive from the work of Jacques Derrida and with varying degrees of acquiescence offer themselves as illustrative of the possibilities of 'deconstructive' criticism.

Deconstructive criticism, like the 'poststructuralism' with which it is routinely (and maybe, by and large correctly) associated, is the product of an intensification of structuralism to a point of instructive catastrophe. Having first established the proposition that language is best understood as a formal system of differences and oppositions, structuralism claimed to be able to derive exact and reliable maps of the ways in which difference is distributed in any particular text. Poststructuralism is the name for what follows from the suspicion that difference may be a more mobile and a more indefinite effect than a structuralist way of looking at things might suggest; for if every element in a differential system derives its meaning from its difference from every other element, then there cannot in principle be any fixed points of reference in such a system, no signs that bear or evidence their meaning in and of themselves. Poststructuralism, we may say, tends to celebrate the delirious dance of relativity, the processual force of difference over and against the notion of difference as fixity or form. Or, to borrow some philosophical terms of more venerable lineage, poststructuralism celebrates the energies of becoming over the fixities of being.

Deconstruction is all too often presented as a simple intensification or writing large of this enthusiasm for the unresolved, the energetic and the contingent, along with all the uncomfortable consequences for notions of truth, meaning, rationality, value and so forth which this involves. But the kind of enquiry encouraged and undertaken by Derrida is hard to assimilate to such an account. If it were possible to reduce Derrida's work to a programme, a crucial part of it would be the sceptical determination to inspect and suspect any such simple opposition as that between fixity and motion, being and becoming, form and force. Derrida's work suggests that we would do well to remain aware of the way in which every such clean distinction ignores or represses the ghostly traces of mutual implication within each term of an opposition. It is no more possible to opt for the alluring interpretative irresponsibility of 'play' than it is to guarantee the claims of 'truth', since each depends on the other for its definition. Deconstruction, on this account, is that kind of thinking which baffles or compromises the simple distinction between the alternatives represented by structuralism and poststructuralism. This is why we should not expect a deconstructive account of Dickens to be a 'destructive' account; simply a substitution for an old daylit vocabulary of absolute truth and meaning of the nocturnal values of the enigmatic, the indeterminate and the subversive.

Two examples of criticism which attempt to represent the strange ways in which meaning and its dissolution haunt each other in Dickens's work are represented in this collection. The central insight offered by the first of these, J. Hillis Miller's essay on *Bleak House*, is that the activity of reading which takes place incessantly *in* the novel perfectly and unsettlingly mirrors the reading *of* the novel by its readers. Deciphering enigmas, following the thread of connections, being moved on from one imperfectly understood appearance to another, the position of the reader is just like that of most of the characters of *Bleak House*. Miller proposes that the novel both allows and disallows the possibility of successful interpretation. *Bleak House* suggests that the evil and stagnation of British life are manifested in its secrecies, its concealments, its thwarting of the process of understanding. But at the same time, suggests Miller, there is a darker suggestion in the novel, that the evil of indecipherability is intrinsic to language itself. This is because language and interpretation rely upon the functioning of difference, in which elements derive their identity from patterns of relative, and therefore impermanent, contrast and association. Language, so to speak, alienates things into their identity. If the real villain or guilty party identified by *Bleak House* is not any particular individual or institution, but rather language and the act of interpretation, then, suggests Miller, 'the evil . . . [Dickens] so brilliantly identifies is irremediable' (pp. 67–8). In a world in which everyone and everything is made to 'move on' from their identity, nothing is likely to supply that firm sense of self-coincidence that is traditionally required and purchased by the realist novel.

Christopher D. Morris's deconstructive reading of *Great Expectations* also concerns the relationship between personal identity and language. It begins by renewing the critical controversy about the question of Pip's moral reliability or responsibility, a controversy initiated by an influential article by Julian Moynahan in 1960.[31] According to Morris, the moral problem for Pip is not just to determine and communicate what is right and just, but also to devise a form to guarantee the authenticity of such insights. For Pip to attain to the status of a justified moral consciousness, it is necessary for him to believe in the ideal of a unified and continuous self and for his narration to exemplify it. Morris's essay examines the effect of certain linguistic forms in actually undermining rather than confirming the coherence and self-identity of the author. His account ends with the image of a narrator struggling against an alien and alienating order of language which is close to that provided in J. Hillis Miller's remarks on Esther Summerson in *Bleak House*; during the nightmarish night that he spends at the Hummums, conjugating Wemmick's words 'Don't Go Home' into every conceivable permutation, Pip has his closest experience of language 'as some order independent of the self, prior to the human' (p. 86), just as Esther does in her nightmare of being strung helplessly like a bead on a flaming necklace, which J. Hillis Miller glosses as 'the figure of a moving ring of substitution, in which each person is not himself but part of a system or the sign for some other thing' (p. 70).

No writer until Joyce had a more strongly developed sense than Dickens of the dissident vitalities of the word, or was as willing to allow the authority of the speaking self to be so imperilled by those energies. Dickens's work is therefore hugely illuminated by a criticism that is attentive to the interior self-thwartings of literary and linguistic form, to the mutual dependency in such forms of authority and subversion, self and other, presence and difference.

The relation between authority and language that is so important for deconstructive criticism has been an important topic in other areas of contemporary literary theory, and nowhere more so than in the criticism that draws on the work of the Soviet critic Mikhail Bakhtin. In a number of essays and books written from the 1920s through to the 1960s, Bakhtin developed a critique of 'monologism', or the belief in the value of linguistic singularity, whether in the idea of the individual voice, the unique authorial style, or the ideal of a single, self-identical language. Bakhtin argues that, on the contrary, all languages, and all individual uses of language, are 'heteroglot' from top to bottom; this is to say, they consist of the drift and strife of different voices, different styles, idioms and registers.

This multiple-voicedness is particularly evident in the novel, in which the legislative authority of the narrative voice is all the time in competition and collusion with other voices, idioms and social styles, and the values impacted in them. For Bakhtin, Dickens's novels belong to a comic tradition which subjects the authority invested in singular voices, or in the notion of the singular voice, to the raking critique of parody and laughter. The discussion of *Little Dorrit* that is reproduced in this collection comes from the essay in which the centrality of the novel to Bakhtin's political aesthetics is displayed most plainly, his 'Discourse in the Novel' of 1935. Dickens's novels are of particular interest to Bakhtin, precisely because of their interior resistance to any finality of form. What remains unresolved in the extract reproduced here, and remains unresolved in Bakhtin's work as a whole, is the question of whether the form of a literary work and the authorial intention that this form is traditionally held to objectify, determine or are secondary effects of this play of discursive forces. At times, Bakhtin seems to accept that, in the final instance, a text is an authorially willed orchestration, and not merely a dynamic of interruption, such that the voice of the 'other' which breaks in upon the authoritative voice of the author is always in the end governed and licensed by a designing purpose. But at other times, the logic of his argument seems to be that the

novel is the form in which the singular authority of the author is
most systematically and valuably jeopardized.

The Bakhtinian reading of *Hard Times* by Roger Fowler that
accompanies the extract from 'Discourse in the Novel' exemplifies
the advantages of paying attention to the productivity of linguistic
difference in Dickens's writing. Fowler carefully analyses the
distribution, conflict and intersection of different personal,
professional and class idioms in *Hard Times*. In contrast to those
who, following Leavis, have praised the concentrated poetic unity of
the novel as well as to those who, disagreeing with Leavis, have
objected to its schematism or thematic weakness, Fowler moves
towards a 'picture of a text articulated in a multitude of voices . . .
[which are] discordant and fluctuating in the kaleidoscope of views
they express' (p. 111). Such a view perhaps suggests an enlargement
rather than a complete overturning of the value of unity of design in
criticism of Dickens. Here, in what is sometimes felt to be Dickens's
most concentrated and worked-out novel, Fowler, like Bakhtin,
detects and applauds the principle of the unfinished in Dickens's work,
a principle which requires the reader to grapple with the complex
issues of the novel rather than having them delivered up sole and
whole for contemplation.

Discourse and Power

In the kind of criticism envisaged and practised by Leavis, language
was both the vehicle of social critique and the utopian promise of a
world of complexity, concentration and immediacy which might
replace the debased and abstract regimes of modern mass society.
For Leavis, it was literary language that kept tenuously alive the ideal
of a social order based on richly complex, intensely embodied
experience. Against this counterfactual ideal of language as the
antagonist and transcendence of modern social life, the work of
Bakhtin and others suggests the need to acknowledge the saturation
of literary language in the concrete experiences of daily life, which
is to say, in the experiences of difference and political conflict.
Nevertheless, the utopian vocation of language survives in Bakhtin's
work, which argues that literary forms like the novel instance and
exhibit an ideal maximum of competing voices. The form of the
comic novel, or perhaps one should say, its exemplary and dissociative
force, stands for Bakhtinian criticism as a proleptic enactment of
some as yet unrealized vision of wholeness-in-plurality. Bakhtin's
work makes it possible for criticism of Dickens to attend to the

social and political force of linguistic forms, as they are both represented and enacted in Dickens's work.

Bakhtin's view of the political force of discourse in literary forms such as the novel accords with other strains of contemporary literary and cultural theory in its enlargement of the question of language beyond the simple function of representation. The long tradition of political readings of Dickens's work has tended previously to be concerned with questions of form, language and structure only where these bear upon questions of the adequacy of Dickens's analysis and representation of various social ills and his implicit suggestion of alternatives to them. This tradition perhaps begins in John Ruskin's ambivalent approval for Dickens's radical social criticism. He declared roundly in 1862 that Dickens 'is entirely right in his main drift and purpose in every book he has written; and all of them, but especially *Hard Times*, should be studied with close and earnest care by persons interested in social questions'.[32] Though acknowledging the melodramatic excesses of his writing, Ruskin believes that these are redeemed by the fundamental correspondence of Dickens's novels to truth.

A similar insistence on novelistic truthfulness is to be found in many other political readings of Dickens. By 1937, Shaw could declare himself in a similar way for the notion of Dickens as intuitive social radical. Like Ruskin, he is unflustered by the fact of Dickens's almost total ignorance of the revolutionary political ideas of his time and his antipathy to nearly every movement of radical popular dissent: 'The difference between Marx and Dickens', he explains, 'was that Marx knew he was a revolutionist whilst Dickens had not the faintest suspicion of that part of his calling.'[33] As a consequence, Shaw is able to declare, famously, that '*Little Dorrit* is a more seditious book than *Das Kapital*'.[34] Writing just a few years later, George Orwell is willing to concede a certain streak of radicalism in Dickens, but is more worried than Shaw by the lack of political concreteness in his work, by the retreat into moral remedies in preference to political analysis of a more developed, and socially encompassing kind. In this, he anticipates the concern of Georg Lukács that Dickens, though at his best he is authentically open to the turbulence of history, always suffers from the tendency 'to separate the "purely human" and "purely moral" from their social basis and to make them, to a certain degree, autonomous'.[35] Lukács and Orwell here are lamenting the fact that Dickens has brought to visibility a potent, but still partial truth. For both of them, the political force of Dickens's writing depends in a similar way on the degree of its faithful and inclusive correspondence to reality. The same attitude governs the more sympathetic estimate that Arnold Kettle gives to Dickens's *Oliver*

Twist. The power of the novel, Kettle assumes, lies in its political realism, though this realism is different from that of the social history on the one hand, or the psychological exploration on the other. *Oliver Twist* does not cause us to participate in the interior life of its characters; rather, it deals 'with something which can without fatuity be called Life. What we get from *Oliver Twist* is . . . a sharpened sense of the large movement of life within which particular problems arise.'[36] This effect is achieved not through documentary realism but by the concentrated force of symbolic presentation 'through which is achieved an objective picture arousing our compassion not through any extraneous comment but through its own validity'.[37] This emphasis on the power or incapacity of the novels to reveal and reflect truth survives in Raymond Williams's *Culture and Society,* which recognizes and applauds the radical energy of Dickens's moral critique of instrumentalist and systematic thinking, but also insists that basing the critique of industrial capitalism in the experience of individuals and in the tenuous claims of pleasure and 'fantasy' mimes the claustrophobic conditions it seeks to escape. Seen in this way, a novel like *Hard Times* is 'more a symptom of the confusion of industrial society than an understanding of it'.[38]

Much contemporary literary theory has been driven by the insight that, rather than simply and more or less accurately representing the world, language – including the language of fiction – might more productively be thought of as doing things in and to the world. This view of language as a kind of action, with certain kinds of measurable and politically palpable effects, has had particular implications for politically accented criticism of Dickens over the last couple of decades. No writer has had more influence in this respect than Michel Foucault, who devoted much of his later work to an exploration of the effects of power exerted through discourse in general and the institutional discourses of particular social groups and professions in particular. Discourse never merely represents the world, for Foucault; it is always also a mode of action on the world, even, indeed, the infliction of a certain kind of violence upon it. The great insight that Foucault's work donates to contemporary political readings of Dickens is that language and discursive forms are never merely the representations of power, but also its very occasion and embodiment.

The essays by Jeremy Tambling and D. A. Miller reprinted in this volume build in particular on Foucault's work on prisons and his account of the growth of what he describes as the 'carceral society' during the nineteenth century. Jeremy Tambling's essay argues that Dickens's novels do not just reflect the concern with prisons and imprisonment that is so general in the nineteenth century, but simultaneously enquire into and enact the ways in which the issues of power, oppression and imprisonment become bound up with language. The effects of power are concentrated in particular in the language of the self employed by autobiography.

Against the critical tradition that would read autobiography as the affirmation of the slow growth into personal autonomy, Tambling sees the autobiographical mode of Pip's narration in *Great Expectations* as instancing the internalization by the subject of an identity imposed from elsewhere. As in Peter Brooks's account of the novel elsewhere in this collection, there is a sense that identity does not arise spontaneously from within, but is derived from without, from narratives and discursive forms that constitute the subject rather than being a vehicle for the subject's self-expression. This means that it is not merely at the level of narrative content that the 'carceral' preoccupations of *Great Expectations* reveal themselves, but also in the very force of its confessional form. Since, following Foucault's account of the internalization of power, it is the very spontaneity of the self and its confessional languages which marks the incision of social power into the most private realms, it may be said that the very mode of writing in Pip's narrative 'belongs to the prison' (p. 129).

Tambling's account of *Great Expectations* offers some interesting parallels and differences with the two other accounts of the novel, psychoanalytic and deconstructive, which feature in this collection. Like Brooks and Morris, Tambling sees the fact that the self is constituted out of the language that it apparently uses as pure instrument or resource as leading to certain instructive forms of paradox or self-division. For Brooks, Hillis Miller and Morris, it is somehow the forms of narrative and language as such that betray the speaking self who relies on them to confer identity, where for Tambling it is the much more specific forms and effects of discourse during this particular moment in the formation of a disciplinary society that bring about this contradiction. An interesting question arises here concerning the authority of critical reading itself. For where both Brooks and Morris imply that no reading is exempt from the paradoxes that afflict the act of narrative writing in the novel, Tambling's account at least implies the possibility of a critical 'seeing-round' of the problem that both thwarts and enables the writing of *Great Expectations*, the possibility of grasping historically what in the other accounts remains merely an instance of the general ungraspability of the self and its languages.

D. A. Miller's account of *Bleak House* shares with Jeremy Tambling's essay a sense that the novels of Dickens can be seen as a powerful and anguished response to the growth of a disciplinary society, conceived in broadly Foucauldian terms both as the imposition from the outside of abstract or institutional power on the oppressed private individual and as the spontaneous conformity from within to the disciplining of society by the very forms and ideas of the private. For D. A. Miller, it is not the exercise of power on its victims that is the real problem, so much as the regulating force of the very distinctions between public and private, social and individual, law and impulse, · which in the nineteenth century were becoming so systematic. Like J. Hillis Miller in the discussion of *Bleak House* reprinted here, D. A. Miller sees a dark and troubling parallelism between form and content in *Bleak House*, between the terrifying endlessness of the Chancery suit that is its narrative subject and the conspicuous length and centrelessness of the narrative form – the fact that 'the representation of length goes on *at* length too' (p. 139). However, D. A. Miller distinguishes himself from J. Hillis Miller by suggesting that it is necessary not merely to note the congruity between the novel's own acts of interpretation and those that are its subject, but also to try to substantiate the historical particularity of this overlap. Thus, even when the novel does bring its complex and disjoined plot to a resolution, this too is to be read, not simply as the affirmation of authentic meaning and purpose in the face of the public world in which those principles are absent, but also as its mimicry of the bureaucratic procedures of Chancery. Even more disquieting is the substantial formal similarity between the novel and the public institution of the police. Miller finds in the congruence between the activities of the police and the processes of investigation, detection and exposure that make up the novel an impulse to order which cuts across the anti-institutional commitment to individual freedom in *Bleak House*. His judgement is that 'the novel's attempt to differentiate its own narrative procedures from those of the institutions it portrays falters, and the effort to disentangle itself from one institution only implicates it in another' (p. 146). Like Jeremy Tambling, therefore, Miller is concerned to investigate the contradiction whereby the very forms of the novel seem simultaneously to protest against and to confirm the operations of social and disciplinary power. In these and other essays, the Bakhtinian sense of the saturation of language by the social does not easily or reliably yield a principle of resistance in the indeterminacies of the novel's own forms or languages. The open-endedness of becoming that is the utopian warrant of the comic novel for Bakhtin, for example, is revealed in D. A. Miller's more wary and sceptical account of *Bleak House* as the very form of bureaucratic paralysis itself. The power of this reading rests rather in its capacity to balance the principle of resistance with the principle of power, or, more accurately perhaps, to remain alert to their mutual implication in one another.

Terry Eagleton's essay is similarly concerned with the ways in which the form of Dickens's novels is related to the social institutions and conditions they attempt to confront. The larger argument of which this is an extract analyses the various ways in which nineteenth- and early twentieth-century literary writing provided, or significantly failed to provide, the organic visions of society which Victorian capitalism increasingly found necessary – 'organic' here meaning self-forming, harmoniously balanced, generously inclusive and reconciling difference in unity. For Eagleton, the most significant fact about Dickens's writing is its failure to live up to these qualities in its own form. The jaggedness, the lopsidedness, the idiosyncrasy of Dickens's writing mark its subversive failure to provide forms of satisfying aesthetic wholeness which would resolve the historical self-divisions of bourgeois society that are Dickens's subject. At the same time, the increasing sense of design and control in Dickens's later work mimics the remorseless but paradoxically decentred systems of control that characterize this society in the later period, for the novels, like society itself, are built around systematic non-relationship, taking as their ordering principles disordering institutions and processes like the Circumlocution Office in *Little Dorrit*, Chancery in *Bleak House* or the elusive movements of investment capital in *Our Mutual Friend*.

One of the most important developments in recent critical theory has been the rise of a diversified range of feminist theories and, more recently, forms of theory and ways of reading concerned with the relations between gender, sexuality and discursive power. The most powerful and sophisticated readings of Dickens's work to have been generated from these two areas focus not so much upon the question of whether Dickens is to be credited with the creation of strong and believable female characters (on the whole, the answer to this question seems to be, not really), as on the ways in which the language and narrative forms of Dickens's novels correlate with the dispositions of gender power. Jean Ferguson Carr's essay suggests that one of the reasons that Dickens's work seemed to his contemporaries and to later readers to be worryingly excessive and undisciplined was that it aligned itself with what the nineteenth century had already distinguished and diminished as 'female' in language and cultural form: romance, melodrama, fancy, sensation, rather than the sterner, more necessary values of realism, truth, imagination and aesthetic discipline. Her essay goes on to measure the duplicity of this identification on Dickens's part. In one sense his work gives voice and visible form to the female experience that nineteenth-century dominant ideology relegated to the condition of the voiceless and formless. This is evident particularly in its association between women and deviant or irregular narrative modes, that 'mark breaks in discursive power' (p. 163), such as stuttering, concealment, allegory, silence and inarticulacy itself. But Dickens's attempt at 'writing as a woman' also appropriates that on to which it so generously opens. Read against the ideological conditions of mid-century, the complexity and overlayering of discourses and idioms in *Hard Times* is not in itself to be seen as a principle of resistance or renewal, as the sunnier kind of Bakhtinian reading might suggest. (Perhaps Roger Fowler's essay in this volume provides an example.) Rather, it must be read as a simultaneous relaxation and tightening of discursive power.

Eve Kosofsky Sedgwick's essay on *Our Mutual Friend* is equally concerned to enlarge the awareness of the dispositions of power. Her focus in this essay, and in *Between Men*, the book from which it is reprinted, is on the distribution and categorization of male sexuality, and especially the complex relations between the insistent, if disavowed, force of male homosocial and homosexual bonding on the one hand and 'normal' male desire on the other. In common with other writers represented in this volume, Sedgwick finds that sexuality in the nineteenth-century novel is to be understood in more dynamic terms than that of a representation of a given set of sociological conditions. Rather, the imagination and projection of sexual desire in narratives is a principal agency whereby desire is both instituted and socially regulated in the nineteenth century and beyond. Sedgwick focuses on the systematic points of connection between what otherwise may seem discrete concerns or thematic areas, especially the nature of male sexual identity and its relationship to class, to the mapping of the body and the energies and imperatives of capitalism and imperialism; for Dickens, she writes, 'the erotic fate of every female or male is also cast in the terms and propelled by the forces of class and economic accumulation' (p. 181). Sedgwick suggests that an organizing centre for the displaced networks of power in *Our Mutual Friend* is the quasi-homosexual relationship between Bradley Headstone and Eugene Wrayburn, a relationship that also mediates class and gender concerns, in the two characters' anxious rivalry over Lizzie Hexam, who is nevertheless not so much the object of male desire as the channel along which it communicates with itself. Sedgwick's essay comes close to D. A. Miller's analysis of the ways in which Dickens's novels replicate the disciplinary forms of the carceral society in its suggestion that *Our Mutual Friend* licenses a certain kind of irregularity of sexual desire and trajectory which is in the interests finally of power relations that diminish and entrap both women and men. For Sedgwick, as for Miller, that which exceeds propriety or official moral norms turns out sinisterly to end up confirming or dissimulating the force of those norms.

Economy and Excess

Sedgwick's approach also has some affinities with that of the two final pieces in this collection, which attempt in different ways to get to grips with the complex relations of economy and excess in Dickens's work. The excessiveness of Dickens's writing which, as we have seen, caused such problems to early readers of his work, manifests itself in the problematic overflowing of categories, the blurring of boundaries, and the promiscuous commingling of what official ideologies wish to promote as naturally distinct. Much contemporary criticism has been drawn to Dickens precisely because of this quality of overflow, the sense of a writing that exceeds or disrupts every coherent economy, or system of calculable relations. However, if such criticism celebrates the principle of excess in Dickens's writing, then it is also forced to take careful note of the ways in which the unbounded 'energetics' of Dickens's writing also shadow and simulate the actions of economic processes during the period of burgeoning industrial capitalism in the nineteenth century, and especially its capacity to render everything exchangeable for everything else, and thus to undermine every fixed distinction. The last two essays in this collection share a concern with the 'economics of narration', as it might be called; a concern with the ways in which narrative itself is drawn into the economic processes which are so often its subject – accumulation, investment, circulation, exchange, expenditure, and so on – as well as the ways in which the novels seem to attempt to resist or transcend the condition of the economic.

John Kucich is drawn to *Our Mutual Friend* because of the paradoxes the novel develops with regard to the question of economy. Kucich bases his analysis on the work of the French philosopher, novelist and cultural analyst, Georges Bataille, who spent a lifetime arguing for the centrality in human life of the principles of excess, intensity, expenditure, negativity and waste as against the more prudent principles of accumulation, profit and conservation of value. Kucich argues that Dickens's novels are generated out of a conflict between what Bataille calls the 'restricted economy' based on the idea of gain and conservation and the less governable splendours and excesses of a 'general economy' which is orientated towards the gratuitous intensity of pure expenditure. Kucich argues that Dickens has a shrewd sense of the deep and systematic complicity between the seeming opposites of violence and repression; *Our Mutual Friend*, for example, sees death, waste and violence not as the opposite, or the simple exterior, of social order and economic utility, but its central principle, death and murder in this novel being a 'financial event'. Against such repressive enlargement of regimes of economic thinking, Kucich discerns within Dickens's writing a desire for excess, or excessive desire, for forms of pure and unrecuperable intensity, instanced for example in violent self-dissolution. Unlike D. A. Miller, Jeremy Tambling and Eve Kosofsky Sedgwick, therefore, Kucich is prepared to see Dickens's novels pushing out of the suffocating circuits of power which turn every form of resistance into a mode of discipline.

My own essay focuses on the relations between politics and space in Dickens's *Barnaby Rudge*. Like other essays in the collection, it attempts to explore the ways in which Dickens's work both represents and replicates dispositions of power. Here the question of power is seen in terms particularly of the question of how to regulate the thronged, self-transforming space of the city. For Dickens, the city is a place in which conventional relations of places to each other, and the social and political orderings that these enact, are both confirmed and threatened with dissolution. The city is the place in which the syntax of place undergoes systematic disturbance, as increasingly through the 1830s, the space of the city is experienced as being *in production*. In his historical account of the Gordon Riots of some 40 years previously, Dickens shows himself fascinated with the convulsions in social space produced under the conditions of riot. His treatment of space in the novel, however, suggests both a conservative desire to defend the regularity of relations between places and a deep and fascinated attentiveness to the riotousness of space itself. The system of space in this novel can also be read in the economic terms employed in Kucich's essay; for, in *Barnaby Rudge*, space is both a regularly and productively organized economy of dynamic differences, and also subject to sudden structural spasms in the very distinctions which are necessary to maintain the functioning of such an economy. Dickens's novel is produced as a kind of simulation of the process whereby the ordered economy of spaces and places is 'systematically' exceeded or deranged.

After Dickens

It would be easy to fall into that form of cultural narcissism which suggests that contemporary theory has at last got Dickens to add up, that the languages and analytic instruments of contemporary modes of thinking about the literary text make us able to avoid the errors, excesses and psychopathological lapses of earlier less-informed critics. In fact, however, it is my sense that what the various contemporary critical approaches to Dickens have been enabled to do is to articulate more clearly the kind of problem that Dickens represents for criticism as such. The effect of this is to make that problem not so much a trauma, to be denied, made up for, or in some way made good in the act of criticism, as an inaugurating opportunity, that makes it possible and necessary for criticism to concern itself in turn with its own nature, values and effects as they bear on the question and the fertile problem that is Dickens. In particular, many of the readings contained in this collection concentrate upon the ways in which the novels of Dickens are concerned with and restlessly enquire into the conditions, powers and effects of their own forms and language; constitute, precisely, the attempt to develop narrative forms which explore the desire and thwarting of the desire for narrative forms. These essays are concerned neither exactly with the force of Dickens's writing, nor exclusively with their form, but with reading the difficulty and significance of the struggle to fix or determine the form of meaning; with reading the force of form.

If I were asked to specify the most productive directions in which Dickens criticism might proceed in the future, I would say that criticism needs now to interrogate the particular histories of the cultural perplexity that Dickens represents for his audiences, professional and non-professional. For the excessiveness of Dickens is not a matter merely of his texts or their forms. Dickens has a centrality in British and English-speaking cultural life partly because, as the first mass-circulation author, his value has never been wholly in the keeping of academic institutions or professional critics. No doubt, this sense of the vulgarity of Dickens's craving for the popular, the sense of the unmasterable spreading of his work outwards from the organizing grasp of cultural legislators of all kinds, is at the bottom of the particular and tenacious problem that Dickens has represented for criticism and the elite culture in whose service it has come ambivalently to act. Like the work of Shakespeare, Dickens's work absconds from or is hijacked out of the safe and manageable condition of textual embodiment, leaking outwards into ideology and mythology, into cultural revision, adaptation and reappropriation. The fact that Dickens himself was the first entrepreneur in the Dickens industry, marketing his own image and product through his public readings in the last years of his life, makes it hard to see this process simply as the corruption of the market-place violating the original integrity of the aesthetic work.

This point of view would suggest that we need to pay more attention not merely to Dickens's work, considered as a completed and authorized oeuvre, but also and especially to the particular kinds of cultural and ideological work that Dickens's work has been made to do over the century and half since it first began to appear. The centrality of Dickens in British cultural life has had a great deal to do, for example, with the use made of his work at different levels of the educational system, to mark and ritually to effect a transition from childhood to adulthood, from illiteracy to literacy, from popular to official culture. The mixed cultural condition of Dickens's work is what allows it both to open and guard the gate of cultural belonging. The uneasiness about precisely these and related questions within the texts is damped and formalized by the use of the texts themselves to facilitate or impede an irreversible passage upwards into identity, mastery and cultural belonging. One might extend this analysis to the reworkings, adaptations and travesties of Dickens into every conceivable form, dramatic and visual, which have taken place since the moment of their appearance, to take account of the complex and conflicted meanings which these works are made to bear and perhaps in themselves determine. This is perhaps the principal sense in which Dickens's works fail to add up, or be identical with themselves. These works resist every attempt to intern them in the unity or closure of a completed text, an authorial oeuvre, or the total recall of an idealized critical reading, because they are always elsewhere than in themselves, always otherwise than *an sich*. His works begin as texts, but almost instantly became 'culture-texts', to borrow a phrase coined by Paul Davis in his study of the different adaptations, parodies and piracies of Dickens's *A Christmas Carol*.[39] As Virginia Woolf observes in her review of a reissue of *David Copperfield*, Dickens's works are so much 'an institution, a monument, a public thoroughfare trodden dusty by a million feet' that it is hard to say when any of Dickens's novels are read for the first time; all readings of Dickens are, from the beginning, rereadings.[40] If in one sense Dickens's work marks the point of division between high art and popular or mass culture, between the aesthetic and the mythical-ideological, then, in another sense, that work evidences the necessary and inescapable liaisons and conflicts between those separated cultural territories. The value of the work lies precisely in the ways in which it refuses to be assimilated wholly and entirely to any of the cultural programmes which it so irresistibly attracts; it is precisely because Dickens has been made to mean so much and so many different things culturally and politically that his work solicits an intense and historically self-aware investigation of the very nature of culture and politics, and the relations of reading and interpretation to them.

Notes

1. *The Diaries of Franz Kafka*, ed. MAX BROD (Harmondsworth: Penguin, 1972), p. 388.
2. HENRY JAMES, 'Our Mutual Friend', in *The House of Fiction: Essays on the Novel by Henry James*, ed. LEON EDEL (London: Rupert Hart-Davis, 1957), p. 255.
3. A. C. SWINBURNE, *Charles Dickens* (London: Chatto and Windus, 1913), p. 45.
4. WALTER BAGEHOT, 'Charles Dickens' (1858), reprinted in *Literary Studies*, 2 vols, 2nd edn. (London: Longmans, Green and Co., 1879), Vol. 2, p. 197.
5. JAMES, 'Our Mutual Friend', p. 254.
6. Ibid.
7. MARGARET OLIPHANT, 'Sensation Novels', *Blackwood's Edinburgh Magazine*, 91 (May, 1862), p. 575.
8. *The English Novel: Form and Function* (New York: Holt, Rinehart and Winston, 1953), p. 128.
9. Ibid., p. 131.
10. *The Craft of Fiction* (London: Jonathan Cape, 1921), p. 213.
11. Ibid., pp. 213–4.
12. Ibid., p. 216.
13. LIONEL TRILLING, *The Opposing Self: Nine Essays in Fiction* (London: Secker and Warburg, 1953), p. 64.
14. Ibid.
15. Ibid.
16. W. J. HARVEY, *Character and the Novel* (London: Chatto and Windus, 1965), p. 90.
17. G. K. CHESTERTON, *Charles Dickens* (London: Methuen, 1906), pp. 78, 80.
18. Ibid., pp. 80–1.
19. Quoted in F. R. LEAVIS and Q. D. LEAVIS, *Dickens the Novelist* (London: Chatto and Windus, 1973), p. viii. References hereafter in the text.
20. I have attempted to follow through some of the forms and consequences of this identification between Gradgrindery and Dickens's own writing in *Charles Dickens* (Oxford: Basil Blackwell, 1985), pp. 89–106.
21. *History of English Literature*, trans. H. VAN LAUN, 2 vols (Edinburgh: Edmonston and Douglas, 1871), vol. 2, p. 344.
22. '*David Copperfield*', in *Collected Essays*, vol. 1 (London: Hogarth Press, 1968), p. 193.
23. Ibid.
24. *Dickens the Novelist*, p. ix.
25. TRILLING, *The Opposing Self*, pp. 63–4.
26. 'Dickens: The Two Scrooges', *The Wound and the Bow: Seven Studies in Literature*

(Cambridge, Mass.: Houghton Mifflin, 1941), p. 102. References hereafter in the text.

27. JOHN FORSTER, *The Life of Charles Dickens* (London: Chapman and Hall, 1879), p. 624.

28. *Charles Dickens: The World of His Novels* (Bloomington and London: Indiana University Press, 1969), p. x.

29. Ibid., pp. 10, 9.

30. *The Dickens Theatre: A Reassessment of the Novels* (Oxford: Clarendon Press, 1965), p. 9.

31. JULIAN MOYNAHAN, 'The Hero's Guilt: The Case of *Great Expectations*', *Essays in Criticism*, 10 (1960), pp. 60–79.

32. *Unto This Last* (1862), in *The Works of John Ruskin*, ed. E. T. COOK and A. WEDDERBURN (London: Grant Allen, 1903–12), vol. 17, p. 31.

33. GEORGE BERNARD SHAW, 'Preface' to Charles Dickens, *Great Expectations* (Edinburgh: R. and R. Clark, 1937), p. ix.

34. Ibid., p. xi.

35. *The Historical Novel*, trans. HANNAH and STANLEY MITCHELL (London: Merlin Press, 1962), p. 244.

36. ARNOLD KETTLE, *An Introduction to the English Novel: Vol 1, To George Eliot* (London: Hutchinson, 1951), p. 125.

37. Ibid., p. 127.

38. *Culture and Society 1780–1950* (Harmondsworth: Penguin, 1963), p. 107.

39. *The Life and Times of Ebenezer Scrooge* (New Haven: Yale University Press, 1990), pp. 3–15. Davis offers 'a celebratory history, one that affirms the excesses of our collective imagination and recognizes all the versions of the Carol as manifestations of an ongoing myth in the consciousness of the industrial era', but misses the opportunity, I think, to examine the significance of the struggles for ownership and the fracturing of collective consciousness that are enacted through the 'culture-text' of *A Christmas Carol*, powerfully cohering though its cultural force may be.

40. WOOLF, *'David Copperfield'*, p. 192; see also pp. 191, 195.

2 Repetition, Repression, and Return: The Plotting of *Great Expectations*

PETER BROOKS*

Peter Brooks is Professor of Comparative Literature at Yale University. He was associated for a time with the Yale school of deconstructive critics, having been taught by Paul de Man; he was joint editor, with Shoshana Felman and J. Hillis Miller, of *The Lesson of Paul de Man* (New Haven: Yale University Press, 1985). His work shows the close attentiveness to the powers of language and rhetoric characteristic of the 'Yale' critics, but his most distinctive contribution has been in his work on the powers and functions of narrative. In a series of works, from *The Novel of Worldliness: Crébillon, Marivaux, Laclos, Stendhal* (Princeton: Princeton University Press, 1969), to *The Melodramatic Imagination: Balzac, Henry James, Melodrama and the Modes of Excess* (New Haven: Yale University Press, 1976) and, more recently, *Reading for the Plot: Design and Intention in Narrative* (Oxford: Clarendon Press, 1984), *Body Work: Objects of Desire in Modern Narrative* (Cambridge, Mass.: Harvard University Press, 1993) and *Psychoanalysis and Storytelling* (Oxford: Blackwell, 1994), Peter Brooks has combined the rigour and clarity of narratological analysis with the more ambitious enquiries into the nature of the self conducted in contemporary psychoanalysis. The essay reprinted below focuses on a category of organisation which critics have tended to ignore or dismiss as part of the exterior mechanics of narrative, namely the question of plot. It does so in order to show that plotting, in all its operative senses, is a matter not just of the ways in which events are connected and developed in the novel, but is also a central preoccupation of the narrative's central character. In an eerie *mise en abîme*, the 'plot' of *Great Expectations* is shown by Brooks to be powered precisely by the desire to establish and sustain a 'plot', which is to say, a coherent narrative of the origin, growth and continuance of the narrating subject. Drawing deeply on Freud's account in *Beyond the Pleasure Principle* of the way in which individual subjects bind and channel painful or unmasterably

---

*Reprinted from *Reading for the Plot: Design and Intention in Narrative* (Oxford: Clarendon Press, 1984), pp. 115–42.

diverse energies into the form of narrative progression or repetitive closure, Brooks's essay coaxes narrative theory into striking cooperation with psychoanalytic theory. The great innovation and reward of this kind of analysis lies in the fact that it is able to discuss the psychic dynamics of repression, repetition and so on, without assuming them to be the mere symptoms, impressed unconsciously upon the text, of a particular psychopathology, whether of a character, or of Dickens himself. The complex dynamics of desire and concealment analysed by Brooks belong both to the individual psyche and to the structure of the novel, insofar as the action of reading draws the reader, resisting and cooperating at once (for, given that the text mimes various kinds of resistance, resistance must here *be* a certain kind of cooperation), into the field of those dynamics.

I

Great Expectations is exemplary for a discourse on plot in many respects, not least of all for its beginning. For what the novel chooses to present at its outset is precisely the search for a beginning. As in so many nineteenth-century novels, the hero is an orphan, thus undetermined by any visible inheritance, apparently unauthored. This clears away Julien Sorel's problems with paternity. There may be sociological and sentimental reasons to account for the high incidence of orphans in the nineteenth-century novel, but clearly the parentless protagonist frees an author from struggle with preexisting authorities, allowing him to create afresh all the determinants of plot within his text. He thus profits from what Gide called the 'lawlessness' of the novel by starting with an undefined, rule-free character and then bringing the law to bear upon him – creating the rules – as the text proceeds. With Pip, Dickens begins as it were with a life that is for the moment precedent to plot, and indeed necessarily in search of plot. Pip when we first see him is himself in search of the 'authority' – the word stands in the second paragraph of the novel – that would define and justify – authorize – the plot of his ensuing life.

The 'authority' to which Pip refers here is that of the tombstone which bears the names of his dead parents, the names that have already been displaced, condensed, and superseded in the first paragraph, where Pip describes how his 'infant tongue' (literally, a speechless tongue: a catachresis that points to a moment of emergence, of entry into language) could only make of the name, Philip Pirrip, left to him by the dead parents, the monosyllabic Pip. 'So, I called myself Pip, and came to be called Pip.'[1] This originating moment of

Pip's narration and his narrative is a self-naming that already subverts whatever authority could be found in the text of the tombstones. The process of reading that text is described by Pip the narrator as 'unreasonable,' in that it interprets the appearance of the lost father and mother from the shape of the letters of their names. The tracing of the name – which he has already distorted in its application to self – involves a misguided attempt to remotivate the graphic symbol, to make it directly mimetic, mimetic specifically of origin. Loss of origin, misreading, and the problematic of identity are bound up here in ways we will further explore later on. The question of reading and writing – of learning to compose and to decipher texts – is persistently thematized in the novel.[2]

The decipherment of the tombstone text as confirmation of loss of origin – as unauthorization – is here at the start of the novel the prelude to Pip's *cogito*, the moment in which his consciousness seizes his existence as other, alien, forlorn:

> My first most vivid and broad impression of the identity of things seems to me to have been gained on a memorable raw afternoon towards evening. At such a time I found out for certain, that this bleak place overgrown with nettles was the churchyard; and that Philip Pirrip, late of this parish, and also Georgiana, wife of the above, were dead and buried; and that Alexander, Bartholomew, Abraham, Tobias, and Roger, infant children of the aforesaid, were also dead and buried; and that the dark flat wilderness beyond the churchyard, intersected with dykes and mounds and gates, with scattered cattle feeding on it, was the marshes; and that the low leaden line beyond was the river; and that the distant savage lair from which the wind was rushing, was the sea; and that the small bundle of shivers growing afraid of it all and beginning to cry, was Pip.
> 'Hold your noise!' cried a terrible voice . . . (p. 1)

The repeated verbs of existence – 'was' and 'were' – perform an elementary phenomenology of Pip's world, locating its irreducible objects and leading finally to the individual subject as other, as aware of his existence through the emotion of fear, fear that then appears as the origin of voice, or articulated sound, as Pip begins to cry: a cry that is immediately censored by the command of the convict Magwitch, the father-to-be, the fearful intrusive figure of future authorship who will demand of Pip: 'Give us your name.'

The scenario is rightly suggestive of the problem of identity, self-consciousness, naming, and language that will accompany Pip throughout the novel, and points to the original decentering of the subject in regard to himself. For purposes of my study of plot, it is important to note how this beginning establishes Pip as an existence without a plot, at the very moment of occurrence of that event which will prove to be decisive for the plotting of his existence, as he will discover only two-thirds of the way through the novel. Alien, unauthorized, self-named, at the point of entry into the language code and the social systems it implies, Pip will in the first part of the novel be in search of a plot, and the novel will recount the gradual precipitation of a sense of plot around him, the creation of portents of direction and intention.

Schematically, we can identify four lines of plot that begin to crystallize around the young Pip, the Pip of Part 1, before the arrival of his 'Expectations':

1. Communion with the convict/criminal deviance.
2. Naterally wicious/bringing up by hand.
3. The dream of Satis House/the fairy tale.
4. The nightmare of Satis House/the witch tale.

These plots, we will see in a moment, are paired as follows: 2/1 = 3/4. That is, there is in each case an 'official' and censoring plot standing over a 'repressed' plot. In terms of Pip's own choices, we could rewrite the formula: 3/4/2/1, to show (in accordance with one of Freud's favorite models) the archaeological layering of strata of repressed material.[3] When the Expectations are announced by Jaggers at the end of part one, they will apparently coincide with Pip's choices ('My dream was out; my wild fancy was surpassed by sober reality' [Chapter 18, p. 130]), and will thus appear to take care of the question of plot. But this will be so only on the level of official plots; the Expectations will in fact only mask further the problem of the repressed plots.

I choose the term 'communion' for the first plot because its characteristic symbolic gesture is Pip's pity for the convict as he swallows the food Pip has brought him, a moment of sympathetic identification which focuses a series of suggestive sympathies and identifications with the outlaw: the bread and butter that Pip puts down his leg, which makes him walk like the chained convict; Mrs Joe's belief that he is on his way to the Hulks; Pip's flight from the Christmas dinner table into the arms of a soldier holding out handcuffs, to give a few examples. Pip is concerned to assure 'his' convict that he is not responsible for his recapture, a point he conveys in a mute exchange of glances which the convict understands and which leads him to make a public statement in exoneration of Pip, taking responsibility for stealing the food. This in turn provokes an overt statement of community with the outlaw, which comes from Joe: 'We don't know what you have done, but we wouldn't have you starved to death for it, poor miserable fellow-creature. – Would us, Pip?' (Chapter 5, p. 36).

The fellowship with the convict here stated by Joe will remain with Pip, but in a state of repression, as what he will later call 'that spell of my childhood' (Chapter 16, p. 114) – an unavowable memory. It finds its official, adult, repressive version in the conviction – shared by all the adults in Pip's life, with the exception of the childlike Joe – that children are naturally depraved and need to be corrected, kept in line with the Tickler, brought up by hand lest their natural willfulness assert itself in plots that are deviant, transgressive. Pumblechook and the Hubbles, in their Christmas dinner dialogue, give the theme a choric statement:

> 'Especially,' said Mr Pumblechook, 'be grateful, boy, to them which brought you up by hand.'
>
> Mrs Hubble shook her head, and contemplating me with a mournful presentiment that I should come to no good, asked, 'Why is it that the young are never grateful?' This moral mystery seemed too much for the company until Mr Hubble tersely solved it by saying, 'Naterally wicious.' Everybody then murmured 'True!' and looked at me in a particularly unpleasant and personal manner. (Chapter 4, pp. 22–23)

The 'nateral wiciousness' of children legitimates communion with the outlaw, but legitimates it as that which must be repressed, forced into other plots – including, as we shall see, 'binding' Pip as an apprentice.

The dream of Satis House is properly a daydream, in which 'His Majesty, the Ego' pleasures himself with the phantasy of social ascension and gentility. Miss Havisham is made to play the role of Fairy Godmother, her crutch become a magic wand, explicitly evoked twice near the close of part 1.[4] This plot has adult sanction; its first expression comes from Pumblechook and Mrs Joe when they surmise that Miss Havisham intends to 'do something' for Pip, and Pip comes to believe in it, so that when the 'Expectations' arrive he accepts them as the logical fulfillment of the daydream, of his 'longings'. Yet to identify Satis House with the daydream is to perform a repression of all else that Satis House suggests and represents – all that clusters around the central emblem of the rotting bride cake and its crawling things. The craziness and morbidity of Satis House repose on desire fixated, become fetishistic and sadistic, on a deviated eroticism that has literally shut out the light, stopped the clocks, and made the forward movement of plot impossible. Satis House, as the circular journeys of the wheelchair to the rhythm of the blacksmith's song 'Old Clem' may best suggest, constitutes repetition without variation, pure reproduction, a collapsed metonymy where cause and effect have become identical, the same-as-same. It is significant that when Pip returns from his first visit to Satis House, he responds to the interrogations of Pumblechook and Mrs Joe with an elaborate lie – the story of the coach, the flags, the dogs fighting for 'weal cutlets' from a silver basket – a phantasy that we can read as his response to what he calls a 'smart without a name, that needed counteraction' (Chapter 8, p. 57). All the attempts to read Satis House as a text speaking of gentility and social ascension may be subverted from the outset, in the passage that describes Pip's first impression of Miss Havisham:

> It was not in the first few moments that I saw all these things, though I saw more of them in the first moments than might be supposed. But, I saw that everything within my view which ought to be white, had been white long ago, and had lost its lustre, and was faded and yellow. I saw that the bride within the bridal dress had withered like the dress, and like the flowers, and had no brightness left but the brightness of her sunken eyes. I saw that the dress had been put upon the rounded figure of a young woman, and that the figure upon which it now hung loose, had shrunk to skin and bone. Once, I had been taken to see some ghastly waxwork at the Fair, representing I know not what impossible personage lying in state. Once, I had been taken to one of our old marsh churches to see a skeleton in the ashes of a rich dress, that had been dug out of a vault under the church pavement. Now, waxwork and skeleton seemed to have dark eyes that moved and looked at me. I should have cried out, if I could. (Chapter 8, p. 53)

The passage records the formation of a memory trace from a moment of unmastered horror, itself formed in repetition of moments of past visual impression, a trace that forces its way through the mind without being grasped by consciousness and is refused outlet in a cry. Much later in the novel, Pip – and also Miss Havisham herself – will have to deal with the return of this repressed.

We have, then, a quadripartite scheme of plots, organized into two pairs, each with an 'official' plot, or interpretation of plot, standing over a repressed plot. The scheme may lead us in the first instance to reflect on the place of repression as one of the large 'orders' of the novel. Repression plays a dominant role in the theme of education which is so important to the novel, from Mrs Joe's bringing up by hand, through Mrs Wopsle's aunt's school-room, to Mr Pocket's career as a 'grinder' of dull blades (while his own children meanwhile are 'tumbling up'). Bringing up by hand in turn suggests Jaggers's hands, representation of accusation and the law, which in turn suggest all the instances of censorship in the name of high authorities evoked from the first scene of the novel onward: censorship is repression in the name of the Law.[5] Jaggers's sinister hand-washings point to the omnipresent taint of Newgate, which echoes the earlier presence of the Hulks, to which Mrs Joe verbally assigns Pip. Then there is the moment when Pip is 'bound' as apprentice blacksmith before the magistrates, in a scene of such repressive appearance that a well-meaning philanthropist is moved to hand Pip a pamphlet entitled *To Be Read in My Cell*. There is a constant association of education, repression, the threat of prison, criminality, the fear of deviance. We might note in passing Dickens's capacity to literalize the metaphors of education – 'bringing up by hand', 'grinding' – in a manner that subverts the order that ought to assure their figural validity. The particularly sinister version of the *Bildungsroman* presented by *Great Expectations* derives in some measure from the literalization of metaphors pertaining to education and upbringing. Societal repression and censorship are, of course, reinforced by Pip's own, his internalization of the law and the denial of what he calls the 'old taint' of his association with the criminal. The whole theme of gentility, as represented by the Finches of the Grove, for instance, or the punishment of Trabb's boy, consistently suggests an aggressivity based on denial. One could reflect here on the splendid name of Pip's superfluous valet: the Avenger.

The way in which the Expectations are instituted, in seeming realization of the Satis House dream, comprehends 'bringing up by hand' (the other official plot) in that it includes the disciplines necessary to gentility: grinding with Mr Pocket, lessons in manners from Herbert, learning to spend one's time and money in appropriate gentlemanly pursuits. There is in this manner a blurring of plot lines, useful to the processes of wish fulfillment in that education and indeed repression itself can be interpreted as agencies necessary to the pursuit of the dream. Realization of the dream permits acceptance of society's interpretations, and in fact requires the abandonment of any effort at personal interpretation: Pip is now enjoined from seeking to know more about the intentions of his donor, disallowed the role of detective which so much animates him in part three of the novel – when the Expectations have proved false – and is already incipiently present in part one.

Taking our terminology from the scene where Pip is bound as apprentice, we may consider that education and repression operate in the novel as one form of 'binding': official ways of channeling and tying up the mobile energies of life. It is notable that after he has become apprenticed to Joe, Pip goes through a stage of purely iterative existence – presented in chapter 14 – where the direction and movement of plot appear to be finished, where all life's 'interest and romance' appear shut out as by a 'thick curtain', time reduced to repetitive duration. Conversely, when the Expectations have arrived, Miss Havisham is apparently identified as the fairy-tale donor, and the Satis House plot appears securely bound, Pip need only wait for the next stage of the plot to become manifest. Yet it is clear that for the reader neither binding as an apprentice (the first accomplishment of an upbringing by hand) nor the tying up of Satis House as a fairy-tale plot constitutes valid and adequate means of dealing with and disposing of the communion with the convict and the nightmare of Satis House. The energy released in the text by its liminary 'primal scene' – in the graveyard – and by the early visits to Satis House, creating that 'smart without a name,' simply is not and cannot be bound by the bindings of the official, repressive plots. As readers we know that there has been created in the text an intensive level of energy that cannot be discharged through these official plots.

In fact, the text has been working simultaneously to bind these disavowed energies in other ways, ways over which Pip's ego, and the societal superego, have no control, and of which they have no knowledge, through repetitions that, for the reader, prepare an inevitable return of the repressed. Most striking are the periodic fragmentary returns of the convict-communion material: the leg iron used to bludgeon Mrs Joe, guns firing from the Hulks to signal further escapes, and especially the reappearance of Joe's file, the dramatic stage property used by Magwitch's emissary in a 'proceeding in dumb show . . . pointedly addressed at me'. His stirring and tasting his rum and water 'pointedly at' Pip suggests the establishment of an aim (Pip calls his proceeding 'a shot'), a direction, an intention in Pip's life: the first covert announcement of another plot which will come to govern Pip's life, but of course misinterpreted as to its true aim. With the nightmare energies of Satis House, binding may be at work in those repetitive journeys around the rotting bridal cake, suggestive of the reproduction or working through of the traumatic neurotic whose affects remain fixed on the past, on the traumatic moment that never can be mastered. For Miss Havisham herself, these energies can never be plotted to effective discharge; and we will have occasion to doubt whether they are ever fully bound for Pip as well. The compulsive reproductive repetition that characterizes every detail of Satis House lets us perceive how the returns of the convict-communion suggest a more significant working through of an unmastered past, a repetition that can alter the form of the repeated. In both instances – but ultimately with different results – the progressive, educative plots, the plots of repression and social advancement, are threatened by a repetitive process obscurely going on underneath and beyond them. We sense that forward progress will have to recover markings from the beginning through a dialectic of return.

II

In my references to the work of repetition as the binding of energies, I have been implicitly assuming that one can make a transfer from the model of psychic functioning proposed in *Beyond the Pleasure Principle* to the literary text, an assumption that no doubt can never be 'proved' and must essentially find its justification in the illumination it can bring to texts. We saw in Chapter 2 [of *Reading for the Plot*] that texts represent themselves as inhabited by energies, which are ultimately images of desire, and correspond to the arousals, expectations, doubts, suspense, reversals, revaluations, disappointments, embarrassments, fulfillments, and even the incoherences animated by reading. If we can accept the idea of a textual energetics, we can see that in any well-plotted novel the energies released and aroused in the text, especially in its early moments, will not be lost: the text is a kind of thermodynamic plenum, obeying the law of the conservation of energy (as well, no doubt, as the law of entropy). Repetition is clearly a major operative principle of the system, shaping energy, giving it perceptible form, form that the text and the reader can work with in the construction of thematic wholes and narrative orders. Repetition conceived as binding, the creation of cohesion – see the French translation of Freud's *Verbindung: liaison*, a word we would commonly use in the description of discourse and argument – may allow us to see how the text and the reader put energy into forms where it can be mastered, both by the logics set in motion by the plot, and by interpretive effort.

Repetition is, of course, a complex phenomenon, and one that has its history of commentary in philosophical as well as psychoanalytic thought. Is repetition sameness or difference? To repeat evidently implies resemblance, yet can we speak of resemblance unless there is difference? Without difference, repetition would be identity, which would not usually appear to be the case, if only because the

chronological context of the repeated occurrence differs from that of
the 'original' occurrence (the 'original' is thus a concept that
repetition puts into question). In this sense, repetition always includes
the idea of variation in time, and may ever be potentially a
progressive act. As Kierkegaard writes near the beginning of
Repetition, 'Repetition and recollection are the same movement, only
in opposite directions; for what is recollected has been, is repeated
backwards, whereas repetition properly is repeated forwards.'[6]
Freud, as we noted, considers repetition to be a form of recollection,
brought into play when conscious mental rememoration has been
blocked by repression. Lacan argues that Freud distinguishes between
repeating (*wiederholen*) and reproducing (*reproduzieren*): reproduction
would be the full reliving, of the original traumatic scene, for instance,
that Freud aimed at early in his career, when he still believed in
'catharsis'; whereas repetition always takes place in the realm of the
symbolic – in the transference, in language – where the affects and
figures of the past are confronted in symbolic form.[7] We can thus
perhaps say that for Freud repetition is a symbolic enactment
referring back to unconscious determinants, progressive in that it
belongs to the forward thrust of desire and is known by way of
desire's workings in the signifying chain, but regressive in its points
of reference.

We cannot and should not attempt to reduce and resolve the
ambiguities of repetition since they are indeed inherent to our
experience of repetition, part of what creates its 'uncanny' effect and
allows us to think about the intractable problem of temporal form,
in our lives and in our fictions. In *Great Expectations*, the repetitions
associated with Satis House, particularly as played out by Miss
Havisham herself, suggest the reproductive in that they aim to restore
in all its detail the traumatic moment – recorded by the clocks
stopped at twenty minutes to nine – when erotic wishes were abruptly
foreclosed by Compeyson's rupture of faith. On the other hand, the
repetitions of the convict material experienced by Pip all imply
something to come – something to come that, as we shall see, will
take him back, painfully, to the primal scene, yet take him back in
the context of difference. Repetition in the text is a return, a calling
back or a turning back. And as I suggested earlier, repetitions are
thus both returns to and returns of: for instance, returns to origins
and returns of the repressed, moving us forward in Pip's journey
toward elucidation, disillusion, and maturity by taking us back, as
if in obsessive reminder that we cannot really move ahead until we
have understood that still enigmatic past, yet ever pushing us
forward, since revelation, tied to the past, belongs to the future.

The novelistic middle, which is perhaps the most difficult of

Aristotle's 'parts' of a plot to talk about, is in this case notably characterized by the return. Quite literally: it is Pip's repeated returns from London to his home town that constitute the organizing device of the whole of the London period, the time of the Expectations and their aftermath. Pip's returns are always ostensibly undertaken to make reparation to the neglected Joe, an intention never realized; and always implicitly an attempt to discover the intentions of the putative donor in Satis House, to bring her plot to completion. Yet the returns also always bring his regression, in Satis House, to the status of the 'coarse and common boy' (Chapter 29, p. 222) whose social ascension is hallucinatorily denied, his return to the nightmare of unprogressive repetition; and, too, a revival of the repressed convict association, the return of the childhood spell. Each return suggests that Pip's official plots, which seem to speak of progress, ascent, and the satisfaction of desire, are in fact subject to a process of repetition of the yet unmastered past, the true determinant of his life's direction.

The pattern of the return is established in Pip's first journey back from London, in Chapter 28. His decision to visit Joe is quickly thrown into the shade by the presence on the stagecoach of two convicts, one of whom Pip recognizes as the man of the file and the rum and water, Magwitch's emissary. There is a renewed juxtaposition of official, genteel judgment on the convicts, voiced by Herbert Pocket – 'What a vile and degraded spectacle' – and Pip's inward avowal that he feels sympathy for their alienation. On the roof of the coach, seated in front of the convicts, Pip dozes off while pondering whether he ought to restore the two one-pound notes that the convict of the file had passed him so many years before. Upon regaining consciousness, the first two words he hears, continuing his dream thoughts, are: 'Two one-pound notes'. There follows the convict's account of his embassy from 'Pip's convict' to the boy who had saved him. Although Pip is certain that the convict cannot recognize him, so changed in age, circumstance, and even name (since Herbert Pocket calls him 'Handel'), the dreamlike experience forces a kind of recognition of a forgotten self, refound in fear and pain.

> I could not have said what I was afraid of, for my fear was altogether undefined and vague, but there was a great fear upon me. As I walked on to the hotel, I felt that a dread, much exceeding the mere apprehension of a painful or disagreeable recognition, made me tremble. I am confident that it took no distinctness of shape, and that it was the revival for a few minutes of the terror of childhood. (Chapter 28, p. 217)

The return to origins has led to the return of the repressed, and vice versa. Repetition as return becomes a reproduction and reenactment of infantile experience: not simply a recall of the primal moment, but a reliving of its pain and terror, suggesting the impossibility of escape from the originating scenarios of childhood, the condemnation forever to replay them.

This first example may stand for the other returns of the novel's middle, which all follow the same pattern, which all double return to with return of and show Pip's ostensible progress in the world to be subverted by the irradicable presence of the convict-communion and the Satis House nightmare. It is notable that toward the end of the middle – as the novel's dénouement approaches – there is an acceleration in the rhythm of these returns, as if to affirm that all the clues to Pip's future, the forward movement of his plot, in fact lie in the past. Repetition as return speaks as a textual version of the death instinct, plotting the text, beyond the seeming dominance of the pleasure principle, towards its proper end, imaging this end as necessarily a time before the beginning. In the moment of crisis before the climax of the novel's action, Pip is summoned back to the marshes associated with his infancy to face extinction at the hands of Orlick – who has throughout the novel acted the role of Pip's 'bad double,' a hateful and sadistic version of the hero – in a threatened short-circuit of the text, as Pip indicates when he thinks how he will be misunderstood by others if he dies prematurely, without explanation: 'Misremembered after death . . . despised by unborn generations' (Chapter 53, p. 404).[8] Released from this threat, Pip attempts to escape from England, but even this voyage out to another land and another life leads him back: the climax of Magwitch's discovery and recapture are played out in the Thames estuary, where 'it was like my own marsh country, flat and monotonous, and with a dim horizon' (Chapter 54, p. 416). We are back in the horizontal perspectives and muddy tidal flats that are so much a part of our perception of the childhood Pip.

But before speaking further of resolutions, I must say a word about the novel's great 'recognition scene,' the moment at which the latent becomes manifest, the repressed convict plot is forcibly brought to consciousness, a scene that decisively re-enacts both a return of the repressed and a return to the primal moment of childhood. The recognition scene comes in chapter 39, and it is preceded by two curious paragraphs at the end of chapter 38 in which Pip as narrator suggests that the pages he has just written, concerning his frustrated courtship of Estella, constitute, on the plane of narration itself, a last binding of that plot in its overt version, as a plot of romance, and that now he must move on to a deeper level of plot – reaching further back – which subsumes as it subverts all the other plots of the novel: 'All the work, near and afar, that tended to the end had been accomplished.' That this long-range plot is presented as analogous to 'the Eastern story' in which a heavy slab of stone is carved out and fitted into the roof in order that it may fall on 'the bed of state in the flush of conquest' seems in coded fashion to suggest punishment for erotic transgression, which we may want to read as return of the nightmare plot of Satis House, forcing its way through the fairy tale, speaking of the perverse, sadistic eroticism that Pip has covered over with his erotic object choice – Estella, who in fact represents the wrong choice of plot and another danger of short-circuit. To anticipate later revelations, we should note that Estella will turn out to be approximately Pip's sister – natural daughter of Magwitch as he is Magwitch's adoptive son – which lends force to the idea that she, like so many Romantic maidens, is marked by the interdict, as well as the seduction, of incest, which, as the perfect androgynous coupling, is precisely the short-circuit of desire.[9]

The scene of Magwitch's return operates for Pip as a painful forcing through of layers of repression, an analogue of analytic work, compelling Pip to recognize that what he calls 'that chance encounter of long ago' is no chance, and cannot be assigned to the buried past but must be repeated, reenacted, worked through in the present. The scene replays numerous details of their earlier encounter, and the central moment of recognition comes as a reenactment and revival of the novel's primal scene, played in dumb show, a mute text which the more effectively stages recognition as a process of return to the inescapable past:

> Even yet I could not recall a single feature, but I knew him! If the wind and the rain had driven away the intervening years, had scattered all the intervening objects, had swept us to the churchyard where we first stood face to face on such different levels, I could not have known my convict more distinctly than I knew him now, as he sat in the chair before the fire. No need to take a file from his pocket and show it to me; no need to take the handkerchief from his neck and twist it round his head; no need to hug himself with both his arms, and take a shivering turn across the room, looking back at me for recognition. I knew him before he gave me one of those aids, though, a moment before, I had not been conscious of remotely suspecting his identity. (Chapter 39, p. 301)

The praeterition on which the passage is constructed – 'no need . . . no need' – marks the gradual retrieval of the past as its involuntary repetition within the present. The repetition takes place – as

Magwitch's effective use of indicative signs may suggest – in the mode of the symbolic, offering a persuasive instance of Freud's conception of repetition as a form of recollection brought into action by repression and resistance to its removal. It becomes clear that the necessity for Pip to repeat and work through everything associated with his original communion with Magwitch is a factor of his 'forgetting' this communion: a forgetting that is merely conscious. The reader has undergone a similar process through textual repetition and return, one that in his case has had the function of not permitting him to forget.

The scene of Magwitch's return is an important one for any study of plot since it demonstrates so well how such a novelist as Dickens can make plotting the central vehicle and armature of meaning in the narrative text. All the issues raised in the novel – social, ethical, interpretive – are here simultaneously brought to climax through the peripety of the plot. Exposure of the 'true' plot of Pip's life brings with it instantaneous consequences for all the other 'codes' of the novel, as he recognizes with the statement, 'All the truth of my position came *flashing* on me; and its disappointments, dangers, disgraces, consequences of all kinds' (Chapter 39, p. 303 – my italics). The return of the repressed – the repressed as knowledge of the self's other story, the true history of its misapprehended desire – forces a total revision of the subject's relation to the orders within which it constitutes meaning.

Magwitch poses unanswerable questions, about the origins of Pip's property and the means of his social ascent, which force home to Pip that he has covered over a radical lack of original authority. Like Oedipus – who cannot answer Tiresias's final challenge: who are your parents? – Pip does not know where he stands. The result has been the intrusion of an aberrant, contingent authorship – Magwitch's – in the story of the self. Education and training in gentility turn out to be merely an agency in the repression of the determinative convict plot. Likewise, the daydream/fairy tale of Satis House stands revealed as a repression, or perhaps a 'secondary revision,' of the nightmare. That it should be the criminally deviant, transgressive plot that is shown to have priority over all the others stands within the logic of the model derived from *Beyond the Pleasure Principle*, since it is precisely this plot that most markedly constitutes the detour from inorganic quiescence: the arabesque of the narratable. One could almost derive a narratological law here: the true plot will be the most deviant. We might be tempted to see this deviant arabesque as gratuitous, the figure of 'pure narration'. Yet we are obliged to remotivate it, for the return of the repressed shows that the story Pip would tell about himself has all along been undermined and rewritten by the more complex history of unconscious desire, unavailable to the conscious subject but at work in the text. Pip has in fact misread the plot of his life.

III

The misreading of plots and the question of authority bring us back to the question of reading with which the novel began. Pip's initial attempt to decipher his parents' appearance and character from the letters traced on their tombstones has been characterized as 'childish' and 'unreasonable'. Pip's decipherment in fact appears as an attempt to motivate the arbitrary sign, to interpret signs as if they were mimetic and thus naturally tied to the object for which they stand. Deriving from the shape of the letters on the tombstones that his father 'was a square, stout, dark man, with curly hair,' and that his mother was 'freckled and sickly,' for all its literal fidelity to the graphic trace, constitutes a dangerously figural reading, a metaphorical process unaware of itself, the making of a fiction unaware of its status as fiction making. Pip is here claiming natural authority for what is in fact conventional, arbitrary, dependent on interpretation.

The question of texts, reading, and interpretation is, as we earlier noted, consistently thematized in the novel: in Pip's learning to read (using that meager text, Mrs Wopsle's aunt's catalogue of prices), and his attempts to transmit the art of writing to Joe; the expressive dumb shows between Pip and Joe; messages written on the slate, by Pip to Joe, and then (in minimum symbolic form) by the aphasic Mrs Joe; the uncanny text of Estella's visage, always reminding Pip of a repetition of something else which he cannot identify; Molly's wrists, cross-hatched with scratches, a text for the judge, and eventually for Pip as detective, to decipher; Mr Wopsle's declamations of *George Barnwell* and *Richard III*. The characters appear to be ever on the watch for ways in which to textualize the world, so that they can give their readings of it: a situation thematized early in the novel, at the Christmas dinner table, as Pumblechook and Wopsle criticize the sermon of the day and propose other 'subjects':

> Mr Pumblechook added, after a short interval of reflection, 'Look at Pork alone. There's a subject! If you want a subject, look at Pork!'
> 'True, sir. Many a moral for the young,' returned Mr Wopsle; and I knew he was going to lug me in, before he said it, 'might be deduced from that text.'

('You listen to this,' said my sister to me, in a severe parenthesis.)
Joe gave me some more gravy.

'Swine,' pursued Mr Wopsle, in his deepest voice, and pointing
his fork at my blushes, as if he were mentioning my christian name,
'Swine were the companions of the prodigal. The gluttony of Swine
is put before us, as an example to the young.' (I thought this pretty
well in him who had been praising up the pork for being so plump
and juicy.) 'What is detestable in a pig, is more detestable in a boy.'

'Or girl,' suggested Mr Hubble.

'Of course, or girl, Mr Hubble,' assented Mr Wopsle, rather irri-
tably, 'but there is no girl present.'

'Besides,' said Mr Pumblechook, turning sharp on me, 'think
what you've got to be grateful for. If you'd been born a Squeaker – '

'He *was* if ever a child was,' said my sister, most emphatically.

Joe gave me some more gravy.

'Well, but I mean a four-footed Squeaker,' said Mr Pumblechook.
'If you had been born such, would you have been here now? Not
you – '

'Unless in that form,' said Mr Wopsle, nodding towards the dish.
(Chapter 4, pp. 23–24)

The scene suggests a mad proliferation of textuality, where literal and
figural switch places, where any referent can serve as an interpretant,
become the sign of another message, in a wild process of semiosis
which seems to be anchored only insofar as all texts eventually speak
of Pip himself as an unjustified presence, a presence demanding
interpretation.

The novel constantly warns us that texts may have no unambiguous
referent and no transcendent signified. Of the many examples one
might choose in illustration of the status of texts and their
interpretation in the novel, perhaps the most telling is the case of
Mr Wopsle. Mr Wopsle, the church clerk, is a frustrated preacher, ever
intimating that if the church were to be 'thrown open,' he would really
'give it out.' This hypothetical case never coming to realization, Mr
Wopsle is obliged to content himself with the declamation of a number
of secular texts, from Shakespeare to Collins's ode. The church indeed
remains resolutely closed (we never in fact hear the word of the
preacher in the novel, only Mr Wopsle's critique of it), and Mr Wopsle
'has a fall': into play-acting. He undertakes the repetition of fictional
texts which lack the authority of that divine word he would like to
'give out.' We next see him playing *Hamlet*, which is of course the text
par excellence about usurpation, parricide, lost regal authority, and
wrong relations of transmission from generation to generation.

Something of the problematic status of textual authority is suggested in Mr Wopsle's rendition of the classic soliloquy:

> Whenever that undecided Prince had to ask a question or state a doubt, the public helped him out with it. As for example: on the question whether 'twas nobler in the mind to suffer, some roared yes, and some no, and some inclining to both opinions said 'toss up for it'; and quite a Debating Society arose. (Chapter 31, p. 240)

From this uncertainty, Mr Wopsle has a further fall, into playing what was known as 'nautical melodrama,' an anonymously authored theater played to a vulgar public in the Surreyside houses. When Pip attends this performance, there occurs a curious mirroring and reversal of the spectacle, where Mr Wopsle himself becomes the spectator, fascinated by the vision, in the audience, of what he calls a 'ghost' from the past – the face of the novel's hidden arch-plotter, Compeyson. The vision leads to a reconstruction of the chase and capture of the convicts, from the early chapters of the novel, a kind of analytic dialogue in the excavation of the past, where Mr Wopsle repeatedly questions: 'You remember?' and Pip replies: 'I remember it very well . . . I see it all before me.' This reconstruction produces an intense visual, hallucinatory reliving of a charged past moment:

> 'And you remember that we came up with the two in a ditch, and that there was a scuffle between them, and that one of them had been severely handled and much mauled about the face, by the other?'
>
> 'I see it all before me.'
>
> 'And that the soldiers lighted torches, and put the two in the centre, and that we went on to see the last of them, over the black marshes, with the torchlight shining on their faces – I am particular about that; with the torchlight shining on their faces, when there was an outer ring of dark night all about us?' (Chapter 47, p. 365)

By an apparently gratuitous free association, from Mr Wopsle's play-acting, as from behind a screen memory, emerges a drama on that 'other stage': the stage of dream, replaying a past moment that the characters have never exorcised, that moment of the buried yet living past which insists on repeating itself in the present.

Mr Wopsle's career as a whole may exemplify a general movement in the novel toward recognition of the lack of authorship and authority in texts: textures of codes without ultimate referent or hierarchy, signs cut loose from their apparent motivation, capable of wandering toward multiple associations and of evoking messages that are entirely other, and that all speak eventually of determinative histories from the past. The original nostalgia for a founding divine word leads to a generalized scene of writing, as if the plotting self could never discover a decisive plot, but merely its own arbitrary role as plotmaker. Yet the arbitrary is itself subject to an unconscious determinant, the reproductive insistence of the past history.

Mr Wopsle's career may stand as a figure for Pip's. Whereas the model of the *Bildungsroman* seems to imply progress, a leading forth, and developmental change, Pip's story – and this may be true of other nineteenth-century educative plots as well – becomes more and more as it nears its end the working through of past history, an attempted return to the origin as the motivation of all the rest, the clue to what must else appear, as Pip puts it to Miss Havisham, a 'blind and thankless' life (Chapter 49, p. 377). The past needs to be incorporated *as past* within the present, mastered through the play of repetition in order for there to be an escape from repetition: in order for there to be difference, change, progress. In the failure ever to recover his own origin, Pip comes to concern himself with the question of Estella's origin, searching for her patronymics where knowledge of his own is ever foreclosed. Estella's story in fact eventually links all the plots of the novel: Satis House, the aspiration to gentility, the convict identity, 'naterally wicious' (the status from which Jaggers rescued her), bringing up by hand, the law. Pip's investigation of her origins as substitute for knowledge of his own has a certain validity in that, we discover, he appeared originally to Magwitch as a substitute for the lost Estella, his great expectations a compensation for the impossibility of hers: a chiasmus of the true situation. Yet when Pip has proved himself to be the successful detective in this quest, when he has uncovered the convergence of lines of plot that previously appeared distinct and indeed proved himself more penetrating even than Jaggers, he discovers the knowledge he has gained to be radically unusable. When he has imparted his knowledge to Jaggers and Wemmick, he reaches a kind of standoff between what he has called his 'poor dreams' and the deep plot he has now exposed. As Jaggers puts it to him, there is no gain to be had from knowledge. We are in the heart of darkness, and the articulation of its meaning must simply be repressed. In this novel full of mysteries and hidden connections, detective work turns out to be both necessary and useless. It can offer no comfort and no true illumination to the detective himself. Like deciphering the letters on the tombstone, it produces no authority for the plot of life.

The novel in fact toward its end appears to record a generalized breakdown of plots: none of the schemes machinated by the characters manages to accomplish its aims. The proof *a contrario* may

be the 'oversuccessful' result of Miss Havisham's plot, which has
turned Estella into so heartless a creature that she cannot even
experience emotional recognition of her benefactress. Miss
Havisham's plotting has been a mechanical success but an intentional
failure, as her final words, during her delirium following the fire,
may suggest:

> Towards midnight she began to wander in her speech, and after
> that it gradually set in that she said innumerable times in a low
> solemn voice, 'What have I done?' And then, 'When she first came,
> I meant to save her from misery like mine.' And then, 'Take the
> pencil and write under my name, "I forgive her"!' She never
> changed the order of these three sentences, but she sometimes left
> out a word in one or other of them; never putting in another word,
> but always leaving a blank and going on to the next word. (Chapter
> 49, pp. 381–82)

The cycle of three statements suggests a metonymic movement in
search of arrest, a plot that can never find satisfactory resolution,
that unresolved must play over its insistent repetitions, until silenced
by death. Miss Havisham's deathbed scene transmits a 'wisdom'
that is in the deconstructive mode, a warning against plot.

We confront the paradox that in this most highly plotted of novels,
where Dickens performs all his thematic demonstrations through
the manipulation of plot, we witness an evident subversion and
futilization of the very concept of plot. If the chosen plots turn out
to be erroneous, unauthorized, self-delusive, the deep plots when
brought to light turn out to be criminally tainted, deviant, and thus
unusable. Plot as direction and intention in existence appears
ultimately to be as evanescent as Magwitch's money, the product of
immense labor, deprivation, and planning, which is in the end forfeit
to the Crown. Like money in its role as universal modern (capitalist)
signifier as described by Roland Barthes in *S/Z*, tied to no referent
(such as land), defined only by its exchange value, capable of unlimited
metonymic circulation, the expectations of fortune, as both plot and
its aim or intention, as vehicle and object of representation, circulate
through inflation to devaluation.

The ultimate situation of plot in the novel may suggest an approach
to the vexed question of Dickens's two endings to the novel: the
one he originally wrote and the revision (substituted at Bulwer
Lytton's suggestion) that was in fact printed. I think it is entirely
legitimate to prefer the original ending, with its flat tone and refusal
of romantic expectation, and find that the revision, with its tentative
promise of reunion between Pip and Estella, 'unbinds' energies that

we thought had been thoroughly bound and indeed discharged from the text. We may also feel that choice between the two endings is somewhat arbitrary and unimportant in that the decisive moment has already occurred before either of these finales begins. The real ending may take place with Pip's recognition and acceptance of Magwitch after his recapture – this is certainly the ethical dénouement – and his acceptance of a continuing existence without plot, as celibate clerk for Clarrikers. The pages that follow may simply be *obiter dicta*.

If we acknowledge Pip's experience of and with Magwitch to be the central energy of the text, it is significant that the climax of this experience, the moment of crisis and reversal in the attempted escape from England, bears traces of a hallucinatory repetition of the childhood spell – indeed, of that first recapture of Magwitch already repeated in Mr Wopsle's theatrical vision:

> In the same moment, I saw the steersman of the galley lay his hand on the prisoner's shoulder, and saw that both boats were swinging round with the force of the tide, and saw that all hands on board the steamer were running forward quite frantically. Still in the same moment, I saw the prisoner start up, lean across his captor, and pull the cloak from the neck of the shrinking sitter in the galley. Still in the same moment, I saw that the face disclosed was the face of the other convict of long ago. Still in the same moment, I saw the face tilt backward with a white terror on it that I shall never forget, and heard a great cry on board the steamer and a loud splash in the water, and felt the boat sink from under me. (Chapter 54, pp. 421–22)

If this scene marks the beginning of a resolution – which it does in that it brings the death of the arch-villain Compeyson and the death sentence for Magwitch, hence the disappearance from the novel of its most energetic plotters – it is resolution in the register of repetition and working through, the final effort to master painful material from the insistent past. Pip emerges from this scene with an acceptance of the determinative past as both determinative and as *past*, which prepares us for the final escape *from* plot. It is interesting to note that where the 'dream' plot of Estella is concerned, Pip's stated resolution has none of the compulsive energetic force of the passage just quoted, but is rather a conventional romantic fairy-tale ending, a conscious fiction designed, of course, to console the dying Magwitch, but possibly also a last effort at self-delusion: 'You had a child once, whom you loved and lost . . . She lived and found powerful friends. She is living now. She is a lady and very beautiful. And I love her!'

(Chapter 56, p. 436). If taken as anything other than a conscious fiction – if taken as part of the 'truth' discovered by Pip's detections – this version of Pip's experience leads straight to what is most troubling in Dickens's revised version of the ending: the suggestion of an unbinding of what has already been bound up and disposed of, an unbinding that is indeed perceptible in the rather embarrassed prose with which the revision begins: 'Nevertheless, I knew while I said these words, that I secretly intended to revisit the site of the old house that evening alone, for her sake. Yes, even so. For Estella's sake' (Chapter 59, p. 458). Are we to understand that the experience of Satis House has never really been mastered? Is its nightmare energy still present in the text as well? The original end may have an advantage in denying to Pip's text the possibility of any reflux of energy, any new aspirations, the undoing of anything already done, the unbinding of energy that has been bound and led to discharge.

As at the start of the novel we had the impression of a life not yet subject to plot – a life in search of the sense of plot that would only gradually begin to precipitate around it – so at the end we have the impression of a life that has outlived plot, renounced plot, been cured of it: life that is left over. What follows the recognition of Magwitch is left over, and any renewal of expectation and plotting – such as a revived romance with Estella – would have to belong to another story. It is with the image of a life bereft of plot, of movement and desire, that the novel most appropriately leaves us. Indeed, we have at the end what could appropriately be called a 'cure' from plot, in Pip's recognition of the general forfeiture of plotting, his renunciation of any attempt to direct his life. Plot comes to resemble a diseased, fevered state of the organism caught in the machinery of a desire which must eventually be renounced. Plot, we come to understand, was a state of abnormality or deviance, suggested thematically by its uneasy position between Newgate and Old Bailey, between criminality and the law. The nineteenth-century novel in general – and especially that highly symptomatic development, the detective story – regularly conceives plot as a condition of deviance and abnormality, the product of cities and social depths, of a world where *récit* is *complot*, where all stories are the result of plotting, and plotting is very much machination. Deviance is the very condition for life to be 'narratable': the state of normality is devoid of interest, energy, and the possibility for narration. In between a beginning prior to plot and an end beyond plot, the middle – the plotted text – has been in a state of *error*: wandering and misinterpretation.

IV

That plot should prove to be deviance and error is fully consonant with Freud's model in *Beyond the Pleasure Principle,* where the narratable life of the organism is seen as detour, a deviance from the quiescence of the inorganic which has been maintained through the dynamic interaction of Eros and the death instinct. What Pip at one point has called his 'ill-regulated aspirations' (Chapter 29, p. 223) is the figure of plot as desire: Eros as the force that binds integers together in ever-larger wholes, totalizing, metaphoric, the desire for possession of the world and for the integration of meaning – whereas, concomitantly, repetition and return have spoken of the death instinct, the drive to return to the quiescence of the inorganic, of the nontextual. Yet the repetitions, which have served to bind the various plots, both prolonging the detour and more effectively preparing the final discharge, have created that delay necessary to incorporate the past within the present and to let us understand end in relation to beginning. Through the erotics of the text, we have inexorably been led to its end, which is precisely quiescence: a time after which is an image of the time before. We have reached the non-narratable. Adducing the argument of 'Remembering, Repeating and Working Through' to that of *Beyond the Pleasure Principle,* we perceive that repetition is a kind of remembering, and thus a way of reorganizing a story whose connective links have been obscured and lost. If repetition speaks of the death instinct, the finding of the right end, then what is being played out in repetition is necessarily the proper vector of the drive toward the end. That is, once you have determined the right plot, plot is over. Plot itself is working-through.

Great Expectations is exemplary in demonstrating both the need for plot and its status as deviance, both the need for narration and the necessity to be cured from it. The deviance and error of plot may necessarily result from the interplay of desire in its history with the narrative insistence on explanatory form: the desire to wrest beginnings and ends from the uninterrupted flow of middles, from temporality itself; the search for that significant closure that would illuminate the sense of an existence, the meaning of life. The desire for meaning is ultimately the reader's, who must mime Pip's acts of reading but do them better. Both using and subverting the systems of meaning discovered or postulated by its hero, *Great Expectations* exposes for its reader the very reading process itself: the way the reader goes about finding meaning in the narrative text, and the limits of that meaning as the limits of narrative.

In terms of the problematic of reading which the novel thematizes from its opening page, we could say that Pip, continuously returning toward origins in order to know the plot whose authority would lead him to the right end but never recovering origins and never finding the authoritative plot, never succeeds in going behind his self-naming to a reading of the missing patronymic. He is ever returned to a rereading of the unauthorized text of his self-given name, Pip. 'Pip' sounded like a beginning, a seed. But, of course, when you reach the end of the name 'Pip,' you can return backward, and it is just the same: a repetitive text without variation or point of fixity, a return that leads to an unarrested shuttling back and forth. The name is in fact a palindrome. In the rereading of the palindrome the novel may offer its final comment on its expectative plot.

What, finally, do we make of the fact that Dickens, master-plotter in the history of the novel, in this most tightly and consistently plotted of his novels seems to expose plot as a kind of necessary error? Dickens's most telling comment on the question may come at the moment of Magwitch's sentencing. The judge gives a legalistic and moralistic version of Magwitch's life story, his violence, his crimes, the passions that made him a 'scourge to society' and led him to escape from deportation, thus calling upon his head the death sentence. The passage continues:

> The sun was striking in at the great windows of the court, through the glittering drops of rain upon the glass, and it made a broad shaft of light between the two-and-thirty [prisoners at the bar] and the Judge, linking both together, and perhaps reminding some among the audience, how both were passing on, with absolute equality, to the greater Judgment that knoweth all things and cannot err. Rising for a moment, a distinct speck of face in this way of light, the prisoner [Magwitch] said, 'My Lord, I have received my sentence of Death from the Almighty, but I bow to yours,' and sat down again. There was some hushing, and the Judge went on with what he had to say to the rest. (Chapter 56, p. 434)

The passage is sentimental but also, I think, effective. It juxtaposes human plots – including those of the law – to eternal orders that render human attempts to plot, and to interpret plot, not only futile but ethically unacceptable. The greater Judgment makes human plots mere shadows. There is another end that recuperates passing human time, and its petty chronologies, to the timeless. Yet despite the narrator's affirmations, this other end is not visible, the other orders are not available. As Mr Wopsle's case suggested, the divine word is barred in the world of the novel (it is suggestive that Christmas dinner is interrupted by the command to repair handcuffs). If there is a divine masterplot for human existence, it is radically unknowable.

In the absence or silence of divine masterplots, the organization and interpretation of human plots remains as necessary as it is problematic. Reading the signs of intention in life's actions is the central act of existence, which in turn legitimizes the enterprise of reading for the reader of *Great Expectations* – or perhaps, vice versa, since the reading of plot within the text and as the text are perfectly analogous, mirrors of one another. If there is by the end of the narrative an abandonment of the attempt to read plot, this simply mirrors the fact that the process of narration has come to a close – or, again, vice versa. But that there should be a cure from the reading of plot within the text – before its very end – and the creation of a leftover, suggests a critique of reading itself, which is possibly like the judge's sentence: human interpretation in ignorance of the true vectors of the true text. So it may indeed be: the *savoir* proposed by Balzac's antique dealer is not *in* the text. But if the mastertext is not available, we are condemned to the reading of erroneous plots, granted insight only insofar as we can gain disillusion from them. We are condemned to repetition, rereading, in the knowledge that what we discover will always be that there was nothing to be discovered. Yet the process remains necessary if we are not to be caught perpetually in the 'blind and thankless' existence, in the illusory middle. Like Oedipus, like Pip, we are condemned to reinterpretation of our names. But it is rare that the name coincides so perfectly with a fullness and a negation of identity as in the case of Oedipus. In a post-tragic universe, our situation is more likely to be that of Pip, compelled to reinterpret the meaning of the name he assigned to himself with his infant tongue, the history of an infinitely repeatable palindrome.

Notes

1. CHARLES DICKENS, *Great Expectations* (London: Oxford University Press, 1975), p. 1. References are to this edition, and will hereafter be given in parentheses in the text. I will include chapter numbers to facilitate reference to other editions.
2. On the theme of reading in the novel, see MAX BYRD, ' "Reading" in *Great Expectations*,' *PMLA* 91, no. 2 (1976), pp. 259–65.
3. On the archaeological model in Freud, see in particular the use he makes of Pompeii in 'Delusions and Dreams in Jensen's *Gradiva*' [*Der Wahn und die Träume in W. Jensens* Gradiva] (1907), in *The Standard Edition of the Complete*

Charles Dickens

Psychological Works of Sigmund Freud, ed. JAMES STRACHEY (London: Hogarth Press, 1953–74), vol. 9, pp. 3–95.

4. See *Great Expectations*, chap. 19, p. 149. Miss Havisham is thus seemingly cast in the role of the 'Donor,' who provides the hero with a magical agent, one of the seven *dramatis personae* of the fairy tale identified by VLADIMIR PROPP in *The Morphology of the Folktale*, trans. Laurence Scott (Austin: University of Texas Press, 1968).

5. On the role of the law as one of the formal orders of the novel, see MOSHE RON, 'Autobiographical Narration and Formal Closure in *Great Expectations,*' *Hebrew University Studies in Literature 5*, no. 1 (1977), pp. 37–66. The importance of criminality in Dickens has, of course, been noted by many critics, including EDMUND WILSON in his seminal essay 'Dickens: The Two Scrooges,' in *The Wound and the Bow* (Boston: Houghton Mifflin, 1941).

6. SØREN KIERKEGAARD, *Repetition*, trans. WALTER LOWRIE (Princeton, N.J.: Princeton University Press, 1941), pp. 3–4. For other discussions of repetition in literature, see GILLES DELEUZE, *Logique du sens* (Paris: Editions de Minuit, 1969); and J. HILLIS MILLER, *Fiction and Repetition* (Cambridge: Harvard University Press, 1982).

7. See Freud, 'The Dynamics of the Transference' and 'Remembering, Repeating and Working Through,' in *Standard Edition*, vol. 12; and JACQUES LACAN, *Le Séminaire, Livre XI: Les Quatre Concepts fondamentaux de la psychanalyse* (Paris: Editions du Seuil, 1973), pp. 49–50.

8. This scene with Orlick brings to the surface much of the aggressivity latent in the novel, aggressivity that is attributed to Orlick, but may in some sense emanate from Pip himself, as Orlick seems to imply when he repeatedly calls Pip 'wolf' and argues that Pip was really responsible for Orlick's bludgeoning of Mrs Joe. One could make a case for conferring greater interpretive importance on this scene, as is done by TERESA GRANT in her excellent essay 'Story vs. Discourse: A Dialectical Perspective' (unpublished MS, University of Texas, Austin), which in part takes issue with some of the emphases of an earlier version of the present chapter, published in *New Literary History* 11, no. 3 (1980). Yet I am not convinced that Orlick 'works' as a character: his evil appears so total and gratuitous that he at times appears too easy a device for deflecting our attention from Pip's more hostile impulses.

9. The pattern of the incestuous couple, where the implication of the brother-sister relation serves as both attraction and prohibition, has been noted by several critics. See especially HARRY STONE, 'The Love Pattern in Dickens' Novels,' in *Dickens the Craftsman*, ed. ROBERT B. PARTLOW, Jr. (Carbondale: Southern Illinois University Press, 1970); and ALBERT J. GUERARD, *The Triumph of the Novel* (New York: Oxford University Press, 1976), p. 70. *Great Expectations* gives particular weight to the figure of the father as source of the law: Magwitch, assuming in different registers the role of father both to Estella and to Pip, becomes not a figure of authority so much as a principle of interdiction, of prohibition.

3 Dickens's *Bleak House*

J HILLIS MILLER*

In his long and prolific career, J. Hillis Miller, who is Professor of Victorian Literature at the University of California, Irvine, has moved through a number of interesting phases. His early book, *Charles Dickens: The World of His Novels* (Cambridge, Mass.: Harvard University Press, 1958), was written under the influence of the phenomenological critic Georges Poulet, and concerned itself with the formation of structures of perception and identity in Dickens's writing. Increasingly, through the 1970s and 1980s, his work registered the influence of Jacques Derrida and Paul de Man, the latter being Miller's colleague at Yale University. The so-called 'Yale' school of deconstruction focused attention on the indeterminacies of rhetorical and literary language and developed the doctrine of what might be called (but mercifully never has been) 'endodeconstructionism'. This would be the notion that deconstruction is not merely a kind of critical vandalism, designed to liquidate the meanings and values sedimented in literary texts; rather, it is a reading that brings to light the energetic self-deconstruction which takes place on the inside of most distinctive and valuable literary works. It is in this conviction that certain texts, often texts central to the traditional canon, possess this quality of self-discomposure to a particularly marked degree, and that this is a measure of their continuing value, that Miller's work serves to rebut the charge that deconstruction is a species of textual nihilism. Another criticism mounted against the Yale critics, especially by critics on the left such as Frank Lentricchia and Terry Eagleton, is that their work overemphasises the textual as opposed to the historical. Miller's essay on *Bleak House* might seem to bear out the kind of argument that Miller has mounted in reply to this, namely that the seemingly concrete realities of history are in fact always made up of discursive forms and operations; in *Bleak House*, the most concrete of social realities and institutions, the law, government, class power, are shown to be matters of language.

*Reprinted from 'Introduction' to *Bleak House*, ed. Norman Page (Harmondsworth: Penguin, 1971), pp. 11, 13–30.

Charles Dickens

This essay first appeared as part of J. Hillis Miller's introduction to the Penguin edition of *Bleak House*. As such, it has a claim to being one of the most widely read pieces of deconstructive criticism, though it nowhere announces for itself any such programme. The virtues of J. Hillis Miller's writing have always been those of directness and sweetly economical lucidity, even when the ideas he is dealing with require of the reader the most athletic kinds of conceptual contortion. This essay demonstrates well perhaps why Miller has been called a 'boa deconstructor'.

Among J. Hillis Miller's many other books are *The Disappearance of God: Five Nineteenth-Century Writers* (Cambridge, Mass.: Belknap Press, 1963); *Fiction and Repetition: Seven English Novels* (Oxford: Blackwell, 1982); *The Ethics of Reading: Kant, de Man, Eliot, Trollope, James, and Benjamin* (New York: Columbia University Press, 1987); *Victorian Subjects* (Hemel Hempstead: Harvester/Wheatsheaf, 1990); *Theory Now and Then* (Durham, NC: Duke University Press, 1991); *Ariadne's Thread: Story Lines* (New Haven: Yale University Press, 1992) and *Topographies* (Stanford: Stanford University Press, 1995).

> forcing, adjusting, abbreviating, omitting,
> padding, inventing, falsifying, and whatever
> else is of the *essence* of interpreting.
> (Nietzsche, *On the Genealogy of Morals*, III, 24).

Bleak House is a document about the interpretation of documents. Like many great works of literature it raises questions about its own status as a text. The novel doubles back on itself or turns itself inside out. The situation of characters within the novel corresponds to the situation of its reader or author.

Bleak House does not easily yield its meaning. It significance is by no means transparent. Both narrators hide as much as they reveal. The habitual method of the novel is to present persons and scenes which are conspicuously enigmatic. The reader is invited in various ways to read the signs, to decipher the mystery. This invitation is made openly by the anonymous, present-tense narrator through rhetorical questions and other devices of language. The invitation to interpret is performed more covertly by Esther Summerson in her past-tense narrative. Her pretence not to understand the dishonesty, hypocrisy or self-deception of the people she encounters, though she gives the reader the information necessary to understand them, is such an invitation, as is her coy withholding of information which she has at the time she writes, but did not have at the time she has reached in her story: 'I did not understand it. Not for many and many a day' (17).[1]

Moreover, the narrators offer here and there examples of the proper way to read the book. They encourage the reader to consider the names, gestures and appearances of the characters as indications of some hidden truth about them. Esther, for example, in spite of her reluctance to read signs, says that Prince Turveydrop's 'little innocent, feminine manner' 'made this singular effect upon me: that I received the impression that he was like his mother, and that his mother had not been much considered or well used' (14). The anonymous narrator can tell from George Rouncewell's way of sitting, walking, and brushing his palm across his upper lip, as if there were a great moustache there, that he must 'have been a trooper once upon a time' (21).

The reader of *Bleak House* is confronted with a document which he must piece together, scrutinize, interrogate at every turn – in short, interpret – in order to understand. Perhaps the most obvious way in which he is led to do this is the presentation, at the beginning of the novel, of a series of disconnected places and personages – the Court of Chancery, Chesney Wold, Esther Summerson as a child, the Jellyby household and so on. Though the relations among these are withheld from the reader, he assumes that they will turn out to be connected. He makes this assumption according to his acceptance of a figure close to synecdoche, metonymy. Metonymy presupposes a similarity or causality between things presented as contiguous and thereby makes storytelling possible. The reader is encouraged to consider these contiguous items to be in one way or another analogous and to interrogate them for such analogies. Metaphor and metonymy together make up the deep grammatical armature by which the reader of *Bleak House* is led to make a whole out of discontinuous parts. At the beginning of the second chapter, for example, when the narrator shifts 'as the crow flies' from the Court of Chancery to Chesney Wold, he observes that both are alike in being 'things of precedent and usage', and the similarity between Krook and the Lord Chancellor is affirmed in detail by Krook himself:

> You see I have so many things here ... of so many kinds, and all, as the neighbours think (but *they* know nothing), wasting away and going to rack and ruin, that that's why they have given me and my place a christening. And I have so many old parchmentses and papers in my stock. And I have a liking for rust and must and cobwebs. And all's fish that comes to my net. And I can't bear to part with anything I once lay hold of ... or to alter anything, or to have any sweeping, nor scouring, nor cleaning, nor repairing

going on about me. That's the way I've got the ill name of Chancery (5).

Such passages give the reader hints as to the right way to read *Bleak House*. The novel must be understood according to correspondences within the text between one character and another, one scene and another, one figurative expression and another. If Krook is like the Lord Chancellor, the various Chancery suitors – Miss Flite, Gridley, Tom Jarndyce and Richard Carstone – are all alike; there are similarities between Tulkinghorn, Conversation Kenge and Vholes; Tom-all-Alone's and Bleak House were both in Chancery; Esther's doll is duplicated with a difference by the brickmaker's baby, by the keeper's child at Chesney Wold and by Esther herself. Once the reader has been alerted to look for such relationships he discovers that the novel is a complex fabric of recurrences. Characters, scenes, themes and metaphors return in proliferating resemblances. Each character serves as an emblem of other similar characters. Each is to be understood in terms of his reference to others like him. The reader is invited to perform a constant interpretative dance or lateral movement of cross-reference as he makes his way through the text. Each scene or character shimmers before his eyes as he makes these connections. Think, for example, how many orphans or neglected children there are in *Bleak House*, and how many bad parents. The Lord Chancellor himself may be included, figuratively, among the latter, since his court was charged in part to administer equity to widows and orphans, those especially unable to take care of themselves. The Chancellor stands *in loco parentis* to Ada and Richard, the 'Wards in Chancery'.

In this system of reference and counter-reference the differences are, it is important to see, as essential as the similarities. Each lawyer in the novel is different from all the others. Esther did not die, like the brickmaker's baby, though her mother was told that she was dead. The relation between George Rouncewell and his mother is an inverse variant of the theme of bad parents and neglected children. Krook is not the Lord Chancellor. He is only a sign for him. The man himself is kindly enough, though certainly a bit eccentric. The Lord Chancellor is a kindly man too, as he shows in his private interview with Ada and Richard. They are sinister only in their representative capacities, Krook as a symbol of the disorder, avarice and waste of Chancery, the Lord Chancellor as the sign of the authority of his court. An emblem is always to some extent incompatible with its referent. A sign with ominous or deadly meaning may be an innocent enough old weather-beaten board with marks on it when it is seen close up, or it may be the absurd painting of 'one impossible

Roman upside down', as in the case of the 'pointing Allegory' on Mr
Tulkinghorn's ceiling (16). The power of a sign lies not in itself but
in what it indicates. *Bleak House* is made up of a multitude of such
indications.

Though many of the connections in this elaborate structure of
analogies are made explicitly in the text, many are left for the reader
to see for himself. One valuable bit of evidence that Dickens took
conscious pains to prepare these correspondences is given in his
plan for Chapter 16. In this chapter Lady Dedlock gets Jo to take her
to see the paupers' graveyard where her lover lies buried. Jo points
through the iron gate at the spot, and Lady Dedlock asks if it is
'consecrated ground'. Dickens's notes show that he was aware, and
perhaps intended the reader to be aware, of the similarity between
Jo's gesture of pointing and the gesture of the pointing Allegory on
Mr Tulkinghorn's ceiling. The latter is mentioned in passing earlier
in the chapter and of course is made much of at the time of
Tulkinghorn's murder. 'Jo – ,' says the note for this chapter,
'shadowing forth of Lady Dedlock in the churchyard./Pointing hand
of allegory – consecrated ground/"Is it Blessed?" ' The two gestures
of pointing are alike, as is suggested by the similarity of pose in the
illustrations of both by 'Phiz' for the first editions: 'Consecrated
ground' and 'A new meaning in the Roman'. Both are examples of
that procedure of indication which is the basic structural principle
of *Bleak House*. This procedure is 'allegorical' in the strict sense. It
speaks of one thing by speaking of another, as Dickens defines the
Court of Chancery by talking about a rag and bottle shop.
Everywhere in *Bleak House* the reader encounters examples of this
technique of 'pointing' whereby one thing stands for another, is a
sign for another, indicates another, can be understood only in terms
of another, or named only by the name of another. The reader must
thread his way through the labyrinth of such connections in order to
succeed in his interpretation and solve the mystery of *Bleak House*.

The situation of many characters in the novel is exactly like that of
its writer or reader. So many people in this novel are engaged in
writing or in studying documents, in attempting to decipher what
one chapter title calls 'Signs and Tokens', in learning to read or
write, in hiding documents or in seeking them out, there are so many
references to letters, wills, parchments and scraps of paper, that the
interpretation of signs or of texts may be said to be the fundamental
theme of the novel. Krook's shop is full of old law papers – one of
them, it turns out, perhaps the authentic will for resolving the case
of Jarndyce and Jarndyce. Krook is obsessed, rightly enough, with
the idea that he possesses documents of value, but he does not trust
anyone to read them or to teach him to read. He tries to teach

himself, forming laboriously with chalk on his wall the letters that spell out 'Jarndyce', rubbing out each letter in turn as he makes it. Miss Flite carries everywhere her reticule full of documents. Richard broods day and night over the papers in his case, as he is drawn deeper and deeper into Chancery. Gridley too pores over documents. Much essential business in this novel, as, to be sure, in many novels, is carried on by means of letters. Tulkinghorn finds out Lady Dedlock's secret by the law writing in her lover's hand which matches the note of instructions Trooper George has from his old officer, Captain Hawdon. Esther teaches her little maid, Charley, how to read and write. Mrs Jellyby's irresponsibility is signified in the way she sits all day writing or dictating letters about Borrioboola-Gha instead of caring for her family. Poor Caddy Jellyby, her mother's amanuensis, is bespattered with ink, and Lawyer Tulkinghorn is a fathomless repository of secrets, all inscribed on the family papers in his strong-boxes.

Some of the most dreamlike and grotesque episodes in the novel involve documents, for example, the chapter in which Grandfather Smallweed, after Krook's death, rummages among the possessions of the deceased, surrounded, in his chair, with great piles of paper, or the chilling scene of the end of Jarndyce and Jarndyce. The latter moves beyond 'realism' in the usual sense toward what Baudelaire in 'The Essence of Laughter' calls the 'dizzy hyperbole' of the 'absolute comic':

> It appeared to be something that made the professional gentlemen very merry, for there were several young counsellors in wigs and whiskers on the outside of the crowd, and when one of them told the others about it, they put their hands in their pockets, and quite doubled themselves up with laughter, and went stamping about the pavement of the Hall ... [P]resently great bundles of papers began to be carried out – bundles in bags, bundles too large to be got into any bags, immense masses of papers of all shapes and no shapes, which the bearers staggered under, and threw down for the time being, anyhow, on the Hall pavement, while they went back to bring out more. Even these clerks were laughing (65).

Not to put too fine a point upon it, as Mr Snagsby would say, what is the meaning of all this hermeneutical and archival activity? The reader of the novel must go beyond surface appearances to the deeper coherences of which these surfaces are the dispersed signs. In the same way, many of the characters are cryptographers. They attempt to fit details together to make a pattern revealing some hidden secret. Like Krook they must put 'J' and 'a' and so on together to spell 'Jarndyce'. They want to identify the buried truth which is the substance behind all the shadowy signs with which they are surrounded, as Richard Carstone believes that there 'is – is – must be somewhere' 'truth and justice' in the case of Jarndyce and Jarndyce (37). Two motives impel these readers of signs. Like Richard, Gridley or even, in spite of herself, Esther, they may want to find out secrets about themselves. Each seeks his unrevealed place in the system of which he is a part. To find out how I am related to others will be to find out who I am, for I am defined by my connections, familial or legal. Esther *is* the illegitimate daughter of Lady Dedlock and Captain Hawdon. Richard *is*, or perhaps is not, a rightful heir to the Jarndyce fortune. Other characters – Mr Tulkinghorn, Guppy, Grandfather Smallweed, Hortense, Mrs Snagsby or Inspector Bucket – want to find out secrets about others. Their motive is the search for power. To find out the hidden place of another in the system is to be able to manipulate him, to dominate him, and of course to make money out of him.

These two versions of the theme of interpretation echo through the novel in melodramatic and parodic forms. Many characters find themselves surrounded by mysterious indications, sinister, threatening or soliciting. Poor Mr Snagsby says, 'I find myself wrapped round with secrecy and mystery, till my life is a burden to me' (47). He is 'a party to some dangerous secret, without knowing what it is. And it is the fearful peculiarity of this condition that, at any hour of his daily life, . . . the secret may take air and fire, explode, and blow up' (25). Most of the characters are more aggressive than Mr Snagsby in their relation to secrets. Mr Tulkinghorn's 'calling is the acquisition of secrets, and the holding possession of such power as they give him, with no sharer or opponent in it' (36). Guppy slowly puts together the evidence of Lady Dedlock's guilt and Esther's parentage. 'It's going on,' he says of his 'case', 'and I shall gather it up closer and closer as it goes on' (29). In the same way, Hortense, Lady Dedlock's maid, is 'maliciously watchful . . . of everyone and everything' (18), and the 'one occupation' of Mrs Snagsby's jealous life 'has been . . . to follow Mr Snagsby to and fro, and up and down, and to piece suspicious circumstances together' (54). She has, says Mr Bucket, 'done a deal more harm in bringing odds and ends together than if she had meant it' (54). Just as Gridley, Richard and Miss Flite are obsessed with the documents in their 'cases', so the Smallweeds carry on Krook's search for valuable papers after his death, 'rummaging and searching, digging, delving, and diving among the treasures of the late lamented' (39). Tom Jarndyce, the original owner of Bleak House, who finally blew out his brains in despair, lived there, 'shut up: day and night poring over the wicked heaps of papers in the suit, and hoping against hope to disentangle it from its mystification and bring it to a close' (8). Even Sir Leicester, when he hears the story of a noble lady unfaithful to her husband, 'arranges a sequence of events on a plan of his own' (4), and Esther, though she makes no detective effort to uncover the facts about her birth, nevertheless finds Lady Dedlock's face, 'in a confused way, like a broken glass to me, in which I saw scraps of old remembrances' (18). She is, in spite of herself, led to put these broken pieces together to mirror the truth about herself, just as, in relation to another secret, she says, 'I observed it in many slight particulars, which were nothing in themselves, and only became something when they were pieced together' (50).

The remarkable fact is that these interpreters for the most part are failures. Sometimes their interpretations are false, fictional patterns thrown over the surface of things like a mirage without relation to any deeper truth. Sometimes authentic secrets are discovered but are found out too late or in the wrong way to be of any use to their discoverers. *Bleak House* is full of unsuccessful detectives. The 'plan of his own' which Sir Leicester constructs does not save him from the revelation which will shatter his proud complacency. Mrs Snagsby is ludicrously mistaken in her idea that her husband has been unfaithful and is the father of Jo. Krook dies before he finds anything of value in his papers, and even Grandfather Smallweed makes little out of his discovery. Guppy finds out Lady Dedlock's secret, but it does not win him Esther's hand. Gridley dies without resolving his suit. The case of Jarndyce and Jarndyce is used up in costs before the revelation of the newly discovered will which might have brought it to a close. Even Tulkinghorn and Bucket, the two most clairvoyant and persistent detectives in the novel, are failures. Tulkinghorn is murdered just before he is going to make use of the secret he has discovered about Lady Dedlock. Bucket, in spite of the fact that 'the velocity and certainty of [his] interpretation . . . is little short of miraculous' (56), does not save Lady Dedlock. The masterly intuition which leads him to see that she has changed clothes with the brickmaker's wife (another lateral displacement) gets Esther to her mother just too late. They find her 'cold and dead' on the steps of Nemo's graveyard. Moreover, the novel is deliberately constructed by Dickens in a way calculated to make the reader a bad detective. Carefully placed clues are designed to lead the reader to believe that either George Rouncewell or Lady Dedlock has murdered Tulkinghorn. Even now, when Dickens's strewing of false clues may seem amateur in comparison with the sophisticated puzzles in modern mystery stories, some readers, one may imagine, are inveigled into thinking that Lady Dedlock is a murderess.

A clue to the meaning of this emphasis on false or fruitless interpretation may be given by what appears to be a fault in the novel. The most salient case of an apparent loose end or inconsistency is the failure to integrate perfectly the two major plots. '[T]he plan, so logical and complete,' says Angus Wilson in his recent lively study of Dickens, 'by which the Jarndyce lawsuit corrupts all who touch it (save Mr Jarndyce, a nonesuch) is quite upset when we discover that Lady Dedlock's fall from virtue has nothing to do with her being a claimant in the case. The fault is the more glaring because Miss Flite, the little, mad suitor at law, specifically tells how her own sister went to the bad as a result of the misery brought to the family by their legal involvement.'[2] This fissure in the novel, a conspicuous reft in its web, seems all the more inexplicable when we consider Dickens's obvious care in other parts of the book to tie together apparently unrelated details. This is done, for example, by the use of a pattern of figurative language which runs throughout the text. One case of this is the apparently trivial metaphor which Dickens uses in the second chapter to describe Lady Dedlock's icy boredom by saying that, unlike Alexander, 'having conquered *her* world [she] fell, not into the melting but rather into the freezing mood' (2). This is picked up in the climactic scenes of her death in the melting snow which lies everywhere and which matches the break in her frigid restraint leading to her death. Surely, the reader supposes, Dickens could have related Lady Dedlock's 'crime' more closely to the corrupting effect of Chancery if he had wanted to do so. Perhaps he did not want to. Perhaps he wanted to mislead the reader into thinking that the revelation of Lady Dedlock's secret is at the same time an explanation of the real mystery in the novel – that is, the question of why English society is in such a sad state. At the same time he may have wanted, by leaving the loose end in the open, to invite the reader to investigate further before he takes the revelation of the one mystery as a sufficient explanation of the other. The larger mystery, the mystery of Chancery or of the degeneration of England, is in fact not explained, or if it is explained this is done in so obscure a manner as to leave things at the end of the novel almost as dark, as mud-soaked and fog-drenched, as they are in the opening pages.

The sombre suggestion toward which many elements of the novel lead, like pointers converging from different directions on a single spot, is that the guilty party is not any person or persons, not correctable evil in any institution. The villain is the act of interpretation itself, the naming which assimilates the particular into a system, giving it a definition and a value, incorporating it into a whole. If this is the case, then in spite of Dickens's generous rage against injustice, selfishness and procrastination, the evil he so brilliantly identifies is irremediable. It is inseparable from language and from the organization of men into society. All proper names, as linguists and ethnologists have recognized, are metaphors. They alienate the person named from his unspeakable individuality and assimilate him into a system of language. They label him in terms of something other than himself, in one form of the differentiating or stepping aside which is the essence of language. To name someone is to alienate him from himself by making him part of a family. Even the orphans or the illegitimate characters in *Bleak House* – Jo, Guster or Esther Summerson – are not free from this alienation. Institutions like Chancery, the workhouse or the Tooting baby-farm where Guster 'grew', or persons like Mrs Pardiggle and the Reverend Chadband, act in place of proper parents for such people and force them into social moulds. Everyone in *Bleak House* is, like Jo, made to 'move on', in one form or another of the displacement which separates so many of the characters of *Bleak House* from themselves.

It is no accident that the names of so many characters in the novel are either openly metaphorical (Dedlock, Bucket, Guppy, Vholes, Smallweed, Summerson, Badger, Clare, Boythorn, Krook, Swills, Flite, Volumnia) or seem tantalizingly to contain some covert metaphor lying almost on the surface of the word (Tulkinghorn, Turveydrop, Chadband, Pardiggle, Jellyby, Rouncewell, Squod, Bagnet, Snagsby, Skimpole). Each of these names, especially those in the last group, seems to shimmer with multiple meanings drawn from various contexts, like the portmanteau words of 'Jabberwocky'. They invite etymological interpretation or 'explication' in the root sense of an unfolding. Turveydrop? Turf? Turd? Curve? Drop of turf? 'Turvey, turvey, clothed in black', as in the children's singing game? An essay could be written exploring the implications of these names. The meaning of names and of naming is, as in Proust's *Remembrance of Things Past*, an important theme in *Bleak House*, though Dickens, unlike Proust, seems to remain in that realm of fiction where names truly correspond to the essence of what they name. He does not appear to move on to the stage of disillusion where the incommensurability of name and person or of name and place appears.[3] Dickens's version of this disillusionment, however, is the implicit recognition that the characters to which he gives such emblematic names are linguistic fictions. The metaphors in their names reveal the fact that they are not real people or even copies of real people. They exist only in language. This overt fictionality is Dickens's way of demystifying the belief, affirmed in Plato's *Cratylus*, that the right name gives the essence of the thing. Along with this goes the recognition throughout *Bleak House* that a man's name is a primary way in which he is separated from his privacy and incorporated into society. 'Lady Dedlock', says Tulkinghorn in a reproachful reminder of her crime and of her responsibility to the name she has wrongly taken, 'here is a family name compromised' (48). Just as Dickens names his characters and helps them do their duty as emblems by borrowing labels for them from other contents, and just as Miss Flite gives her birds allegorical names which juxtapose the victims of Chancery (Hope, Joy, Youth and so on), its effects (Dust, Ashes, Waste, Want, Ruin, etc.), and its qualities or the instruments of its deadly fictions (Folly, Words, Wigs, Rags, Sheepskin, Plunder, Precedent, Jargon, Gammon and Spinach), so the characters have been appropriated by society, named members of it, and cannot escape its coercion.

If the metaphors in the names in *Bleak House* are functional, it is also significant that so many characters have more than one name – nicknames, aliases or occupational names. The effect of these nominal displacements, as the reader shifts from one to another, is to mime in the permutations of language that movement within the social system which prevents each person from being himself and puts him beside himself into some other role. Young Bartholomew Smallweed is 'metaphorically called Small and eke Chick Weed, as it were jocularly to express a fledgling' (20). Captain Hawdon takes the alias of 'Nemo', 'nobody', as if he were trying to escape the involvement in society inevitable if one has any name at all. Gridley is known in the court he haunts as 'The man from Shropshire'. Tony Jobling takes the alias of Mr Weevle. Jo is called 'Toughey' or 'The Tough Subject', names pathetically inappropriate. George Rouncewell is 'Trooper George'. Mr Bagnet is 'Lignum Vitae', and Mr Kenge the lawyer has been given the splendid name of 'Conversation Kenge'. Ada and Richard are 'the Wards in Jarndyce', and Miss Flite calls Esther 'Fitz-Jarndyce', suggesting thereby not only her relationship to her guardian, John Jarndyce, but also the figurative similarity between her situation as an illegitimate child and the situation of Ada and Richard as wards of the court.

In the context of the sinister connotation of multiple naming in *Bleak House* there is something a little disquieting, in spite of its loving intent, in the way Mr Jarndyce gives Esther a multitude of nursery rhyme and legendary pseudonyms, including the name of a fifteenth-century witch: 'Old Woman', 'Little Old Woman', 'Cobweb', 'Mrs Shipton', 'Mother Hubbard', 'Dame Durden'. To give someone a nickname is to force on him a metaphorical translation and to appropriate him especially to oneself. This is precisely Jarndyce's selfishness in planning to make Esther his wife, which after all would be another form of renaming. Nor can he protect Esther from her involvement in society by way of her birth. Perhaps her first experience of this is her receipt of a letter from Kenge and Carboy which takes her, as so many characters in the novel are taken, into the legal language which turns her into an object: 'We have arrnged for your being forded, carriage free, p'eight o'clock coach from Reading . . .' (3). A fit emblem for the violence exercised over the individual by language and other social institutions is that terrifying form of helplessness Esther endures when she lies ill with the smallpox caught from Jo, who caught it from Tom-all-Alone's, the Jarndyce property ruined because it is in Chancery, or perhaps from the place where her unknown father lies buried, 'sown in corruption' (11). 'Dare I hint', asks Esther, 'at that worse time when, strung together somewhere in great black space, there was a flaming necklace, or ring, or starry circle of some kind, of which *I* was one of the beads! And when my only prayer was to be taken off from the rest, and when it was such inexplicable agony and misery to be a part of the dreadful thing?' (35).

Perfect image of the alienation the characters of *Bleak House* suffer by being named members of society! The figure of a moving ring of substitution, in which each person is not himself but part of a system or the sign for some other thing, is used throughout the novel to define those aspects of society Dickens attacks. The evil of Mrs Jellyby's 'telescopic philanthropy' or of Mrs Pardiggle's 'rapacious benevolence' is that they treat people not as individuals but as elements in a system of abstract do-gooding. Mrs Pardiggle has 'a mechanical way of taking possession of people', 'a show . . . of doing charity by wholesale, and of dealing in it to a large extent', and a voice 'much too business-like and systematic' (8). The world of aristocratic fashion is a 'brilliant and distinguished circle' (12), 'tremendous orb, nearly five miles round' (48), just as London as a whole is a 'great tee-totum . . . set up for its daily spin and whirl' (16). Within her circle Lady Dedlock lives imprisoned 'in the desolation of Boredom and the clutch of Giant Despair': substituting one place for another in a perpetually unsuccessful attempt to escape from her consciousness of the false self she has assumed. 'Weariness of soul lies before her, as it lies behind . . . but the imperfect remedy is always to fly, from the last place where it has been experienced' (12).

A similar metaphor is used in the satire of representative government. It underlies that brilliant chapter in which the ruling classes gather at Chesney Wold to discuss the dissolution of Parliament and the formation of a new Government. Representative government is another form of delegation. Each Member of Parliament acts as the synecdochic sign for his constituents. Dickens, as is well known, had little faith in this form of government. The relation between representative and represented is always indirect. Any authentic correspondence between sign and signified is lost in the process of mediation. When Sir Thomas Doodle undertakes to form a new ministry he 'throw[s] himself upon the country', but this throwing is only figurative, 'chiefly in the form of sovereigns and beer'. This has the advantage over direct appeal to the voters that 'in this metamorphosed state he is available in a good many places simultaneously, and can throw himself upon a considerable portion of the country at one time' (40). In the practice of Parliamentary government the People are no more than 'a certain large number of supernumeraries, who are to be occasionally addressed, and relied upon for shouts and choruses, as on the theatrical stage' (12). The actual business of governing is carried on by a small group of leaders of the two parties, Lord Coodle, Sir Thomas Doodle and so on down to Poodle and Quoodle on one side, Buffy, Cuffy, Duffy, Fuffy, Guffy and so on on the other. The comic names admirably suggest not only the anonymity of these men but the fact that each may replace any of the others. They exist, like the letters of the alphabet which Krook or Charlie Neckett so painfully learn, as the possibility of an inexhaustible set of permutations and combinations in which Noodle would replace Moodle; Puffy, Muffy; Puffy, Poodle; or Nuffy, Noodle, and nothing would be change at all. Government is a circular game of substitutions like the nursery rhyme based on the letters of the alphabet beginning 'A was an apple-pie'.

This nursery rhyme, incorporated into another reference to the basic elements of language and to naming as the absorption of the particular into a system, is referred to in John Jarndyce's analysis of the Court of Chancery. Chancery, he says, is a dance or round. It proceeds through interminable linguistic substitutions replacing one declaration by another and never getting closer to any end. People, once they are named parties to a suit, are swept into the ring, as Esther is caught in her dream necklace, and can never hope to escape. No other text identifies so well the structure of *Bleak House* as a work of literature and also the structure of the society it describes. 'It's about a Will, and the trusts under a Will – or it was, once,' says Jarndyce.

> It's about nothing but Costs, now. We are always appearing, and disappearing, and swearing, and interrogating, and filing, and cross-filing, and arguing, and sealing, and motioning, and referring, and reporting, and revolving about the Lord Chancellor and all his satellites, and equitably waltzing ourselves off to dusty death, about Costs ... Law finds it can't do this, Equity finds it can't do that; neither can so much as say it can't do anything, without this solicitor

instructing and this counsel appearing for A, and that solicitor instructing and that counsel appearing for B; and so on through the whole alphabet, like the history of the Apple Pie. And thus, through years and years, and lives and lives, everything goes on, constantly beginning over and over again, and nothing ever ends. And we can't get out of the suit on any terms, for we are made parties to it, and *must be* parties to it, whether we like it or not (8).

'Nothing ever ends' – an important thematic strand of the novel is the special mode of temporal existence in an unjust society, or perhaps under any social order. Such an order has replaced realities by signs, substances by shadows. Each sign, in such a 'system', refers not to a reality but to another sign which precedes it and which is pure anteriority in the sense that it refers back in its turn to another sign. A sign by definition designates what is absent, something which may exist but which at present is not here, as the cross on the top of St Paul's Cathedral, 'so golden, so high up, so far out of his reach', is a 'sacred emblem' indicating the apparent absence of God from Jo's life (19). A sign which refers back to another sign designates what is in its turn another absence. Gridley, the 'Man from Shropshire', protests against the explanation of his suffering which blames it all on that code of equity which Conversation Kenge calls 'a very great system, a very great system' (62). 'There again!' says Gridley. 'The system! I am told, on all hands, it's the system. I mustn't look to individuals. It's the system. I mustn't go into Court, and say, "My Lord, I beg to know this from you – is this right or wrong? Have you the face to tell me I have received justice, and therefore am dismissed?" My Lord knows nothing of it. He sits there, to administer the system' (15).

In spite of Dickens's sympathy for Gridley's indignant outrage, the whole bent of *Bleak House* is toward indicating that it is in fact the systematic quality of organized society which causes Gridley's suffering – not a bad system of law, but any system, not a bad representative government, but the institution itself, not the special evil of aristocratic family pride, but any social organization based on membership in a family. As soon as a man becomes in one way or another part of such a system, born into it or made a party to it, he enters into a strange kind of time. He loses any possibility of ever having a present self or a present satisfaction, loses any possibility of ever going back to find the origin of his present plight, loses the possibility of ever escaping from his present restless state or of making any end to it other than 'dusty death'. This intolerable experience of time is dramatized with admirable explicitness, not only in the Chancery suit which can never end except in its consumption in costs, but also in the unhappy life of Richard Carstone. If no proper 'Will' or explicable origin of Jarndyce and Jarndyce can ever be found (there are in fact three wills in the case), Richard as a result lives in perpetual deferring or postponement, never able to settle down to a profession or to commit himself to a present project. He dwells in a continual expectation of a settlement which can never come: 'Everything postponed to that imaginary time! Everything held in confusion and indecision until then!' (37). 'The uncertainties and delays of the Chancery suit' have made him unlike his natural self and have 'imparted to his nature something of the careless spirit of a gamester, who [feels] that he [is] part of a great gaming system' (17). 'Now?' asks Richard. 'There's no now for us suitors' (37). If there is no now there is also no past or future for people who have been forced to accept their membership in a pattern of signs without substance. Each element in such a game refers to other elements in it, in a perpetually frustrated movement which can hope for no end. The other nightmare of Esther's dream expresses this perfectly: 'I laboured up colossal staircases, ever striving to reach the top, and ever turned, as I have seen a worm in a garden path, by some obstruction, and labouring again' (35).

Miss Flite, mad as she is, is close to the truth about Chancery when she says, 'I expect a Judgement. On the day of Judgement. And shall then confer estates' (14). The only escape from the circle of signs would be the end of the world or death, that 'beginning the world' which Richard undertakes at the moment he dies, but 'Not this world, O not this! The world that sets this right' (65). Dickens here, as in his work throughout, suggests an absolute incompatibility between this world and the far-off supernatural world. The many deaths in *Bleak House* have a significance somewhat different from that in many novels. In fiction generally, according to Walter Benjamin, the reader enjoys vicariously a finality he can never experience directly in his own life, my death being on principle an end I shall never be able to view in retrospect. In a novel, says Benjamin, the 'meaning' of each character's life 'is revealed only in his death', and 'what draws the reader to the novel is the hope of warming his shivering life with a death he reads about'.[4] Certainly there are in *Bleak House* many details to read about. Their peculiarity is that they are not satisfactory ends for the lives of those who die. Each character who dies passes suddenly from one world to another, leaving his affairs in this world as unsettled and as unfinished as ever. Krook dies without discovering the secrets in his papers. Gridley dies without resolving his suit, as Richard is killed by the final frustration of his hopes for an end to his case. Tulkinghorn dies without being able to use the power he has gained over Lady Dedlock. Jo's death is elaborately portrayed as the final example of his 'moving on'. The deaths in *Bleak House* constitute only in a paradoxical way 'ends' which establish the destinies of those who die. Their deaths define them once and for all as people whose lives were unfinished, as people who never achieved the peace of a settlement. Their lives had meaning only in reference to the perpetually unsettled system of which they were part.

Bleak House itself has exactly the same structure as the society it exposes. It too assimilates everything it touches into a system of meaning. In the novel each phrase is alienated from itself and made into a sign of some other phrase. If the case of Jarndyce and Jarndyce is a 'masterly fiction' (3, 65), and if many characters in the novel spend their time reading or writing, *Bleak House* is a masterly fiction too, and Dickens too spent his time, like Miss Jellyby, covering paper with ink, his eye fixed not on his immediate surroundings but on an imaginary world. The novel too has a temporal structure without proper origin, present or end. It too is made up of an incessant movement of reference in which each element leads to other elements in a constant displacement of meaning. *Bleak House* is properly allegorical, according to a definition of allegory as a temporal system of cross references among signs rather than as a spatial pattern of correspondence between signs and referents. Most people in the novel live without understanding their plight. The novel, on the other hand, gives the reader the information necessary to understand why the characters suffer, and at the same time the power to understand that the novel is fiction rather than mimesis. The novel calls attention to its own procedures and confesses to its own rhetoric, not only, for example, in the onomastic system of metaphorical names already discussed, but also in the insistent metaphors of the style throughout.

Each character in *Bleak House* is not only named in metaphor but speaks according to his own private system of metaphors. Moreover, he is spoken of by the narrators in metaphors which recur. Nor are these metaphors allowed to remain 'buried'. In one way or another they are brought into the open. Their figurative quality is insisted upon. In this way the reader has constantly before him one version of the interpretative act whereby nothing is separately itself, but can be named only in its relation to some other thing. Dickens is master of an artificial style which makes its artifice obvious. Among the innumerable examples of this the following contains the linguistic texture of the novel in miniature: 'The Mercuries, exhausted by looking out of window, are reposing in the hall; and hang their heavy heads, the gorgeous creatures, like overblown sun-flowers. Like them too, they seem to run to a deal of seed in their tags and trimmings' (48). The nominal metaphor (Mercuries) has been used throughout to label the Dedlock footmen. To this is here added a second figure, a metaphor of a metaphor. These Mercuries are like gorgeous sunflowers. To name them in this way has a double effect. It invites the reader to think of real footmen being described by the narrator in ornately witty language. This language names them as something other than themselves, but it also calls attention to its own wit, uncovers it by playing with it and extending it. The reader knows it is 'just a figure of speech'. The footmen are not Mercuries, nor are they sunflowers. These are ways of talking about them which bring them vividly before the reader and express the narrator's ironic scorn for aristocratic display. At the same time, the figures and figures within figures remind the reader that there are no real footmen in the novel. The Mercuries have only a linguistic existence. They exist as metaphors, and the reader can reach them only through Dickens's figurative language. This is true for all the characters and events in the novel. The fabric of Dickens's style is woven of words in which each takes its meaning not from something outside words, but from other words. The footmen are to be understood only in terms of Mercury, Mercury only in terms of sunflowers. This way of establishing a fictional reality matches the kind of existence the characters in the novel have. They too are helpless parts of a structure based on words.

Notes

1. Numbers in parentheses refer to chapters in the novel.
2. ANGUS WILSON, *The World of Charles Dickens* (London: Secker and Warburg, 1970), p. 234.
3. See ROLAND BARTHES, 'Proust et les noms', in *To Honor Roman Jakobson: Essays on the Occasion of His Seventieth Birthday* (The Hague: Mouton, 1967), pp. 150–8.
4. WALTER BENJAMIN, *Illuminations*, trans. HARRY ZOHN (New York: Schocken, 1969), p. 101.

4 The Bad Faith of Pip's Bad Faith: Deconstructing *Great Expectations*

CHRISTOPHER D. MORRIS*

Christopher D. Morris teaches in the department of English at Norwich University, Vermont. He has been the editor of *Michigan Quarterly Review,* and has published articles on Hawthorne and the Marx brothers, as well as *Models of Misrepresentation: On the Fiction of E. L. Doctorow* (Jackson: University Press of Mississippi, 1991). The sense of the interdependence of the textual centre and the decentring play of textuality displayed in his reading of *Great Expectations* is similar to that shown by J. Hillis Miller in his reading of *Bleak House.* Indeed, Morris takes as his point of departure the description which J. Hillis Miller has given in later work of the process of 'varnishing', or, as Morris glosses it, 'the authorial establishment of some putative centre for a work which simultaneously conceals evidence that would invalidate such a center' (below p. 77). The central issue of Morris's essay is not the reliability of signification as such, so much as the challenges to the centring ideals of personal identity and continuity which are posed by the aberrance of certain textual forms, which the novel as a whole both constrains and, against its own interest, indulges. Morris considers in particular the use of allusion, to popular and literary narratives and to religious or culturally central texts, showing that such allusion is both a means of asserting the authority and competence of the narrator and, to the degree that these allusions generate ironies and illegitimate associations, also a means of undermining them. Morris looks also at the function of letters in *Great Expectations,* stressing the ways in which Pip ignores the self-referential functions of their language. The recurring critical disagreement about whether Pip authentically makes, or inauthentically mistakes his true nature in his narration is thus neatly projected into the structure of the novel itself, which is shown to be organised around the undecidable question of how the self is made in language.

---

*Reprinted from *English Literary History,* 54 (1987), 941–55.

The problem of Pip's moral bad faith, both in his actions and in his narrative assessment of his past conduct, has long troubled critics, so much so that in recent years very probing questions have been asked about the depiction of his moral character, even about his self.[1] In this essay I want to extend the direction of this recent questioning by considering Pip's bad faith as an instance of what J. Hillis Miller calls 'varnishing,' that is, the authorial establishment of some putative center for a work which simultaneously conceals evidence that would invalidate such a center.[2] Pip's bad faith works this way in *Great Expectations*: because we so often attend to the serpentine maneuvers of his conscience, we accept without question that this conscience is functioning within an autonomous, continuous, achieved, created self. And yet analysis of the varnished side of *Great Expectations* shows that it is precisely these assumptions that have been called into question, even in the very attempt to establish Pip's conscience as a center. After a discussion of the general relation between narration and bad faith, I examine, in turn, the novel's famous opening, the allusions Pip makes as narrator, and the letters sent in the novel. The polemical connotations of 'deconstruction' are nothing to the purpose here, but I do hope to show the existence of fundamental contradictions in the novel, aporia whose logical reconciliation seems impossible to articulate.

I

Pip's relation with all characters is self-serving, even when he claims to be acting altruistically, and in his narration he occasionally covers this seemingly irreducible egotism with a veneer of disingenuous contrition. One example is his relation with Joe. As narrator, Pip claims to have developed a solicitude for Joe, but that claim is everywhere contradicted by his actions. After learning the selfless rationale for Joe's acquiesence in Mrs Joe's 'government,' Pip writes:

> Young as I was, I believe that I dated a new admiration of Joe from that night. We were equals afterwards, as we had been before; but afterwards, at quiet times when I sat looking at Joe and thinking about him, I had a new sensation of feeling conscious that I was looking up to Joe in my heart.
>
> (7, 52)[3]

But nowhere afterwards are they 'equals'. On the contrary, at the end of the novel, Pip still condescends to Joe even as he benefits from his ransoming, even as he egocentrically worries what 'little Pip,' his only posterity, will think of him. Similarly distorted appraisals of his past conduct surface in his comments on Biddy, Estella, Pumblechook, and Magwitch. The pervasive pattern of Pip's distortions raises the question of whether there might be some inherent discontinuity between the narrating and the narrated self. Peter Brooks hints at such a contradiction when he cites Sartre's remark that all autobiographies are obituaries, excluding the margins of experience.[4] But Pip's bad faith runs deeper than that phenomenological *mauvaise foi* described by Sartre: it is not that Pip distorts by reifying the For-Itself in language. Instead, as we will see, there never was an original self apart from language to suffer such distortion. Selfhood has always already been the narrator's fictive construct, and Pip's moral bad faith serves to varnish that fact.

This deeper contradiction within the process of narration is discernible in other retrospective judgments. After concluding the account of his first visit to Satis House and his new perception of Joe's thick boots and coarse hands, Pip writes:

> That was a memorable day to me, for it made great changes in me. But it is the same with any life. Imagine one selected day struck out of it, and think how different its course would have been. Pause you who read this, and think for a moment of the long chain of iron or gold, of thorns or flowers, that would never have bound you, but for the formation of the first link on one memorable day.
>
> (9, 76)

The admonitory tone of the passage makes it resemble an epitaph on a tombstone: narration itself may be only the substitution of a new set of dead letters for old. But in this paragraph, too, Pip struggles to articulate the determinative value of this first exposure to class, to wealth, to humiliation. In retrospect Pip speaks as a developmental psychologist, a Piaget, who believes in formative events and irrevocable stages of development. (We may note in passing that the metaphor of the chain also serves to exculpate Pip: after this point, he is no longer responsible for his actions.) Yet even more important than the passage's self-serving function are its contradictory metaphors for life. The chain is the privileged metaphor here, implying absolute continuity, formative events, historical determinism and a narration that could transparently trace these. And yet a life is also a 'course,' a movement through time, that lacks the capacity to 'bind'. The problem is not simply one of mixed metaphors. Instead, language seems incapable of articulating both diachrony and synchrony simultaneously. Words mark the conversion of the synchronic into the diachronic; to articulate is to be caught in a signifying chain; what Pip struggles to express cannot be expressed: the act of narration already excludes it. It is against this background that we should understand the novel's famous opening, in which Pip reads his name from the dead letters of the tombstones.

II

The first page of *Great Expectations*, especially the process by which the name Pip is arrived at, has been the subject of extended critical commentary. Nearly all agree that the process is alienating and that Dickens emphasizes the arbitrary nature of language. Brooks's analysis is one of the most astute in this vein: 'This originating moment of Pip's narration and his narrative is a self-naming that already subverts whatever authority could be found in the text of the tombstones.'[5] Other critics have also noticed this subversion at the novel's origin; misconceptions may be perpetuated, however, by the use of the phrase 'self-naming' for this process. It is true the narrating Pip says 'I called myself Pip,' but his doing so is not a wholly free act, nor should it presume the existence of some self apart from language. Instead, the name must be formed – as all names must – out of signifiers that exist prior to and independent of their subsequent combination. Rightly considered, then, Pip's action is a trope, a syncope, a substitution of one group of signifiers for another through the omission of mediate letters.[6] The idea that the process of naming can never be a free act generated out of some autonomous subjectivity is reinforced by the words, less often cited, that follow Pip's assertion: 'I called myself Pip, *and came to be called Pip*' (emphasis added). The sentence forces us to understand the Janus-like nature of signifiers, which derive their signifying capacity not from the individual, but from a prior linguistic order of which they form a part.

I stress this point because part of Pip's bad faith throughout the novel is his belief in his own freedom to name – that by naming or narrating he is imparting some truth, defining some center or signified, if only himself. Such is the lure or ruse that has seduced not only Pip, but so many critics of *Great Expectations*, who see its triumph as the construction of a self. Joseph Gold's view is typical: 'Pip is made by Pip in the telling . . . By using the first person Dickens eliminates himself and this makes clear his moral-psychological conviction that the remaking of oneself by the confrontation with the past and one's own nature is essential to being fully alive and aware in the present.'[7] Brooks's assessment seems more defensible than such a claim because it presumes less: Pip's experience shows us that we are 'condemned to repetition, re-reading, in the knowledge that what we discover will always be that there was nothing to be discovered . . . Like Oedipus, like Pip, we are condemned to reinterpretation of our names.'[8]

Brooks is right, too, to emphasize the circularity of Pip's name, a palindrome whose emptiness reflects the futility of his quest for meaning. In general, following Jakobson's distinction between the referential and poetic functions of language, we can distinguish two sets of meanings for that name.[9] The first set is oriented toward the referent: thus, a pip is a seed, a unitary origin whose growth is presumably as continuous as that of the organic world. The narrating Pip fills his story with imagery of gardens and cultivation, language that has been analyzed at length for the light it sheds on Pip's moral and ethical education.[10] But a pip is also a disease or the symptom of a disease, so the semantic values of the word begin to cancel or contradict each other: a seed that is a disease, a growth that is a dying. A pip is also a mark on a deck of cards, distinguishing one value from another. Yet this third message-oriented, or referential, meaning also subverts the first, organic definition: the sequence of numbers is less self-evidently continuous than the growth of plants. In any case, the deck of cards figures prominently in Estella's game of 'beggar your neighbor' and other alienating power relations in the novel. The possibility is raised that Pip's self may be but one card manipulated in a game subordinated to some order outside himself.

But if the referent-oriented meanings of the name Pip suggest ultimate aporia, the two 'poetic' meanings (in Jakobson's terms) – those that focus on the message for its own sake – yield even more startling contradictions. A pip can, more generally, be any mark, step, or degree that signifies a difference. Here 'pip' could be merely sensory evidence of a possible meaning, like an alaphone, which at the same time cannot mean without the juxtaposition of some other sound or silence. Therefore Pip's name suggests an unrealized potential for signification, truly a deferral, in Derrida's sense. This poetic meaning of the word further calls into question the already problematic semantic meanings. And the final referent of 'Pip' is its allusion to *Sartor Resartus*. Given the chronology of *Great Expectations*, neither the narrating nor the narrated Pip could be aware of Carlyle's use of the word to denote an inarticulate cry. Therefore, this sense of the protagonist's name can only call attention to Dickens, to his readers in and after 1860, and ultimately to the fictitiousness of the novel *Great Expectations*. There is one other such self-reflective device in the novel – the capitalized words that conclude each third of the book. The importance of these legends, which almost resemble intermittent epitaphs for the novel itself, will be more fully analyzed later. But here we can observe that the novel's opening is more complex even than Brooks allows. Pip's 'self-naming' conceals a fallacy. It holds out hopes for signification in general and for some continuously stable self in particular, but it simultaneously denies these hopes by emphasizing the arbitrary and fictive nature of its language and of language in general.

III

Pip's allusions continue the double play of language noted in the aporia of his 'self-naming': they reflect the narrating Pip's desire to stand outside his narration, to make his words objective, independent tracings of an autonomous self, a continuous life; at the same time, however, they undermine these very expectations by exposing the narrated Pip as merely a fictive entity constructed from discontinuous signs. The allusions, then, serve that 'varnishing' purpose that J. Hillis Miller finds at work in narrative since Oedipus.[11]

At first glance Pip's allusions show mild urbanity: his knowledge of the Bible, of the classics, and of recent literature confers upon his narration a veneer of sophistication in keeping with his ostensible 'maturation' from blacksmith's apprentice to clerk at Clarriker's. Yet the status of any such maturation is immediately called into question by these allusions: is the clerk who can quote from Collins superior in any way to the world of illiteracy from which he emerged? Has education enabled him to some qualitatively new stage of perception barred to characters without the ability to allude? That the answer to these questions should be 'no' is implicit not only in the limited range and relative accessibility of the passages to which Pip alludes, but also in his persistent misapprehension of them, which leaves the reader to decide between mutually contradictory interpretations.

An early example is Pip's recollection of a sermon on the morning after he learns of his expectations: 'I went to church with Joe, and thought, perhaps the clergyman wouldn't have read that about the rich man and the kingdom of Heaven, if he had known all' (20, 157). The blatant bad faith of Pip's wish to exempt himself from the applicability of New Testament parables is of course in keeping with the morally repugnant condescension he begins to show here to Joe, Biddy, and the townspeople. But more disquieting is the narrating Pip's failure to correct his earlier opacity.[12] Of course the irony of the passage may be interpreted differently: Pip's silence, his apparent inability to see his own bad faith, may merely be his grimly wry commentary, full of the wisdom of experience, on an earlier egotism too obvious for later remark. The point is not that one interpretation can be shown to be more tenable, but that it is impossible to decide between the two. Both coexist and cancel each other. According to the first, Pip has not learned and persists in his folly. According to the second, Pip's learning, his grasp of the allusion, is complete. The issue, which finally distinguishes the two traditions of the novel's interpretation discussed in notes 1 and 7 below, turns upon the interpretation of a silence, and cannot be decided.

The most extended allusion is Pip's recounting of this episode in which Wopsle and Pumblechook read 'at him' George Lillo's *The History of George Barnwell*. Several elements of the scene show that Pip as retrospective narrator uses this literary work to protest his innocence even as he misinterprets its purport. Traditionally the play had served as a cautionary role for apprentices, warning them of the evils of rising up against masters. Pip protests against the application of this theme to his own case: 'What stung me, was the identification of the whole affair with my unoffending self' (15, 125). Yet Pip's claim to innocence is belied by the undeniable fact that he *has* grown restive with his apprenticeship to Joe, ever since his first visit to Satis House (see 14, 114). But even more disingenuous is his response to Pumblechook's admonition 'take warning!' which prompts Pip to observe sarcastically: 'as if it were a well-known fact that I contemplated murdering a near relation, provided I could only induce one to have the weakness to become my benefactor' (15, 125). But quite clearly, Pip has resented a near relation (his sister); he has also contemplated murdering a benefactor (his surreal vision of Miss Havisham hanging from a wooden beam [8, 68]). Pumblechook and Wopsle are of course in error to interpret the play as applying exclusively and directly to Pip; but Pip is in error (and as narrator compounds this error by refusing to correct it) by assuming that the allusion is without any application to him. And it never occurs to either the narrated or narrating Pip to forge the obvious parallel between the prostitute Millwood (seducing Barnwell and exacting her revenge on men) and Estella.

Our confidence in the narrating Pip's perspicuity in allusion may also be shaken by his idiosyncratic adaptation of the parable known as 'The Pharisee and the Publican'. At Magwitch's death Pip 'thought of the two men who went into the Temple to pray, and I knew there were no better words that I could say beside his bed, than "O Lord, be merciful to him, a sinner" ' (56, 498). The point of the parable in Luke is that the Publican's simple confession of his own unworthiness is preferable to the Pharisee's lengthy self-justifications. But Pip's twist of the parable into a prayer for Magwitch rather than a confession of his own unworthiness disingenuously allows him to preserve an altruistic sense of his own selfhood. In fact it is always impossible to separate Pip's apparent solicitude for Magwitch from his own self-interest. For example, he has much to gain from Magwitch's escape from England, since it would prevent the convict's wealth from escheating to the crown. And even after Magwitch's imprisonment Pip's actions remain self-serving, especially his withholding from Magwitch until the moment before he dies the news that Estella lives. In short, it is Pip, not Magwitch, who continues to be a 'sinner' up to the very moment their relation ends.[13] Pip's inversion of the parable's applicability is another instance of the persistent misreadings by which he surreptitiously affirms his own selfhood.

Two other allusions may deepen our sense of Pip's narrative duplicity. As he reads in foreign languages to an uncomprehending Magwitch, he compares his situation to Victor Frankenstein's: 'The imaginary student pursued by the misshapen creature he had impiously made, was not more wretched than I, pursued by the creature who had made me, and recoiling from him with a stronger repulsion, the more he admired me and the fonder he was of me' (40, 365). In this allusion Pip once more exonerates himself as he interprets a text. The allusion first claims Pip is more wretched than Victor Frankenstein. But the second comparison contradicts the first: Pip is pursued by the 'creature who had made me,' thereby aligning himself with the creature and Magwitch with Victor. Pip finds in Shelley's text the idea of the 'double': especially in view of the final evocation of Victor brutalized by his need for revenge, Pip's oxymoron – that the creature created its creator – makes sense. But by making himself parallel to both characters, Pip takes on only the sympathetic attributes of each: like Victor he is made 'wretched' by the pursuit, the existence, the reappearance of the misshapen Magwitch; and like the creature, his life is threatened in the pursuit. Pip's dual roles serve his purposes: whether maker or made, possessor of free will or determined by the action, the narrated Pip is given the status of a pure object of sympathy, independent of his 'true' creator, the narrating Pip. Through the allusion to Frankenstein, Pip attempts to establish his own innocence as both character and narrator.

The allusion that most explicitly indicates the narrating Pip's varnishing duplicity is the long comparison, just before Magwitch's return, between the peripeteia of his story and the 'Eastern story' he paraphrases from 'The History of Mahoud' in Sir James Ridley's *Tales of the Genii*. In that story a Sultan cuts a rope which held a slab above the bed of two of his enemies. Pip explains the meaning of this allusion: 'So, in my case; all the work, near and afar, that tended to the end, has been accomplished; and in an instant the blow was struck, and the roof of my stronghold dropped on me' (38, 338). For the narrating Pip, the rope is an excellent figure for absolute continuity, from the beginning of his tale until this very moment (though the discontinuities of the novel are everywhere apparent, most conspicuously in the sentences that begin the very next chapter, which allude to a gap of about two years). The severing of the rope makes Magwitch like Sultan Misnar, unaware of the far-off, catastrophic result of his action, and Pip like his two sleeping enemies. In other words, like the reference to *Frankenstein*, this allusion depicts Pip as pure victim and Magwitch as destructive avenger – albeit, problematically, an unconscious one – of his enemy's illusory triumph. That assignment of roles varnishes Pip's responsibility for his own misinterpretation of events. This allusion, like the others, attempts to cover previous misinterpretations with new signifiers.

But the varnishing function here is also evident in the allusion's placement just prior to the narration of Magwitch's return. The narrating Pip is in a hurry to fix the significance of this episode even before narrating it. Pip's haste betrays his desire to be the sole interpreter, the master interpreter, of his narration. But the novel shows us many times that such a wish is a delusion. For example, a dumbfounded Pip listens to his own story being told by the innkeeper, who sees in it Pip's ingratitude to Pumblechook; Pip of course rejects the innkeeper's interpretation, but doing so leads him to a new interpretation of his own: 'I had never been struck at so keenly, for my thanklessness to Joe, as through the brazen imposter Pumblechook. The falser he, the truer Joe; the meaner he, the nobler Joe' (52, 425). The innkeeper's 'false' narration changes Pip's interpretation of his own life, thereby demonstrating the deficiencies of his prior narration. Surely Pumblechook is not the only 'brazen imposter'. Such an incident subverts the notion of some privileged or master interpretation that will fix the course of a life; instead, interpretation in the book is interminable, constantly modified by new interpretations.

This survey of Pip's allusions shows that they work in the same way as his putative 'self-naming'. Both are, in fact, renamings, substitutions of one set of signifiers for another. The texts to which Pip alludes precede him, just as do those other 'dead letters' in the graveyard. And, of course, allusions create an initial effect of enhanced verisimilitude: the created life of Pip seems more real when it is interpreted next to lives described in parables, novels, and tales. Yet as we have seen, instead of validating Pip's claims to autonomy, continuity, and moral innocence, his allusions expose the

groundlessness of these expectations: no assertion is completely
explicit or unfolded; all enfold some hollow; narration is Ariadne's
thread.[14]

IV

Many letters are sent and received in *Great Expectations,* and their
equivocal status has often been remarked. Murray Baumgarten,
crediting John Jordan and Garrett Stewart, notes than in Pip's first
letter, to Joe, the complimentary close 'inF xn' can mean either 'in
affection' or 'infection' or 'in fiction'.[15] Thus, like the meaning of the
word 'Pip,' the letters in *Great Expectations* may be understood in
both of Jakobson's senses – they convey some content from sender to
recipient, and they refer to themselves, to other letters, to the signifying
chain.

Like most readers, Pip attends mainly to the first sense. For
example, in his letter insisting that Pip meet him at the lime kiln,
Orlick writes 'bring this letter with you,' perhaps to ensure that Pip
will come alone. But Pip forgets this self-referential part of the letter;
ironically, his negligence is rewarded when he is rescued by Herbert.

Beyond its plot function, Pip's indifference to the second sense of
letters perpetuates his bad faith, a cover-up that can be seen in his
reaction to Biddy's letter, in which she asks Pip on behalf of Joe if he
will receive him on the following Tuesday (chapter 27). The letter's
content is simple, yet there is a subtext, created by Biddy's treatment
of the letter as letter, which Pip gives no indication of
comprehending. (More accurately, as in his reaction to the parable
of the rich man, the issue is undecidable, since Pip doesn't in
retrospect correct his prior silent misreading.) Biddy tells Pip in a
postscript that she had read to Joe 'all excepting only the last little
sentence' in which she had expressed her own hope that 'even though
a gentleman' Pip will receive Joe. Both contents of the letter are
important, but Pip grasps only the first, the semantic content
concerning Joe's imminent arrival. The second – Biddy's growing
perception of Pip's inhumanity and her resolve to protect Joe – is
expressed through her ellipsis, which Pip does not read. This
instance of misunderstanding may serve as a template for Pip's bad
faith: attending to the diachronic, semantic content of *parole* and
forgetting that letters are arbitrary signifiers, Pip assumes the
existence of a unitary, necessary connection between signifier and
signified. His missing Biddy's delicate criticism is only a local instance
of that universal misapprehension – great expectations – which finds

its major manifestation, of course, in Pip's assumption that Jaggers's signifiers must correspond to Miss Havisham.

On the one occasion Pip does attend to the self-referential component of language, he is nearly driven mad. Approaching his room at the Temple after leaving Estella for what he believes is the last time, Pip is given a message with the superscription, 'Please Read This Here.' The message itself, from Wemmick, is 'Don't Go Home.' This message leads Pip to spend the night in Hummums, where he experiences a kind of dark night of the soul: 'What a doleful night! How anxious, how dismal, how long!' (45, 395). In this anguish he is led to perceive Wemmick's message only in its self-referential sense. The result is the conversion of the physical world into a meaningless prison house of language:

> When I had lain awake a little while, those extraordinary voices with which silence teems, began to make themselves audible. The closet whispered, the fireplace sighed, the little washing-stand ticked, and one guitar-string played occasionally in the chest of drawers. At about the same time, the eyes of the wall acquired a new expression, and in every one of those staring rounds I saw written, DON'T GO HOME.
>
> (45, 395–96)

In a nightmare frenzy, Pip comes to his closest experience of language as some order independent of the self, prior to the human. Far from being a neutral or transparent medium with which to capture or define reality, words finally come to suggest that Lacanian discourse of the Other. Pip refers to Wemmick's message as 'this' or 'it':

> Whatever night-fancies and night-noises crowded on me, they never warded off this DON'T GO HOME. It plaited itself onto whatever I thought of, as a bodily pain would have done.
>
> (45, 396)

Of course there is a semantic content to Wemmick's message, and when morning comes Pip will be ready to act on it. Yet in the light of Pip's extraordinary meditation on these words, the semantic value of the message may be considered apart from its function in the plot. This is the effect of Pip's falling to sleep by conjugating the 'vast shadowy verb' in the imperative mood, present tense:

> Do not thou go home, let him not go home, let us not go home, do not ye or you go home, let not them go home. Then, potentially: I may not and I cannot go home; and I might not, could not, would

not, and should not go home; until I felt that I was going distracted, and rolled over on the pillow, and looked at the staring rounds upon the wall again.

Pip's conjugation of Wemmick's message converts its meaning into a statement of pure exclusion. The ultimate meaning of the words, in both of Jakobson's senses, suggests inexorable separation, apartness, exile, lack of connection. Pip as narrator has shown us, despite himself, that such exclusion is inherent in his acts of articulation. In order to proceed with life – to obey the message, to help the convict, to fall in love, to rectify wrongs – we must, like Pip, ignore the insoluble, inescapable contradictions woven into 'plaited' or folded language. Terrified, Pip remembers that a gentleman had recently committed suicide at Hummums, and that nightmare place, also a word that resembles 'humans,' may provide the only alternative to life amid the contradictions of *Great Expectations*.

V

Each volume of *Great Expectations* ends with a legend capitalized, like 'DON'T GO HOME'; these legends refer to Pip in the third person and, twice, to the 'stages' of his expectations. The voice of the omniscient narrator thus writes epitaphs for his fiction in the very act of envisioning his protagonist's life developmentally. As if in some recognition of the novel's aporia, the legend that ends the third volume attempts to terminate both the novel and the metaphor of stages: 'THE END OF GREAT EXPECTATIONS'. The syntactical ambiguity here – whether misinterpretations end only with the end of language – is in keeping with the contradictions elsewhere in the novel, seams in its texture whose existence could only with difficulty be regarded as deliberately created or even foreseen. And yet not even this conclusion could end interpretation.

Dickens's revision of the ending of *Great Expectations* ensured that doubleness of interpretation would remain the novel's legacy. Such doubleness, summarized in the notes below that recount the two contradictory traditions of critical reaction to the novel, marks the persistence of authorial bad faith intertextually, that is, beyond even the expected limits of the three-volume novel: to the extent that interpretation of *Great Expectations* follows one of its major critical traditions or chooses one of the two endings, it has already succumbed to the lure through which Dickens, by unfolding language and varnishing its contradictions, seeks to sustain the illusion of a signified.

Notes

An early version of this paper was read at the Eleventh Annual Colloquium on Literature and Film, sponsored by the Department of Foreign Languages, West Virginia University, September 25–27, 1986.

1. JULIAN MOYNAHAN, in 'The Hero's Guilt: The Case of *Great Expectations*,' *Essays in Criticism*, 10 (1960): 60–79, analyzed the ambivalence of Pip's troubled relations with all characters. Moynahan's study was one of the first thoroughgoing accounts of Pip's persistent bad faith: he sees Pip as 'implicated in violence' and brought, finally, to a point of 'alienation from the real world' (77, 78). More recently, COLIN MANLOVE, in 'Neither Here Nor There: Uneasiness in *Great Expectations*,' *Dickens Studies Annual*, 8 (1980): 61–70, cautioned that 'any simple view of Pip's career in terms only of spiritual amelioration and the finding of his selfhood may require considerable qualification' (69). JUDITH WEISSMAN and STEVEN COHAN, in 'Dickens's *Great Expectations*: Pip's Arrested Development,' *American Imago*, 38 (1981): 105–26, hold that Pip's delusions persist through the last chapter because he 'does not confront the sorrow and emptiness that make him need to lie' (124). In 1984, two studies of the novel saw Pip's bad faith as rooted in the conditions of narrative itself: MICHAEL GINSBURG's 'Dickens and the Uncanny: Repression and Displacement in *Great Expectations*,' *Dickens Studies Annual* 13 (1984): 115–24, a Freudian reading, argued that the very possibility of Pip's storytelling is dependent on a repression which 'manifests itself as something other than itself' (123). Fiction-making is therefore inherent in the guilt and desire of existence. PETER BROOKS's study in *Reading for the Plot: Design and Intention in the Narrative* (New York: Alfred A. Knopf, 1984), also fundamentally psychoanalytic, argues that repression causes Pip to 'misread the plot of his life' (130) and that the return of Magwitch, the repressed, dramatizes Freud's dynamic tension between eros and thanatos (139). Taken together with the recent deconstructive readings of Dickens by DIANNE F. SADOFF ('Storytelling and the Figure of the Father in *Little Dorrit*,' *PMLA* 95 [1980]: 234–45) and ALISTAIR M. DUCKWORTH ('*Little Dorrit* and the Question of Closure,' *Nineteenth Century Fiction*, 33 [1978]: 110–30), this critical tradition which calls into question the status of Pip's 'self' seems well established; however, an alternative tradition, which sees the novel as finally valorizing the self, continues. See note 7.
2. J. HILLIS MILLER, 'The Ethics of Reading: Vast Gaps and Parting Hours,' in *American Criticism in the Poststructuralist Age*, ed. IRA KONIGSBERG (Ann Arbor: Michigan Studies in the Humanities, 1981), 34.
3. All references to *Great Expectations* are from the Oxford Edition (London: Oxford University Press, 1953). Chapter and page numbers are given in parentheses.
4. Brooks, 114.

5. Brooks, 114.

6. MAX BYRD, in 'Reading in *Great Expectations,*' *PMLA* 91 (1976): 260–65, writes: 'Pip begins his story making a metaphorical name for himself, then by making a metaphor about the names on his parents' tombstone, in each case the beginning of a fiction of identity' (260). Like Brooks's interpretation, Byrd's sees Pip's naming as free, hence ultimately transcendable: 'Pip's tyrannical fictions, like his illiteracy, yield to time' (261). On the other hand, my thesis is that Pip never escapes fiction-making.

7. JOSEPH GOLD, *Charles Dickens: Radical Moralist* (Minneapolis: University of Minnesota Press, 1972), 244. Despite the strength of the critical tradition discussed in note 1, other readers, like Gold, continue to see the novel as affirming some sense of selfhood in Pip. WILLIAM H. NEW, in 'The Four Elements in *Great Expectations,*' *Dickens Studies* 3 (1967): 111–21, sees Pip's development as a movement 'from the false fortune of life in London to an understanding of the value of love, from childhood ignorance to mature wisdom, and from disharmony to peace' (120). DONALD H. ERIKSON, in 'Demonic Imagery and the Quest for Identity in Dickens' *Great Expectations,*' *Illinois Quarterly,* 33 (1970): 4–11, believes Pip relinquishes the existential Hell of London to find 'the greater values of love and community' (11). HARRY STONE, in *Dickens and the Invisible World: Fairy Tales, Fantasy, and Novel-Making* (Bloomington: Indiana University Press, 1979) sees Pip's maturing and rising 'to further regeneration and ultimate rebirth' (335). Even critics who grant that Dickens radically undermined the stability of the ego in *Great Expectations* still see the novel's conclusion as valorizing the ego. Thus JOHN KUCICH, in *Excess and Restraint in the Novels of Charles Dickens* (Athens: University of Georgia Press, 1981) links Dickens's theme to Bataille's celebration of erotic energy, and sees Pip achieving a genuine liberation by actively, violently overcoming his rivals, Miss Havisham and Orlick. Through such self-assertion Pip insures the 'survival of virtue' (114). DOUGLAS H. THOMSON, in 'The Passing of Another Shadow: A Third Ending to *Great Expectations,*' *Dickens Quarterly,* 3 (1984): 94–6, finds that the novel's tragic spirit 'affirms man's ability to know himself' (96). DAVID GERVAIS, in 'The Prose and Poetry of *Great Expectations,*' *Dickens Studies Annual,* 13 (1984): 85–114, claims that 'moral awareness liberates Pip by the end' (109). And Brooks, as part of a brilliant analysis of Pip outgrowing the 'disease of plot' to reach, at the novel's end, the 'non-narratable' (139), still sees Pip's narration as fundamentally therapeutic: 'The past needs to be incorporated *as past* within the present, mastered through the play of repetition in order for there to be an escape from repetition: in order for there to be difference, change, progress' (134). Brooks finds in Pip's narration, then, the same value he praises in the analyst's task of 'construction' (320), which is more 'dynamic and dialogic than the archeologist's' (321).

8. Brooks, 142.

9. For a discussion of the relevance of Jakobson's distinction to Dickens's early fiction, see Miller's account in 'The Fiction of Realism: *Sketches by Boz, Oliver Twist,* and Cruikshank's Illustrations,' in *Dickens Centennial Essays,* ed. ADA NISBET and BLAKE NEVINS (Berkeley: University of California Press, 1971), 85–153. I am indebted to Miller for this general idea, which I apply here to *Great Expectations.*

10. For example, see JOSEPH A. HYNES's argument, in 'Image and Symbol in *Great*

Expectations,' *ELH* 30 (1962): 258–92, that the garden imagery suggests an 'anti-Paradise' of 'belated growth and renewal' (286).

11. Miller, 'The Ethics of Reading,' 34. Dickens's allusions have also been studied recently by MICHAEL WHEELER, in *The Art of Allusion in Victorian Fiction* (New York: Barnes and Noble, 1979). Wheeler argues that the eschatological references in *Hard Times* support a Carlylean theme that denounces the ascendency of utilitarianism in England. But even Wheeler's thematic analysis raises puzzling questions as to the allusions' stability of reference: 'Dickens's comments on Harthouse as the very devil offer two possible interpretations, one flippant and the other profoundly serious, which, disturbingly, merge in the character's "what will be, will be" philosophy' (70). Wheeler believes it is possible to reconcile these seemingly incompatible interpretations; my thesis is that the choice between alternatives is undecidable.

12. Others have found Pip's refusal to comment, as narrator, on the moral problems raised by his narration to be symptoms of his persistence in delusion. See Weissman and Cohan (note 1), 108.

13. For a convincing account of Pip's inability to extricate himself from his bad faith, even in the fevered dreams that follow Magwitch's death, see Moynahan (note 1), 77–8.

14. Dickens gives warrant for these Derridean metaphors for narration, most particularly in two key passages that could not be easily analyzed in the text. In the novel's first sentence Pip tells us that his infant tongue could make of both names nothing 'longer or more explicit than Pip.' Explicitness in language is, interestingly, a relative matter, but more important, to be explicit means to be 'folded out-from.' Therefore, Pip is a partly unfolded name. If, following Brooks, we see the action of the novel as a reinterpretation of Pip's name, we learn it is never fully unfolded. And, in his meditation on the words 'DON'T GO HOME,' Pip says his phase 'plaited itself onto whatever I thought of' (45, 396). Language thus folds itself into the speaking subject, narration is thus an unfolding that is always a new folding. Derrida discusses Ariadne's thread and other metaphors for writing/narration as an endless unfolding in 'Tympan,' in *Margins of Philosophy*, trans. ALAN BASS (Chicago: University of Chicago Press, 1982), ix–xxix.

15. MURRAY BAUMGARTEN, 'Calligraphy and Code: Writing in *Great Expectations*,' *Dickens Studies Annual*, 11 (1983), 72.

5   Heteroglossia in the Novel: *Little Dorrit*

MIKHAIL BAKHTIN*

The work of Mikhail Bakhtin has had more influence on Anglo-American literary criticism than that of almost any other single writer, though that influence has been of a curiously delayed kind. Writing in Soviet Russia through the 1920s, 1930s and 1940s under the increasingly unpromising conditions of Stalinism, Bakhtin mounted a sustained critique of the abstraction and idealizing of Saussure's structural linguistics that has come to seem uncannily premonitory of the poststructuralist reaction against structuralism that gathered force during the 1970s. Indeed, the rediscovery and translation of many of Bakhtin's works from early in the century contributed considerably to that critical and theoretical shift. What follows is an extract from 'Discourse in the Novel', a long essay of 1935 which concentrates many of the leading themes of Bakhtin's work, especially his claim that the novel is the form which enacts most faithfully and energetically the 'dialogic' condition of all language. By this term, Bakhtin means to evoke the complex systems of relatedness in which individual styles, idioms and even vocabularies jostle congestedly together, such that 'my' language is always inhabited by and orientated to the language of others. In the pages from this essay which are reproduced here, Bakhtin discusses a number of examples from *Little Dorrit* of the 'hybrid construction' of voices in conflict and collusion. The discussion shows how the mechanics of stylistic analysis, with the distinguishing and distributing of different stylistic forms and markers, is allied in Bakhtin's work to a sense of the necessary priority of flux, movement and becoming, over the stasis of being or identity.

Among Bakhtin's other works are *Problems of Dostoevsky's Poetics*, ed. and trans. Caryl Emerson (Manchester: Manchester University Press, 1984); *Rabelais and His World*, trans. Hélène Iswolsky

---

*Reprinted from 'Discourse in the Novel', in *The Dialogic Imagination*, trans. Caryl Emerson and Michael Holquist (Austin: University of Texas Press, 1981), pp. 301–8. A number of footnotes giving cross-references to other parts of the essay have been omitted.

(Bloomington: Indiana University Press, 1984) and *Speech Genres, and Other Late Essays*, trans. Caryl Emerson and Michael Holquist (Austin: University of Texas Press, 1986). Writing under the names of others, or in close collaboration with them, Bakhtin is also usually taken to be largely responsible for P. N. Medvedev and M. M. Bakhtin, *The Formal Method in Literary Scholarship*, trans. Albert J. Wehrle (Baltimore: Johns Hopkins University Press, 1978) and V. N. Voloshinov, *Marxism and the Philosophy of Language*, trans. Ladislav Matejka and I. R. Titunik (New York: Seminar Press, 1973).

The compositional forms for appropriating and organizing heteroglossia in the novel, worked out during the long course of the genre's historical development, are extremely heterogeneous in their variety of generic types. Each such compositional form is connected with particular stylistic possibilities, and demands particular forms for the artistic treatment of the heteroglot 'languages' introduced into it. We will pause here only on the most basic forms that are typical for the majority of novel types.

The so-called comic novel makes available a form for appropriating and organizing heteroglossia that is both externally very vivid and at the same time historically profound: its classic representatives in England were Fielding, Smollett, Sterne, Dickens, Thackeray and others, and in Germany Hippel and Jean Paul.

In the English comic novel we find a comic-parodic re-processing of almost all the levels of literary language, both conversationally and written, that were current at the time. Almost every novel we mentioned above as being a classic representative of this generic type is an encyclopedia of all strata and forms of literary language: depending on the subject being represented, the storyline parodically reproduces first the forms of parliamentary eloquence, then the eloquence of the court, or particular forms of parliamentary protocol, or court protocol, or forms used by reporters in newspaper articles, or the dry business language of the City, or the dealings of speculators, or the pedantic speech of scholars, or the high epic style, or Biblical style, or the style of the hypocritical moral sermon or finally the way one or another concrete and socially determined personality, the subject of the story, happens to speak.

This usually parodic stylization of generic, professional and other strata of language is sometimes interrupted by the direct authorial word (usually as an expression of pathos, of Sentimental or idyllic sensibility), which directly embodies (without any refracting) semantic and axiological intentions of the author. But the primary source of language usage in the comic novel is a highly specific treatment of 'common language'. This 'common language' – usually the average norm of spoken and written language for a given social group – is taken by the author precisely as the *common view*, as the verbal approach to people and things normal for a given sphere of society, as the *going point of view* and the going *value*. To one degree or another, the author distances himself from this common language, he steps back and objectifies it, forcing his own intentions to refract and diffuse themselves through the medium of this common view that has become embodied in language (a view that is always superficial and frequently hypocritical).

The relationship of the author to a language conceived as the common view is not static – it is always found in a state of movement and oscillation that is more or less alive (this sometimes is a rhythmic oscillation): the author exaggerates, now strongly, now weakly, one or another aspect of the 'common language,' sometimes abruptly exposing its inadequacy to its object and sometimes, on the contrary, becoming one with it, maintaining an almost imperceptible distance, sometimes even directly forcing it to reverberate with his own 'truth,' which occurs when the author completely merges his own voice with the common view. As a consequence of such a merger, the aspects of common language, which in the given situation had been parodically exaggerated or had been treated as mere things, undergo change. The comic style demands of the author a lively to-and-fro movement in his relation to language, it demands a continual shifting of the distance between author and language, so that first some, then other aspects of language are thrown into relief. If such were not the case, the style would be monotonous or would require a greater individualization of the narrator – would, in any case, require a quite different means for introducing and organizing heteroglossia.

Against this same backdrop of the 'common language,' of the impersonal, going opinion, one can also isolate in the comic novel those parodic stylizations of generic, professional and other languages we have mentioned, as well as compact masses of direct authorial discourse – pathos-filled, moral-didactic, sentimental-elegiac or idyllic. In the comic novel the direct authorial word is thus realized in direct, unqualified stylizations of poetic genres (idyllic, elegiac, etc.) or stylizations of rhetorical genres (the pathetic, the moral-didactic). Shifts from common language to parodying of generic and other languages and shifts to the direct authorial word may be gradual, or may be on the contrary quite abrupt. Thus does the system of language work in the comic novel.

We will pause for analysis on several examples from Dickens, from his novel *Little Dorrit*.

(1) The conference was held at four or five o'clock in the afternoon,

when all the region of Harley Street, Cavendish Square, was resonant of carriage-wheels and double-knocks. It had reached this point when Mr Merdle came home *from his daily occupation of causing the British name to be more and more respected in all parts of the civilized globe capable of the appreciation of worldwide commercial enterprise and gigantic combinations of skill and capital.* For, though nobody knew with the least precision what Mr Merdle's business was, except that it was to coin money, these were the terms in which everybody defined it on all ceremonious occasions, and which it was the last new polite reading of the parable of the camel and the needle's eye to accept without inquiry. [book 1, ch. 33]

The italicized portion represents a parodic stylization of the language of ceremonial speeches (in parliaments and at banquets). The shift into this style is prepared for by the sentence's construction, which from the very beginning is kept within bounds by a somewhat ceremonious epic tone. Further on – and already in the language of the author (and consequently in a different style) – the parodic meaning of the ceremoniousness of Merdle's labors becomes apparent: such a characterization turns out to be 'another's speech,' to be taken only in quotation marks ('these were the terms in which everybody defined it on all ceremonious occasions').

Thus the speech of another is introduced into the author's discourse (the story) in *concealed form,* that is, without any of the *formal* markers usually accompanying such speech, whether direct or indirect. But this is not just another's speech in the same 'language' – it is another's utterance in a language that is itself 'other' to the author as well, in the archaicized language of oratorical genres associated with hypocritical official celebrations.

(2) In a day or two it was announced to all the town, that Edmund Sparkler, Esquire, son-in-law of the eminent Mr Merdle of worldwide renown, was made one of the Lords of the Circumlocution Office; and proclamation was issued, to all true believers, that this admirable *appointment was to be hailed as a graceful and gracious mark of homage, rendered by the graceful and gracious Decimus, to that commercial interest which must ever in a great commercial country – and all the rest of it, with blast of trumpet.* So, bolstered by this mark of Government homage, the *wonderful* Bank and all the other *wonderful* undertakings went on and went up; and gapers came to Harley Street, Cavendish Square, only to look at the house where the golden wonder lived. [book 2, ch. 12]

Here, in the italicized portion, another's speech in another's (official-ceremonial) language is openly introduced as indirect discourse. But it is surrounded by the hidden, diffused speech of another (in the same official-ceremonial language) that clears the way for the introduction of a form more easily perceived *as* another's speech and that can reverberate more fully as such. The clearing of the way comes with the word 'Esquire,' characteristic of official speech, added to Sparkler's name; the final confirmation that this is another's speech comes with the epithet 'wonderful.' This epithet does not of course belong to the author but to that same 'general opinion' that had created the commotion around Merdle's inflated enterprises.

(3) It was a dinner to provoke an appetite, though he had not had one. The rarest dishes, sumptuously cooked and sumptuously served; the choicest fruits, the most exquisite wines; marvels of workmanship in gold and silver, china and glass; innumerable things delicious to the senses of taste, smell, and sight, were insinuated into its composition. *O, what a wonderful man this Merdle, what a great man, what a master man, how blessedly and enviably endowed –* in one word, what a rich man! [book 2, ch. 12]

The beginning is a parodic stylization of high epic style. What follows is an enthusiastic glorification of Merdle, a chorus of his admirers in the form of the concealed speech of another (the italicized portion). The whole point here is to expose the real basis for such glorification, which is to unmask the chorus' hypocrisy: 'wonderful,' 'great,' 'master,' 'endowed' can all be replaced by the single word 'rich'. This act of authorial unmasking, which is openly accomplished within the boundaries of a single simple sentence, merges with the unmasking of another's speech. The ceremonial emphasis on glorification is complicated by a second emphasis that is indignant, ironic, and this is the one that ultimately predominates in the final unmasking words of the sentence.

We have before us a typical double-accented, double-styled *hybrid construction*.

What we are calling a hybrid construction is an utterance that belongs, by its grammatical (syntactic) and compositional markers, to a single speaker, but that actually contains mixed within it two utterances, two speech manners, two styles, two 'languages,' two semantic and axiological belief systems. We repeat, there is no formal – compositional and syntactic – boundary between these utterances, styles, languages, belief systems; the division of voices and languages takes place within the limits of a single syntactic whole, often within the limits of a simple sentence. It frequently happens that even one and the same word will belong simultaneously to two languages, two belief systems that intersect in a hybrid construction – and, consequently, the word has two contradictory meanings, two accents (examples below). As we shall see, hybrid constructions are of enormous significance in novel style.

(4) But Mr Tite Barnacle was a buttoned-up man, and *consequently* a weighty one. [book 2, ch. 12]

The above sentence is an example of *pseudo-objective motivation*, one of the forms for concealing another's speech – in this example, the speech of 'current opinion'. If judged by the formal markers above, the logic motivating the sentence seems to belong to the author, i.e., he is formally at one with it; but in actual fact, the motivation lies within the subjective belief system of his characters, or of general opinion.

Pseudo-objective motivation is generally characteristic of novel style, since it is one of the manifold forms for concealing another's speech in hybrid constructions. Subordinate conjunctions and link words ('thus,' 'because,' 'for the reason that,' 'in spite of' and so forth), as well as words used to maintain a logical sequence ('therefore,' 'consequently,' etc.) lose their direct authorial intention, take on the flavor of someone else's language, become refracted or even completely reified.

Such motivation is especially characteristic of comic style, in which someone else's speech is dominant (the speech of concrete persons, or, more often, a collective voice).

(5) As a vast fire will fill the air to a great distance with its roar, so the sacred flame which the mighty Barnacles had fanned caused the air to resound more and more with the name of Merdle. It was deposited on every lip, and carried into every ear. There never was, there never had been, there never again should be, such a man as Mr Merdle. Nobody, as aforesaid, knew what he had done; but *everybody knew him to be the greatest that had appeared.* [book 2, ch. 13]

Here we have an epic, 'Homeric' introduction (parodic, of course) into whose frame the crowd's glorification of Merdle has been inserted (concealed speech of another in another's language). We then get direct authorial discourse; however, the author gives an objective tone to this 'aside' by suggesting that 'everybody knew' (the italicized portion). It is as if even the author himself did not doubt the fact.

(6) That illustrious man and great national ornament, Mr Merdle, continued his shining course. It began to be widely understood that one who had done society the admirable service *of making so much money out of it*, could not be suffered to remain a commoner. A baronetcy was spoken of with confidence; a peerage was frequently mentioned. [book 2, ch. 24]

We have here the same fictive solidarity with the hypocritically ceremonial general opinion of Merdle. All the epithets referring to Merdle in the first sentence derive from general opinion, that is, they are the concealed speech of another. The second sentence – 'it began to be widely understood,' etc. – is kept within the bounds of an emphatically objective style, representing not subjective opinion but the admission of an objective and completely indisputable fact. The epithet 'who had done society the admirable service' is completely at the level of common opinion, repeating its official glorification, but the subordinate clause attached to that glorification ('of making so much money out of it') are the words of the author himself (as if put in parentheses in the quotation). The main sentence then picks up again at the level of common opinion. We have here a typical hybrid construction, where the subordinate clause is in direct authorial speech and the main clause in someone else's speech. The main and subordinate clauses are constructed in different semantic and axiological conceptual systems.

The whole of this portion of the novel's action, which centers around Merdle and the persons associated with him, is depicted in the language (or more accurately, the languages) of hypocritically ceremonial common opinion about Merdle, and at the same time there is a parodic stylization of that everyday language of banal society gossip, or of the ceremonial language of official pronouncements and banquet speeches, or the high epic style or Biblical style. This atmosphere around Merdle, the common opinion about him and his enterprises, infects the positive heroes of the novel as well, in particular the sober Pancks, and forces him to invest his entire estate – his own, and Little Dorrit's – in Merdle's hollow enterprises.

(7) Physician had engaged to break the intelligence in Harley Street. Bar could not at once return to his inveiglements of the most enlightened and remarkable jury he had ever seen in that box, with whom, he could tell his learned friend, no shallow sophistry would go down, and no unhappily abused professional tact and skill prevail (this was the way he meant to begin with them); so he said he

would go too, and would loiter to and fro near the house while his friend was inside. [book 2, ch. 25]

Here we have a clear example of hybrid construction where within the frame of authorial speech (informative speech) – the beginning of a speech prepared by the lawyer has been inserted, 'The Bar could not at once return to his inveiglements . . . of the jury . . . so he said he would go too . . .', etc. – while this speech is simultaneously a fully developed epithet attached to the subject of the author's speech, that is, 'jury'. The word 'jury' enters into the context of informative authorial speech (in the capacity of a necessary object to the word 'inveiglements') as well as into the context of the parodic-stylized speech of the lawyer. The author's word 'inveiglement' itself emphasizes the parodic nature of the re-processing of the lawyer's speech, the hypocritical meaning of which consists precisely in the fact that it would be impossible to inveigle such a remarkable jury.

(8) It followed that Mrs Merdle, as a woman of fashion and good breeding *who had been sacrificed to wiles of a vulgar barbarian* (for Mr Merdle was found out from the crown of his head to the sole of his foot, the moment he was found out in his pocket), must be actively championed by her order for her order's sake. [book 2, ch. 33]

This is an analogous hybrid construction, in which the definition provided by the general opinion of society – 'a sacrifice to the wiles of a vulgar barbarian' – merges with authorial speech, exposing the hypocrisy and greed of common opinion.

So it is throughout Dickens' whole novel. His entire text is, in fact, everywhere dotted with quotation marks that serve to separate out little islands of scattered direct speech and purely authorial speech, washed by heteroglot waves from all sides. But it would have been impossible actually to insert such marks, since, as we have seen, one and the same word often figures both as the speech of the author and as the speech of another – and at the same time.

Another's speech – whether as storytelling, as mimicking, as the display of a thing in light of a particular point of view, as a speech deployed first in compact masses, then loosely scattered, a speech that is in most cases impersonal ('common opinion', professional and generic languages) – is at none of these points clearly separated from authorial speech: the boundaries are deliberately flexible and ambiguous, often passing through a single syntactic whole, often through a simple sentence, and sometimes even dividing up the main parts of a sentence. This varied *play with the boundaries of speech types*, languages and belief systems is one of the most fundamental aspects of comic style.

Comic style (of the English sort) is based, therefore, on the stratification of common language and on the possibilities available for isolating from these strata, to one degree or another, one's own intentions, without ever completely merging with them. *It is precisely the diversity of speech, and not the unity of a normative shared language, that is the ground of style.* It is true that such speech diversity does not exceed the boundaries of literary language conceived as a linguistic whole (that is, language defined by abstract linguistic markers), does not pass into an authentic heteroglossia and is based on an abstract notion of language as unitary (that is, it does not require knowledge of various dialects or languages). However a mere concern for language is but the abstract side of the concrete and active (i.e., dialogically engaged) understanding of the living heteroglossia that has been introduced into the novel and artistically organized within it.

6   Polyphony and Problematic in *Hard Times*

ROGER FOWLER*

Roger Fowler is Professor of Linguistics at the University of East Anglia. He was one of the earliest British critics to recommend and explore in his own work a number of different linguistic approaches to the study of literature. His early work, such as *The Languages of Literature* (London: Routledge and Kegan Paul 1971), promoted the claims of stylistics in the understanding of literary language, while his *Linguistics and the Novel* (London: Methuen, 1977), offered a lucid, compelling case for the extension of forms of linguistic description and analysis to the study of the novel. In his more recent work, such as *Literature as Social Discourse: The Practice of Linguistic Criticism* (London: Batsford, 1981), *Language in the News: Discourse and Ideology in the British Press* (London: Routledge, 1991) and the revised edition of his *Linguistic Criticism* (Oxford: Oxford University Press, 1996) Roger Fowler has become more interested in the study of language in its concrete social uses. He is also the author of *The Language of George Orwell* (Basingstoke: Macmillan, 1995).

This essay was an early attempt to exemplify in a practical way the difference that might be made by a Bakhtinian reading of Dickens's work. Fowler's method works against the tendency to read the language of *Hard Times* as Dickens's own – a tendency exemplified, for example, in David Lodge's reading of the novel, which works from the assumption that 'the author's voice [is] always insistent in his novels' and that, therefore, '*Hard Times* succeeds where its rhetoric succeeds and fails where its rhetoric fails' (*The Language of Fiction: Essays in Criticism and Verbal Analysis*, 2nd edn (London: Routledge and Kegan Paul, 1984), p. 147). Fowler urges us in this essay to attend to the coordinated multiplicity of voices that are heard through the novel, voices that embody 'unresolved contrary ideologies . . . conflicting worldviews [which] resist submersion or cancellation' (p. 103). Seen from this point of view, the

*Reprinted from *The Changing World of Charles Dickens*, ed. Robert Giddings (London: Vision, 1983), pp. 91–108.

success or failure of the novel rests not so much on the kind of solution to contradiction which the novel arrives at, as with the intensity with which it registers and sustains contradiction. Roger Fowler's Bakhtinian reading of *Hard Times* may usefully be compared and contrasted with Jean Ferguson Carr's deployment of Bakhtin for a reading of the same novel, in Chapter 10 of this volume.

The polarization of critical response to *Hard Times* is familiar enough to make detailed reporting unnecessary, but since this polarization is a fact relevant to my argument, I will recapitulate it briefly.

Popular reception of the novel has been largely antagonistic or uninterested. The character of the earlier novels has led to the formation of a cheerful and sentimental 'Dickensian' response which finds *Hard Times*, like the other later novels, cold and uncomfortable, lacking in the innocent jollity, sentimentality and grotesquery of the earlier writings. When Dickens's anniversary was mentioned in a T.V. spot on 7 February 1983, the novelist was identified through a list of his works which totally excluded the later 'social' novels.

In other circles, there has been a keenly appreciative response to *Hard Times*: in some quarters more academic, and in some quarters more socialist. Committedly positive evaluation is found as early as 1860 in Ruskin and then in this century in Shaw, whose appreciation of the book as 'serious social history' initiated a line of evaluation more recently reflected in, for example, Raymond Williams and in David Craig. Then there is a famous and extravagant essay by Leavis:

> Of all Dickens's works it is the one that has all the strength of his genius, together with a strength no other of them can show – that of a completely serious work of art.[1]

If Leavis was over-enthusiastic, others, some such as John Holloway and David M. Hirsch provoked by Leavis's surplus of commendation, have insisted on faults in the novel both as art and as social history. Even that majority of modern academic critics who accept and praise *Hard Times* concede some faults. Among the flaws cited by both camps are the following. A failure of a documentary kind is the presentation of the demagogue Slackbridge – 'a mere figment of the middle-class imagination. No such man would be listened to by a meeting of English factory hands' (Shaw). Similarly, the use of a professional circus to represent Fancy as opposed to Fact has been faulted on the grounds that Dickens might have found Fancy in the native recreations of working people (Craig). A more 'ideological' criticism would allege that Dickens's *concept* of Fancy was, judging from the symbols by which he represented it, too trivial to weigh effectively against the Fact of Utilitarian economic theory and philosophy of education (Holloway, Lodge).[2] Other critics have admitted faults of characterization – the girl Sissy is sentimentally presented and emerges as inadequate: her childhood attributes do not ground her later strength on Louisa's behalf. Again, Stephen and Rachael are said to be too good to be true; Stephen's martyrdom to a drunken wife is a cliché; his refusal to join the union is not motivated and therefore puts him into a weak, contradictory position in relation to his fellow-workers. Now these allegations of faults of construction are not naïve 'Dickensian' complaints. There is real evidence that many things are not quite right with the book, for whatever reason: because of the unfamiliar constraints of small-scale writing for weekly parts, because of the secondhand nature of Dickens's experience?

Since *Hard Times* has gained a very positive reputation in this century, we should beware of condemning it by totting up 'faults'. Perhaps the yardstick which we unconsciously apply, the tradition of the humanistic novel already well established by 1850, is not entirely relevant. It might be preferable to revise our conception of what type of novel this is, or at least to suspend preconception. *Hard Times* is problematic for the critics, and that response itself is perhaps evidence of peculiarities of form. And what we know about the genesis of the novel suggests that it was problematic for Dickens too, involving him in compositional innovations. By this I do not refer merely to the structural consequences of weekly serialization (a discipline he had experienced only once before, in writing *Barnaby Rudge* (1841)), though this mode undoubtedly imposed constraints on episodic and thematic structure, and demanded compression. I mean by 'compositional innovations' new and defamiliarizing dispositions of language in response to new themes and unprecedented *and unresolved* ideological complexity.

A possible model for the structure of *Hard Times* is provided by Mikhail Bakhtin's theory of the 'polyphonic' novel; a theory which has the great benefit, for my purpose, of being interpretable in linguistic terms.[3] In a complex argument, partly theoretical and partly historical, Bakhtin proposes that there have existed two modes of representational fiction: monologic on the one hand and polyphonic or dialogic on the other. The monologic novel, which he claims has been the dominant traditional form, is authoritarian in essence: the author insists on the particular ideology which he voices, and the characters are 'objectified', dependent on the authorial position, and evaluated from the point of view of that position. In the polyphonic novel, on the other hand, the characters (or the 'hero', according to Bakhtin) are more liberated: they achieve voices, and points of view, which challenge the validity of the authorial position. The musical metaphor of polyphony refers to the co-presence of independent but interconnected voices. 'Dialogue' means implicit dialogue, not turn-by-turn speeches: it refers to the fact that one person's speech-forms reflect consciousness of the actual or potential response of an interlocutor, orientation towards a second act of speech. But there is a stronger meaning which Bakhtin seems to have in mind for 'dialogic', and that is 'dialectical'. The dialogic relationship confronts unresolved contrary ideologies, opposing voices in which conflicting world-views resist submersion or cancellation. The dialectical nature of Bakhtin's aesthetic can best be seen in his discussion of *carnival*, which was in his view the medieval forerunner of the polyphonic novel.[4] Carnival, with its boy kings and other multifarious travesties, mediates opposites, associates them while preserving their autonomous identities. It rejoices in extremes, negation, inversion, subversion, antithesis. The rhetorical figures generated by the logic of carnival are clear: they include prominently hyperbole, litotes, negation, syntactic inversions, paradox, contradiction. In social terms, the carnivalistic dialectic is the tension between mutually supportive but antithetical partners such as ruler and subject, employer and worker, teacher and pupil, husband and wife. And we would expect these differences of role, and antagonisms, to be articulated in the language of carnivalistic structures.

At a superficial level, the application of these ideas to *Hard Times* seems well justified. Three of the role-clashes just mentioned (employer/worker, teacher/pupil, husband/wife) figure directly and importantly in the plot. Then the novel contains a large number of diverse characters and groups of characters of very different social origins and affiliations, putting forward many and clashing points of view. The circus performers are an almost literal case of carnival: their diversity and deviance are strongly emphasized, as is their challenge to the authority of Gradgrind and Bounderby (Bk. I, Ch. 6). But polyphonic or dialogic structure is by no means limited to these circus artistes, but exists in the ensemble of numerous voices of opinion and conflict: Slackbridge, Bounderby, Stephen Blackpool, Harthouse, Louisa, Sissy, etc. The task for the analyst who wishes to make sense of this medley of voices is twofold. First, it is necessary to show in detail the linguistic and semiotic characteristics of the various voices (including the narrating voice) which participate in the dialogic structure. Second, the polyphonic structure, the multiplicity of voices, needs to be interpreted in terms of the author's ideology. A plurality of voices does not in itself mean a non-authoritarian narrative stance.

Turning to language itself, Bakhtin does not give a very clear guide as to how the structure of language contributes to the dialogic aesthetic. In fact, he appears to be quite negative on the dialogic value of stylistic variety. But this caution is strategic. He has to concede that Dostoyevsky, his main subject, is stylistically flat, but he must claim, of course, that this thesis works even in this linguistically undifferentiated case. He observes that marked linguistic individuation of fictional characters may lead to an impression of closure, a feeling that the author has definitively analysed a character and placed a boundary around its imaginative or moral potential: 'characters' linguistic differentiation and clear-cut "characteristics of speech" have the greatest significance precisely for the creation of objectivized, finalized images of people.' This seems to me not so much a limitation as an illumination, specifically an insight into our response to Dickens's grotesques: Peggotty, Micawber, Mrs Gamp, and here, Slackbridge. All such characters seem to be clearly delineated, completely known, striking but uncomplicated. But we also need Bakhtin's more positive concession concerning the dialogic potential of speech styles; this potential is effective under certain conditions:

> the point is not the mere presence of specific styles, social dialects, etc., . . . the point is the dialogical *angle* at which they . . . are juxtaposed or counterposed in the work . . .

and

> dialogical relationships are possible among linguistic styles, social dialects, etc., if those phenomena are perceived as semantic positions, as a sort of linguistic *Weltanschauung*.

That is to say, speech styles need not be just caricaturing oddities, but to transcend caricature they must encode characters' worldviews as dialectical alternatives to the world-view of the author and/or, I would suggest, other characters. Thus we might investigate whether, say, Stephen Blackpool's speech, or Bounderby's, encodes in its specific linguistic form a world-view, a set of attitudes; and how the two attitudes relate – in this case, antithetically. Similarly, and perhaps easier to demonstrate, we can look at the dialogic relationships between Gradgrind and Sleary on the one hand, and Gradgrind and the author on the other.

How to proceed in this project? The examples just mentioned are merely striking instances of many, perhaps dozens, of semiotically significant stylistic oppositions which permeate *Hard Times*. To provide a full account would require a book, not a chapter. As essential as space, however, is analytic methodology. Bakhtin provides no tools for analysing linguistic structure, but there is one linguistic theory which explicitly covers Bakhtin's condition that speech styles should be treated as embodying world-views: M. A. K. Halliday's 'functional' theory of language. I must send my readers elsewhere for details,[5] but Halliday's main premise is that linguistic varieties within a community, or 'registers', encode different kinds of meaning, different orientations on experience. Halliday offers a number of analytic systems such as 'transitivity', 'mood', 'cohesion', 'information structure' which I and others have found very valuable in analysing texts for the world-views which they embody.[6] I will use some of these categories below, but my analysis is constrained by space to be largely untechnical.

A list of distinct speech styles in the novel would show that there is an exceptional range of clearly differentiated voices: Sissy, Sleary, Slackbridge, Harthouse, Childers, Bounderby, Stephen, Gradgrind, etc. The length and diversity of the list are of less importance than the specific meanings of the voices and of their structural relationships, but sheer diversity is of some significance for the notion of polyphony. It could be argued merely on the basis of this multiplicity and variousness of voices and people that *Hard Times* makes a *prima facie* claim to be a polyphonic novel. The case would be putative as a global observation, more concrete and demonstrable in relation to specific sections which are explicitly carnivalistic in conduct. The best instance of the latter is the scene at the Pegasus's Arms in Book I, Chapter 6, when Gradgrind and Bounderby, in search of Sissy's father, are confronted by the members of the circus troupe, who speak 'in a variety of voices' (p. 82)[7] and who are combative and subversive in their address to these gentlemen. This scene, which is both challenging and farcical, threatens an anarchic overriding of utility and authority, and touches on antitheses which are more thoroughly debated elsewhere in the book.

I shall now look more closely at how the multiple languages of *Hard Times* signify and intersect by examining samples under three headings: *idiolect*, *sociolect*, and *dialogue*.

An idiolect is the characteristic speech style of an individual. Like dialect, it is a set of background features of language, supposedly constant and permanent characteristics which distinguish a person linguistically. In its most sophisticated realization it is the complex of features, most phonetic, by which we recognize our acquaintances' voices on the telephone. Now idiolects apply to literature in two ways. First, the elusive 'style of an author' might be thought of as an idiolect. I mention this only to observe that *Hard Times* had no consistent authorial idiolect (unlike, to cite a comparable example, Mrs Gaskell's *North and South*). Second, in fiction foregrounding of idiolect produces caricature; and although caricature is a fixing, objectifying process as Bakhtin has indicated, it is a device for making statements, and that is something we are looking for in *Hard Times*. The two sharp instances in this novel are the union demagogue Slackbridge and the circus-master Sleary. Each has a mode of speech which is quite idiosyncratic (with a qualification in the case of Sleary, below) and absolutely self-consistent. Slackbridge conducts himself with a violent, biblical rhetoric:

> Oh my friends, the down-trodden operatives of Coketown! Oh my friends and fellow countrymen, the slaves of an iron-handed and a grinding despotism! Oh my friends and fellow-sufferers, and fellow-workmen, and fellow-men! I tell you that the hour is come, when we must rally round one another as One united power, and crumble into dust the oppressors that too long have battened upon the plunder of our families, upon the sweat of our brows, upon the labour of our hands, upon the strength of our sinews, upon the God-created glorious rights of Humanity, and upon the holy and eternal privileges of Brotherhood!

It has been objected that no trades unionist of the time would have spoken like that (although, apparently, this is not beyond question). But fidelity to the language of the delegates' platform is only part of the issue. The point is that Dickens does not represent *any* social role in a focused way. He has created a symbolic language for his conception of 'Slackbridges', but this language signifies nothing precise: it is a generalized bombast which might inhabit the pulpit, the House of Lords, or any kind of political or public meeting. Conventionally, of course, this sort of language connotes vacuousness and insincerity, and presumably it does so here; but Slackbridge's appearance is an intervention in a complex moral dilemma (Stephen's refusal to 'combine', and his subsequent ostracism by the work-mates who know and respect him) and the signification of his speech style is inadequate to the situation. So Dickens is forced to comment directly on what Slackbridge represents:

> He was not so honest [as the assembled workmen], he was not so manly, he was not so good-humoured; he substituted cunning for their simplicity, and passion for their safe solid sense.

These judgements cannot be read off from the language in which Slackbridge is presented. His role remains puzzling, and since he is dramatically foregrounded as the main speaker against Stephen in this scene, the troubling nature of the scene (stemming largely from the unclarity of Stephen's motives and therefore of his relations with others at the meeting) remains provocatively unresolved.

Sleary is the second linguistic grotesque in the novel. Whereas Slackbridge's language is dominated by a bombastic rhetoric, Sleary's speech is submerged under brandy-and-water. Sibilants are drowned: [s, z, tʃ, ʃ, dʒ ts] all reduce to a sound spelled *th*:

> Tho be it, my dear. (You thee how it ith, Thquire!) Farewell, Thethi-lia! My lath wordth to you ith thith, Thtick to the termth of your engagement, be obedient to the Thquire, and forget uth. But if, when you're grown up and married and well off, you come upon any horthe-riding ever, don't be hard upon it, don't be croth with it, give it a Bethspeak if you can, and think you might do wurth. People mutht be amuthed, Thquire, thomehow, . . . they can't be alwayth a working, nor yet they can't be alwayth a learning. Make the betht of uth; not the wortht.

But Sleary's function in the plot and in the thematic structure of the novel make him more than a comic drunk. In his first appearance (Bk. I, Ch. 6), he is a firm leader of the circus-people in their challenge to the bullying of Gradgrind and Bounderby, and effectively presides over the passage of Sissy into the care of Gradgrind. At the end of the novel, he has been harbouring Gradgrind's criminal son Tom, and (carnivalistically, through the good offices of a dancing horse) manages Tom's flight from apprehension. He is then given virtually the last word, an almost verbatim repetition of the sentiment just quoted. His interventions in the story are directly implicated in Gradgrind's fortunes, and he is the philosophical antithesis to Gradgrind's utilitarian educational thesis: Sleary's Horse-Riding stands for Fancy. This notion of Fancy may well be too trivial for Dickens's purpose, as has been conceded; but at least Sleary is so constituted as to demand attention. The idiolect is insistently defamiliarizing: it 'make[s] forms difficult . . . increase[s] the difficulty and length of perception' as Shklovsky puts it.[8] It takes effort to determine what Sleary is saying, because of the completeness and the whimsicality of the phonological transformation which has been applied to his speech. The reader is compelled to decipher a radical, and not entirely consistent, code which deforms everyday English words into momentarily unrecognizable spellings: *bitterth, prentitht*. These difficulties do not guarantee that what Sleary says is of any great interest; but the fact that Dickens has placed these difficulties in our way indicates that

Sleary is *meant* to be listened to, that he is designed as a significant voice against Gradgrindism in the polyphonic structure of the book.

There is another interesting aspect of Sleary's speech, and one which further distinguishes his discourse from that of Slackbridge. Beneath the idiolect, there are markers which suggest a social dialect or sociolect. Dickens builds into Sleary's speech hints of working-class morphology and lexis: eathy (easily), ath (who), wouldn't . . . no more, took (taken), plain (plainly), winder, lyin', etc. (plus some odd spellings which suggest deviance from the middle-class code, but obscurely: natur, fortun, wurthst, conwenienth); and slang and oaths: morrithed (morrissed, 'fled'), cut it short, damned, mith'd your tip (missed your tip, 'jumped short'), cackler, pound ('wager'), etc. These characteristics link Sleary with the working class – in this novel, the interests of the 'hands' – and with the circus fraternity – the spokespeople for Fancy. These links not only 'naturalize' Sleary by providing him with social affiliations, but also broaden the basis of opposition to the Utilitarian philosophies embodied in Gradgrind (whom Sleary first meets in a confrontation).

The novel contains many other contrasts of speech style, and on the whole they can be explained sociolectally rather than idiolectally: Dickens seems to have accepted the principle that now provides the theoretical basis for Hallidayan linguistics, namely that registers of language characterize social groups and encode their values. Consider, for example, the contrasting speech of Harthouse and of Stephen Blackpool. The former is first introduced as an idle waster ('carelessly lounging') with a languid, verb-less, fragmented speech (Bk. II, Ch. 1). When he is established in Louisa's favours, however, this affectation is replaced by the syntax of 'elaborated code':

Mrs Bounderby, though a graceless person, of the world worldly, I feel the utmost interest, I assure you, in what you tell me. I cannot possibly be hard upon your brother. I understand and share the wise consideration with which you regard his errors. With all possible respect both for Mr Gradgrind and for Mr Bounderby, I think I perceive that he has not been fortunate in his training. Bred at a disadvantage towards the society in which he has to play, he rushes into these extremes for himself, from opposite extremes that have long been forced – with the very best intentions we have no doubt – upon him. Mr Bounderby's fine bluff English independence, though a most charming characteristic, does not – as we have agreed – invite confidence. If I might venture to remark that it is the least in the world deficient in that delicacy to which a youth mistaken, a character misconceived, and abilities misdirected, would turn for relief and guidance, I should express what it presents to my own view.

Hypotaxis – the use of multiple subordinate clauses – dominates the syntax, which is further complicated by parenthetical clauses such as ' – as we have agreed—'. Main clauses are delayed by preposed adjective clauses ('Bred at a disadvantage . . .') and by suspect protestations of diffidence or sincerity ('If I might venture . . .'). Nouns are liberally modified by adjectives, many of them evaluative and evocative of extremes (*graceless, worldly, utmost, wise, opposite, very best,* etc.). Modals are also prominent, emphasizing the speaker's claim to epistemic and deontic involvement in what he says: *cannot possibly, all possible, very best, no doubt, most, least.* Touches of rhetoric of more identifiable origin than Slackbridge's are present: 'a youth mistaken, a character misconceived, and abilities misdirected' is a literary, educated form associated with writing, not oratory – the key to this literariness being the inverted structure N + Adjective (there is only one inversion, Verb + Subject, in all of Slackbridge's speeches: p. 173). Harthouse's speech in this episode is marked as middle-class, elaborated, evasive.[9]

At the other pole, socio-economically and linguistically, is Stephen Blackpool. There is a detailed effort to make Stephen's language indicate his representativeness of a class. A number of different features of his language combine to make his language suggest the regional, uneducated and oral properties of the language of the Hands. He is first shown in an intimate conversation with Rachael, an introduction which makes an immediate point that his speech style is shared, not idiosyncratic. I must quote a sizeable extract, including some commentary by the narrator which offers a clear contrast of style:

'Ah, lad! 'Tis thou?' When she had said this, with a smile which would have been quite expressed, though nothing of her had been seen but her pleasant eyes, she replaced her hood again, and they went on together.

'I thought thou wast ahind me, Rachael?'

'No.'

'Early t'night, lass?'

"Times I'm a little early, Stephen; 'times a little late. I'm never to be counted on, going home.'

'Nor going t'other way, neither, t'seems to me, Rachael?'

'No, Stephen.'

He looked at her with some disappointment in his face, but with a respectful and patient conviction that she must be right in whatever she did. The expression was not lost upon her; she laid her hand lightly on his arm a moment, as if to thank him for it.

'We are such true friends, lad, and such old friends, and getting to be such old folk, now.'

'No, Rachael, thou'rt as young as ever thou wast.'

'One of us would be puzzled how to get old, Stephen, without t'other getting so too, both being alive,' she answered, laughing; 'but, any ways, we're such old friends, that t'hide a word of honest truth fro' one another would be a sin and a pity. 'Tis better not to walk too much together. 'Times, yes! 'Twould be hard, indeed, if 'twas not to be at all,' she said, with a cheerfulness she sought to communicate to him.

''Tis hard, anyways, Rachael.'

'Try to think not; and 'twill seem better.'

'I've tried a long time, and 'ta'nt got better. But thou'rt right; 'tmight mak fok talk, even of thee. Thou has been that to me, through so many year: thou hast done me so much good, and heartened of me in that cheering way, that thy word is a law to me. Ah lass, and a bright good law! Better than some real ones.'

'Never fret about them, Stephen,' she answered quickly, and not without an anxious glance at his face. 'Let the laws be.'

'Yes,' he said, with a slow nod or two. 'Let 'em be. Let everything be. Let all sorts alone. 'Tis a muddle, and that's aw.'

A minimum of deviant spellings here serves to hint at the vowel sounds and the elisions of a northern accent. Elsewhere, Dickens indicates the accent by a more radical set of orthographic, lexical and morphological peculiarities:

'My friends,' Stephen began, in the midst of a dead calm; 'I ha' hed what's been spok'n o' me, and 'tis lickly that I shan't mend it. But I'd liefer you'd hearn the truth concernin myseln, fro my lips than fro onny other man's, though I never cud'n speak afore so monny, wi'out bein moydert and muddled.'

Detailed analyses of these dialect notations are unnecessary. Different novelists (e.g. Mrs Gaskell, Emily Brontë) use different notational devices: some use more archaisms, others more 'non-standard' morphology, and there is variation in the spelling conventions for vowels. There are two simple points to grasp in all such cases. First, these are not to be judged as realistic transcriptions where fidelity might be an issue – they are simply conventional signals of socio-linguistic difference. Second, only a very slight deviance, as in the conversation between Stephen and Rachael, is needed to persuade middle-class readers that they are in the presence of a social group below their own.

More significant is the syntax, which is in sharp contrast to Harthouse's elaborated forms. Halliday maintains that speech and writing have different information structures, and therefore different modes of syntactic organization. Writing, which can be scanned and re-scanned for complexities and qualifications of meaning, is a medium which can accommodate the kinds of indirections which we noted in Harthouse's language. Speech, according to Halliday, is more straightforwardly linear, and it releases its meanings in a sequence of short chunks or 'information units'; these units are segmented off by intonation patterns, rises and falls in the pitch of the voice. Syntactically, they need not be complete clauses, but are often phrases or single words, and often loosely linked by apposition or concatenation. The overall style is not strictly speaking paratactic, because the conjoined constituents are not clauses of equal weight; but in its avoidance of clause subordination it is much more like parataxis than hypotaxis.

Once the existence of this mode of speech has been pointed out, it takes no great analytic expertise to recognize that the description fits the conversation of Stephen and Rachael. The point is that Dickens has – in *writing*, of course – deliberately constructed a very *oral* model of language for these two humble characters, contrasting with the formal, written model used for some unsympathetic middle-class speakers such as Harthouse. I think there is a contrast of values intended here: solidarity and naturalness on the one hand, deviousness and insincerity on the other. I cannot prove this by reference to the language alone; I simply suggest that Dickens is using speech style stereotypes to which his readers, on the basis of their socio-linguistic competence and of their knowledge of the novel's plot, assign conventional significances.

So far I have offered examples of significant individual voices, and of speech styles which seem to take the imprint of social values ('social semiotic' in Halliday's term). Other examples could be discussed; together they would assemble a picture of a text articulated in a multitude of voices. These voices are, overall, discordant and fluctuating in the kaleidoscope of views they express. Furthermore, the opposing points of view do not neatly align. Though Sleary confronts Gradgrind directly, so that the symbol of Fancy and that of Fact are in direct opposition, Harthouse and Stephen are not immediately opposed, nor many other significant antitheses of voices. Dickens's intellectual scheme for the book does not seem to have been symmetrical: his socio-linguistic symbols embodied in characters do not relate diagrammatically, and so the relationships among theoretical issues such as factual education, exploitive capitalism, statistics, social reform, play, etc., are not dramatized neatly in the linguistic or narrative relationships between the characters. The story and the language figure the ideological debates in an unsettled, troubled way. I think this raggedness is a strength. But before commenting on it directly, I want to refer to other areas of linguistic instability, different from the 'unpatternedness' of the global canvas. These areas involve dialogue, explicit or implicit, and figure shifting organization in the style of the voice.

Stephen Blackpool visits Bounderby's house on two occasions, and each time finds himself in a stand-up argument. The debates start with each speaker using his characteristic speech style. Bounderby is blustery and bullying, his speech packed with commands and demands:

> Well Stephen, what's this I hear? What have these pests of the earth being doing to *you*? Come in, and speak up ... Now, speak up! ... Speak up like a man ...

Bounderby continues in this register (which is his constant idiolect, or a major part of it), while Stephen's responses begin quiet and polite, in a language heavily marked for the dialectal phonology, and based on the short information units noticed earlier:

> 'What were it, sir, as yo' were pleased to want wi' me?' ...
> 'Wi' yor pardon, sir, I ha' nowt to sen about it.' ...
> 'I sed as I had nowt to sen, sir; not as I was fearfo' o' openin' my lips.'
> 'I'm as sooary as yo, sir, when the people's leaders is bad. They taks such as offers. Haply 'tis na' the sma'est o' their misfortuns when they can get no better.' ...

Pressed to state how he would solve the troubles of the weaving industry, Stephen moves into a sequence of five long speeches; their sheer length is a sign of departure from character, against the norm of his conversation with Rachael. The spelling peculiarities are maintained to a large degree, as is the syntax of spoken information; this from the third long speech:

> Look round town – so rich as 'tis – and see the numbers of people as has been broughten into bein heer, fur to weave, an to card, an to piece out a livin', aw the same one way, somehows, twixt their cradles and their graves.

The fifth of these speeches has Stephen, under intense provocation, voicing sentiments of 'man' against 'master' which on independent evidence, as well as the evidence of the novel, can be associated with Dickens's own humanitarian point of view. Stephen cannot say what will right the world, but he can say what will not: the strong hand of the masters, *laissez-faire*, lack of regard for the humanity of the mill-workers, and so on. When Stephen gives voice to these sentiments, the overall structure of his language changes to the parallelistic rhetoric of a public speech: a succession of balanced sentences, steadily increasing in length, is used to enumerate his arguments; here are two of them:

> Not drawin' nigh to fok, wi' kindness and patience an cheery ways, that so draws nigh to one another in their monny troubles, and so cherishes one another in their distresses wi' what they need themseln – like, I humbly believe, as no people the genelman ha seen in aw his travels can beat – will never do't till th'Sun turns t'ice. Most of aw, ratin 'em as so much Power, and reg'latin 'em as if they was figures in a soom, or machines: wi'out loves and likeins, wi'out memories and inclinations, wi'out souls to weary and souls to hope – when aw goes quiet, draggin on wi' 'em as if they'd nowt o' th'kind, an when aw goes onquiet, reproachin 'e, for their want o' sitch humanly feelins in their dealins wi' you – this will never do't, sir, till God's work is onmade.

Some of the elaborated syntax noticed in Harthouse's language can be found here in the internal structure of clauses, in the qualifications and self-interruptions. And the overall format of repetitive structure recalls the insistent harangue of the book's opening scene, in the schoolroom.

When Stephen engages with the moral issues which concern Dickens centrally, then, his language deviates sharply from what had earlier been offered as his own characteristic socio-linguistic style. I do not point this out as an inconsistency of characterization, but as an application of the dialogic principle in the language through which Stephen is constituted. The stylistic shift shows strain in Dickens's use of a voice to express an ideological position that has become problematic through being assigned to that speaker. Stephen as originally set up by Dickens is inadequate to occupy the place in debate in which he has become situated: his language strains towards the rhetoric of a more public form of disputation than his social role warrants.

Surprising shifts of register occur in the speech of other characters, although none so remarkable as the transformation from tongue-tied weaver to articulate orator. I have no space to demonstrate any more of these changes; nor, most regrettably, can I show any selection of the range of styles of the narrative voice. Dickens ranges from subversive parody (Bk. I, Ch. 1, on Gradgrind on Fact), to complex animating and de-animating metaphors (Bk. I, Ch. 5, the superb evocation of Coketown) to pathos, and to simple direct judgement ('He was a good power-loom weaver, and a man of perfect integrity'). David Lodge has analysed some varieties of the narrative rhetoric of *Hard Times* in an excellent chapter of *Language of Fiction*: analysis which readers can consult to fill out this gap in my account. Lodge also relates these variations to uncertainties in Dickens's own position, as I do. But his judgement is essentially based on a monologic norm: '*Hard Times* succeeds where its rhetoric succeeds and fails where its rhetoric fails.' Generally, Lodge argues, this rhetoric is successful when Dickens is being antagonistic or ironic, but fails when he is trying to celebrate his fictional positives.

But it is more complex than that. The various styles are not just 'successful' or 'failed', but transcend a two-term set of values: it is the plurality of codes, their inconstancy, and their frequent stridency, which all together constitute a fruitful and discordant polyphony. Any account of Dickens's 'argument' in this novel is bound to come to the conclusion that he attacks an unmanageably large and miscellaneous range of evils (utilitarianism in education and economics, industrial capitalism, abuse of unions, statistics, bad marriage, selfishness, etc.); that he mostly over-simplifies them (e.g. fails to see the beneficial relationship between some fact-gathering activities and real social reforms); that he is unclear on what evil causes what other evil. On the other side, his proposed palliatives are feeble, misconceived in terms of purely individual initiatives and responsibilities, and sentimentally formulated. Most of this conceptual muddle stems from the crucial inadequacy of Dickens's idealized solution of tolerant rapprochement of the two parties to the industrial situation:

> 'I believe,' said I, 'that into the relations between employers and employed, as into all the relations of this life, there must enter something of feeling and sentiment; something of mutual expla-nation, forbearance, and consideration; something which is not to be found in Mr McCulloch's dictionary, and is not exactly stateable in figures; otherwise those relations are wrong and rotten at the core and will never bear sound fruit.'[10]

Translation of all Dickens's insecurely based theses and antitheses into elements and structural relationships of this novel's form has

produced the asymmetries and dissonances which my stylistic
analysis has begun to display. But few people today would condemn
Hard Times as a ragged failure. The inconsistencies and discords are
an indication of the problematic status of the social and theoretical
crises in question for a great imagination like Dickens who could not
articulate unequivocally in fiction the (unknown to him) facile solutions
which were consciously available to him as theory. The novel's lack
of monologic authority fits Bakhtin's description, I believe; and the
stylistic polyphony is provocative and creative, compelling the reader
to grapple uneasily with the tangle of issues that Dickens
problematizes.

Notes

1. JOHN RUSKIN, 'A note on *Hard Times*', *Cornhill Magazine*, 2 (1860), reprinted in
   GEORGE FORD and SYLVÈRE MONOD (eds.), *Hard Times* (New York: W. W.
   Norton and Co., 1966), pp. 331–32; GEORGE BERNARD SHAW, *Introduction to
   Hard Times* (London: Waverley, 1912), reprinted Ford and Monod, ed. cit.,
   pp. 332–39; RAYMOND WILLIAMS, *Culture and Society 1780–1950*
   (Harmondsworth: Penguin, 1968).
2. JOHN HOLLOWAY, '*Hard Times*: a history and a criticism', in *Dickens and the
   Twentieth Century*, eds. JOHN GROSS and GABRIEL PEARSON (London:
   Routledge and Kegan Paul, 1962), reprinted Ford and Monod, ed. cit.,
   pp. 361–66; DAVID LODGE, *Language of Fiction* (London: Routledge and Kegan
   Paul, 1966).
3. MIKHAIL BAKHTIN, trans. R. W. ROTSEL, *Problems of Dostoyevsky's Poetics* (Ann
   Arbor: Ardis, 1973).
4. MIKHAIL BAKHTIN, trans. H. ISWOLSKY, *Rabelais and his World* (Cambridge,
   Mass.: MIT Press, 1968).
5. M. A. K. HALLIDAY, ed. G. R. KRESS, *Halliday: System and Function in Language*
   (London: Oxford University Press, 1976); Halliday, *Language as Social Semiotic*
   (London: Edward Arnold, 1978). Most of the works cited in note 6 below give
   accounts of relevant aspects of Halliday's theory.
6. A seminal literary application by Halliday is his paper 'Linguistic function
   and literary style', in SEYMOUR CHATMAN (ed.), *Literary Style, A Symposium*
   (New York and London: Oxford University Press, 1971). Relevant applications
   by others include R. FOWLER, *Linguistics and the Novel* (London: Methuen,
   1977); R. FOWLER, 'Anti-language in fiction', *Style*, 13 (1979), 259–78; R. FOWLER,
   R. HODGE, G. R. KRESS and A. TREW, *Language and Control* (London: Routledge
   and Kegan Paul, 1979); R. FOWLER, *Literature as Social Discourse* (London:
   Batsford, 1981); G. N. LEECH and M. H. SHORT, *Style in Fiction* (London:
   Longman, 1981).
7. Quotations from *Hard Times* follow David Craig's edition (Harmondsworth:
   Penguin, 1969), with a very few minor apparent printing errors corrected.
8. VIKTOR SHKLOVSKY, 'Art as technique', in LEE T. LEMON and MARION J. REIS

(ed. and trans.), *Russian Formalist Criticism* (Lincoln, Nebraska: University of Nebraska Press, 1965), p. 12.

9. On 'elaborated code' and its connotations see BASIL BERNSTEIN, *Class, Codes and Control*, Vol. I (London: Routledge and Kegan Paul, 1971); WILLIAM LABOV, 'The logic of non-standard English', in P. P. GIGLIOLI (ed.), *Language and Social Context* (Harmondsworth: Penguin, 1972).

10. Reprinted in FORD and MONOD, ed. cit.

7 Prison-bound: Dickens and Foucault
Great Expectations

JEREMY TAMBLING*

Jeremy Tambling teaches in the Department of Comparative Literature at the University of Hong Kong. He is a versatile critic, who
has written about the relations between opera and contemporary
media, in *Opera, Ideology and Film* (Manchester: Manchester University Press, 1987) and in *A Night In At the Opera: Media Representations
of Opera* (London: John Libbey, 1994), which he edited; about the
work of Dante, in *Dante and Difference: Writing in the Commedia*
(Cambridge: Cambridge University Press, 1988); as well as works
on the nature of narrative and literary language, in *What is Literary
Language?* (Milton Keynes: Open University Press, 1988) and *Narrative and Ideology* (Milton Keynes: Open University Press, 1991). His
Confession: Sexuality, Sin and the Subject (Manchester: Manchester
University Press, 1990) extends the Foucauldian analysis offered in
this essay to a number of other nineteenth-century literary works.
His current work concerns the relations between Dickens and modernity. This essay investigates *Great Expectations* in the light of Michel
Foucault's account of the internalization of structures of surveillance
and power in the forming of the modern disciplinary society.
Against the grain of those conventional accounts of the novel which
would see it as showing the growth into freedom and autonomy of
the narrating Pip, Tambling shows how closely bound up the narration of individuality is with the exercise of power. Finally, the
autobiographical impulse itself is shown to have become an agency
of voluntary self-incarceration.

Great Expectations has been called an analysis of 'Newgate London',[1]
suggesting that the prison is everywhere implicitly dominant in the
book, and it has been a commonplace of Dickens criticism, since
Edmund Wilson's essay in *The Wound and the Bow* and Lionel
Trilling's introduction to *Little Dorrit*, to see the prison as a metaphor

*Reprinted from *Essays in Criticism*, 36 (1986), 11–31. The ordering of the notes has
been adjusted and some bibliographical information added for the purposes of
clarification.

throughout the novels. Not just a metaphor, of course: the interest that Dickens had in prisons themselves was real and lasting, and the one kind of concern leads to the other, the literal to the metaphorical. Some earlier Dickens criticism, particularly that associated with the 1960s, and Trilling's 'liberal imagination', stressed the second at the expense of the first, and Dickens became the novelist of the 'mind forg'd manacles' of Blake, where Mrs Clennam can stand in the Marshalsea 'looking down into this prison as it were out of her own different prison' – *Little Dorrit* pt. 2 ch. 31. This Romantic criticism became a way of attacking the historical critics who emphasized the reformist Dickens, interested in specific social questions: Humphry House and Philip Collins, the last in *Dickens and Crime* and *Dickens and Education*, (1962 and 1964). With Foucault's work on the 'birth of the prison' – the subtitle of his book *Discipline and Punish*, (1976) – it may be possible to see how the physical growth of the modern prison is also the beginning of its entering into discourse and forming structures of thought, so that the literal and the metaphorical do indeed combine, and produce the Dickens whose interest is so clearly in both ways of thinking about the prison.

Discipline and Punish is the first of Foucault's books about modes of power operating in western societies, and it succeeds his inaugural address at the Collège de France in 1970, the 'Discourse on Language', where his interest is in showing the way that knowledge is a form of manipulation, and must be thought of in the same breath as the word 'power'. Power in the absolutist state takes its bearings on the body, illustrated in the first part of the book, but the 'gentle way in punishment', associated with late 18th-century enlightenment thought, leads to a change in the way power is exercised – from 'a right to take life or let live to a form of power that fosters life, the latter being described as a power over life, in contrast to the former sovereign power, which has been described as a power over death'.[2] At the end of the 18th century, penal codes were drawn up which addressed themselves to the mind of the criminal, not defined as such, nor as an offender, but as a 'delinquent' (p. 251).[3] A personality type is thus created: the change Foucault marks is one towards the creation of an entity: a mind to be characterized in certain ways, (whereas earlier the body was directly marked), to produce the 'docile body' – 'one that may be subjected, used, transformed and improved' – and thus fitted for new modes of industrial production. A 'technology of subjection' comes into use: Foucault refers to Marx's discussion of the division of labour in this context (p. 221). The arrangement of the bodies of individuals for productive and training purposes is facilitated by the renewed attention given to the mind, to the prisoner as personality.

Foucault's subject is thus the 'disciplinary technology' engineered in western societies, but perhaps the most compelling image in the book is the very utopist idea of the Panopticon – that which would have been the appearance of the superego in time, if it had been realized, not merely been left on paper by Bentham. The Panopticon, with its central tower where the unseen warders may or may not be looking at the several storeys of individually divided-off prisoners, who can see neither their controlling agency, nor the others in the cells, but are arranged in a circle around this surveillance tower, presents the possibility of total and complete control being exercised over the prison's inmates. Philip Collins discusses it in *Dickens and Crime* – a book still useful for its donkey work, though very undertheorized, and not able to question the role of the prison in western society – and Collins stresses that the Panopticon, while it was itself not to be recognized as a project, was to provide the model for all other types of institution: the birth of the prison means the birth of all kinds of normalizing procedures, carried out in buildings still very familiar today, that all look exactly like the exterior of the 19th-century prison. Collins quotes Bentham: 'Morals reformed, health preserved, industry invigorated, instruction diffused, public burdens lightened, economy seated, as it were, upon a rock, the Gordian knot of the Poor Laws not cut, but untied, – all by a simple idea of Architecture!'[4] Something of the Panoptical method is at work in *Hard Times* too: the idea being thought suitable for schools and factories. In Gradgrind's school, the pupils are so raked that each can be seen at a glance, and each is individuated, though with a number, not a name. Leavis's influential account of this book stresses how Benthamism in Coketown stifles individuality, and life and emotions, but Foucault's argument implies that the Panopticon idea stressed individuality, though not in the idealist manner that the Romantic poets, themselves contemporary with this 'birth of the prison', saw that concept of the individual. The Panopticon's rationale was the sense that each subject of care was to be seen as an individual mind. Alongside this creation of separate sentiences, goes a discourse to sustain it – in the formation of the 'sciences of man . . . these sciences which have so delighted our 'humanity' for over a century . . . (which) . . . have their technical matrix in the petty, malicious minutiae of the disciplines and their investigations' (p. 226). The social sciences emerge out of what Foucault calls the 'constitution' of this individual with an individual mind, as 'a describable, analysable object', (p. 190), the origins of the sciences of man may have their origin, Foucault suggests, in the files of prisons and institutions, 'these ignoble archives, where the modern play of coercion over bodies, gestures and behaviour has its beginnings'

(p. 191). This new carceral framework 'constituted one of the armatures of power-knowledge that has made the human sciences historically possible. Knowable man, (soul, individuality, consciousness, conduct, whatever it is called) is the object-effect of this analytical investment, of this domination-observation' (p. 305). It is a retreat from this positivist conception that stresses 'man's unconquerable mind' – the conclusion to a poem significantly written to a man in prison – and that invests the mind with unknowable, unfathomable qualities – as both Dickens and Leavis-like criticism do. The two stresses run together.

Bentham, more than just the inspirer of Mr Gradgrind, is a voice behind a whole new 'disciplinary technology', then, and the Panopticon becomes a metaphor, or, to quote Foucault,

> the diagram of a mechanism of power reduced to its ideal form; its functioning, abstracted from any obstacle, resistance or friction, must be represented as a pure architectural and optical system: it is, in fact, a figure of political technology that may and must be detached from any specific use. It is polyvalent in its applications; it serves to reform prisoners, but also to treat patients, to instruct school children, to confine the insane, to supervise workers, to put beggars and idlers to work. It is a type of location of bodies in space, of distribution of individuals in relation to one another, of hierarchical organization, of disposition of centres and channels of power, which can be implemented in hospitals, workshops, schools, prisons. (p. 205).

As a metaphor, what is implied is that the prison will enter, as both reality and as a 'type' that will form the discourse of society. Trilling's discussion of the prevalence of the prison motif in 19th-century literature finds its explanation here: the sense that metaphysically the prison is inescapable, – reaching even to a person's whole mode of discourse, and creating Nietzsche's 'prison-house of language', so that nothing escapes the limitations of the carceral, – is objectively true in the domination of the prison in other 19th-century forms of discourse.

What is in question is normalizing delinquent mentalities and preserving them as abnormal, for Foucault makes it clear that normalizing powers succeed best when they are only partially successful, when there can be a marginalization of certain types of personality, and the creation of a stubborn mentality that resists educative and disciplinary processes. 'The prison, and no doubt punishment in general, is not intended to eliminate offences, but rather to distinguish them, to distribute them, to use them . . .' (p.

272). On such bases, the vocabulary of power is sited, where, for additional prop, not the law, but the norm is the standard, and where not acts, but identities are named. The law was however involved as well: police surveillance grew especially in the 1850s, with as a result the nearly inevitable criminalizing of so many sections of the population, due to the growth in the number of penal laws.[5] In the Panopticon, that 'mill grinding rogues honest and idle men industrious',[6] identity is created and named: while the model prison (i.e. solitary confinement, either partial, and belonging merely to the prisoner's leisure time, or total, as in Philadelphia) is discussed by Foucault in terms of the way isolation becomes a means of bringing prisoners to a state where they will carry on the reform work of the prison in their own person, where the language of the dominating discourse is accepted and internalized.

To come with these insights of Foucault to *Great Expectations* is to discover two things. It is to see how far a 19th-century text is aware of this creation of power and of oppression that Foucault has charted so interestingly: to examine the text's relation to this dominant ideology as Foucault has described it. It is also to read the book, as having itself to do with 'the power of normalization and the formation of knowledge in modern society', which is how Foucault describes what *Discipline and Punish* is concerned with (p. 308). The issue of seeing the prison as an essential condition of Victorian society, as also of the generation that was pre-Victorian, turns on the libertarian notion of the prison as inherently oppressive; that much is clear in the novel, with its Hulks, Newgate, and transportation, and prisonous houses, such as Satis House and even Wemmick's castle. It also has to do with Dickens's registering of the prison being bound up with questions of language and the control of language – which, of course, entails ways of thinking, a whole discourse. In other words, the book shows an awareness of the fact that to learn a language is connected with the control of knowledge. In the Panopticon, the knowledge of a person is both coloured and colouring, and to acquire knowledge, by entering into the dominant discourse, is to learn the language of oppression.

In Dickens there is a move from literal treatment of the prison from *Sketches by Boz* onwards, including the visits to the isolation penitentiaries in the United States in 1842, where he saw the 'Auburn system' at work – based on the prison at Gloucester (which Foucault refers to, p. 123) at both Boston and Connecticut;[7] his accounts of both appear in *American Notes*, chs. 3 and 5. The 'silent association' system there – partial solitary confinement only – he preferred to the Eastern Penitentiary at Philadelphia. It is not hard to see both systems as relations of the Panopticon dream.[8] Dickens found what he saw distasteful. He questioned, in a letter to Forster, whether the controllers 'were sufficiently acquainted with the human mind to know what it is they are doing': while *American Notes* finds 'this slow and daily tampering with the mysteries of the brain to be immeasurably worse than any torture of the body'. The person must be returned from this state 'morally unhealthy and diseased'. It is halfway to Foucault's gathering of criticisms of the prison that were made in France between 1820–45: indeed, Dickens's comments are sited within those criticisms, commented on in *Discipline and Punish* (pp. 265–8).

But, as criticism, it isn't free from the point that the thinking about the nature of the prison has not gone far enough to question its rationale, as a social fact, as the product of a type of thinking. The point may be made from *Great Expectations*, at a moment where Pip (the moment is almost gratuitous – Dickens is moving away from treatment of literal prisons) is invited by Wemmick to visit Newgate:

> At that time, jails were much neglected, and the period of exagger-ated reaction consequent on all public wrong-doing – and which is always its heaviest and longest punishment – was still far off. So, felons were not lodged and fed better than soldiers (to say nothing of paupers) and seldom set fire to their prisons with the excusable object of improving the flavour of their soup.[9]

Collins links this observation to the riots that took place at Chatham Convict prison early in 1861,[10] and makes it clear that Chatham represented a heavily reactionary kind of discipline, certainly no 'better' than the Newgate Pip is describing. I put 'better' in quotation-marks to suggest that the concept of progress in prison discipline and order cannot be assumed: in Foucault's terms, the more enlightened the prison, the more subtle its means of control, that is all. Can much be said in favour of this passage? Many readers of Dickens will assume it to be part of the dominant mode to be noted in Dickens's speeches and letters: the voice of the liberal consensus, wanting prisons as simply neither too hard nor too easy. But the quotation also gives the register of Pip, who is historically at the moment when he is furthest away from his knowledge about the criminal basis of society; most alienated from his own associations with criminality – hence, of course, the irony that the chapter closes with the facial resemblance that Estella has to Molly. In terms of writing, he is looking back ('at that time') and seems to have learned nothing: at least he still wishes to place prisoners as below soldiers and paupers, not seeing that both these groups endure the same oppression that makes people prisoners – a conclusion that the novel

often comes to, not least in giving Magwitch the significant name of
Abel and so making him the original innocent and hunted down
figure. Pip's language, then, is still part of that of a 'brought-up
London gentleman' (p. 339): it belongs to a Victorian dominant
discourse. (And 'brought-up' also suggests 'bought-up' and goes
along with the equations of property and personality that go on
throughout; compare Havisham – Have-is-sham, even Have-is-am;
the last the latest development of the Cartesian cogito. The dominators,
no less than the dominated, receive their individuality from their
position in the carceral network.)

Those who identify Pip's attitude with Dickens's assume there is
nothing in the text to qualify what is said here, or else that a plurality
in the text allows Dickens to engage in a journalistic point in the
middle of Pip's narration. Either may be right, but I would rather
regard the utterance as being ironic rather than sincere – a disavowal,
in this most confessional and disavowing of books, of a way of
thinking once held. Pip's mode is autobiographical and confessional
almost in the Catholic sense of that last word: the book reveals
Dickens's autobiography and self-revelation of disgust in the same
way. The reader of *Great Expectations* is able to reject the opinions
expressed at the start of chapter 32 in the light of the reading of the
rest of the book. Behind the narrator, the author asks for a similar
dismissal. Behind Pip's confession, lies Dickens's own: or Dickens's
as the representative of a precisely positioned class, of the liberal
petit-bourgeoisie. The novel distances itself from Pip's confessions
perhaps in order to listen to Dickens's. But then that one – Dickens's
– may itself be refused, be shown to be as relative as the one that it
shadows.

What is clear is the prevailing confessional note of *Great
Expectations*. TO BE READ IN MY CELL (p. 132) is apt
metalinguistically. That is to say, it comments on the text's sense of
the way it should be read, and what Pip thinks it is about. This is
not the fictional Augustinian mode of confessions, though a 'cell'
would well suit the Catholic form of confession: it is rather that the
mode of autobiography fits with Protestant thought. Trilling
comments on the late 18th-century 'impulse to write autobiography'
and says that 'the new kind of personality which emerges . . . is what
we call an individual: at a certain point in history men became
individuals'.[11] The ability to confess in autobiography is constitutive
of the subject for him-herself – but as Foucault would add, it would
be 'subject "in both senses of the word" ',[12] for confession would be
the means whereby the dominant discourse is internalised. Foucault
continues: 'The obligation to confess is now relayed through so many
different points, is so deeply ingrained in us, that we no longer

perceive it as the effect of a power which constrains us; on the contrary, it seems to us that truth, lodged in our most secret nature, "demands" only to surface'. *The History of Sexuality* is the continuation of that theme of power as constitutive of knowledge that runs through *Discipline and Punish* and it is a keypoint of the novel that Pip is ready always to confess: such is his autobiography, a disavowal. The interest in the prison and the interest in autobiographical confession: these two things converge.

For *Great Expectations* certainly recognizes itself to be about the creation of identities, imposed from higher to lower, from oppressor to oppressed. From the first page there is the 'first most vivid and broad impression of the identity of things', where a considerable amount of naming goes on – 'I called myself Pip and came to be called Pip'; where the 7–year-old child names 'this bleak place overgrown with nettles' as 'the churchyard' and similarly characterizes the marshes, the river, the sea, and himself as 'that small bundle of shivers growing afraid of it all and beginning to cry' who 'was Pip'. The phrasing of the last part suggests that the act of naming the self and nature is a rationalization, an incomplete and unsatisfactory way of labelling what resists formulation. It fits with that pejorative way of describing the self just quoted: that too fits the confessional position. The self is mis-named from the beginning, minimised; and gross acts of naming take place thenceforth, from Mrs Hubble's belief that the young are never grateful, not to say 'naturally vicious' (p. 57) to Jaggers saying that boys are 'a bad set of fellows' (p. 111). Wopsle and company identify an accused with the criminal (ch. 18), Pip sees himself as George Barnwell, and receives a number of descriptions and names – Pip, Handel, 'the prowling boy' (p. 199), 'you young dog' (p. 36), 'my boy' (p. 50), 'you boy' (p. 91), 'you visionary boy' (p. 377). Anonymity, though not the absence of naming, hangs over Mrs Joe (defined, absurdly, through the husband), Orlick, whose name Dolge is 'a clear impossibility' (p. 139), Magwitch – Provis at all times to Jaggers, Trabb's boy, Drummle – the Spider -, the Aged P and Mr Waldengarver. The power of naming confers identity: Q. D. Leavis's analysis sees the power as one that implants guilt.[13] That guilt-fixing belongs to Foucault's Panopticon society, and indeed the sense of being looked at is pervasive – whether by the young man who hears the words Pip and Magwitch speak, by the hare hanging up in the larder – an early execution image – or by the cow that watches Pip take the wittles on Christmas Day. Pip expects a constable to be waiting for him on his return; has the sensation of being watched by relatives at Satis House, has his house watched on the night of Magwitch's return, has Compeyson sit behind him in the theatre (where he himself is watching), and is watched by the coastguard and the river police in the attempt to take off Magwitch (none of the friendship here with the police implied in the 1853 article 'Down with the Tide': the Dickensian hero is shown here as in flight from the agents of law). Where such spying is an integral part of the book, the sense of being someone constituted as having a secret to hide is not far away. Pip feels himself a criminal, early and late; and Orlick tells him he is: 'It was you as did for your shrew sister' (p. 437) – this coming from the man who has tracked Pip constantly, and shadowed Biddy, too. Reflecting the first chapters' growth of self-awareness, – where the child is crying over his parents' grave, as though not just feeling himself inadequate, but as already guilty, already needing to make some form of reparation – Magwitch says that he 'first became aware of himself down in Essex a thieving turnips for his living' (p. 360). Jaggers identifies Drummle as criminal – 'the true sport' (p. 239) – and encourages him in his boorishness and readiness to brain Startop. His method of cross-examination is to criminalize everyone, himself resisting classification, no language being appropriate for one as 'deep' as he. 'You know what I am, don't you?' is the last comment he makes after the dinner party where he has hinted that Molly (whom he seems to own) is a criminal type. The question is to be answered negatively, for he is like the unseen watcher in the central tower of the Panopticon, naming others, but not named himself (his centrality is implied in the address of his office), in the position, as criminal lawyer, of power, conferring identities, controlling destinies – not for nothing are those criminals in Newgate compared to plants in the greenhouse, and regarded with the scientific detachment that for Foucault is part of the 'discourse of truth' of 19th-century positivism.

Identities all become a matter of social control and naming: Estella might have turned out one way as one of the 'fish' to come to Jaggers's net, yet she is constituted differently from Miss Havisham's hands. Pip remains the passive victim whose reaction is to blame himself for every action he is in: his willingness to see himself as his sister's murderer (chapter 16) is of a piece with his final ability to see himself as characteristically unjust to Joe. Q. D. Leavis's account works against those which see the book as 'a snob's progress'; her emphases are useful in suggesting that it is *Pip* who sees himself thus; and that now he is 'telling us dispassionately how he came to be the man who can now write thus about his former self'.[14] The 'us', by eliding the 1860s readers of the text with these who come a century later, implies that there is a central, ahistorical way of taking the text: a strong liberal-humanist ideology underwrites the assumption which also implies that there is some decent norm Pip could approximate to, which would untie all his problems. It thus assimilates all historical differences, at the least, to the notion of the free subject, who is at all times accessible to decent human feelings – and capable of reaching a central normality.

If what Q. D. Leavis said were the case, it would mean Pip had reached some degree of 'normality' by the end of what has happened to him, before he starts narrating. He is not a central human presence, but a writer whose text needs inspection for its weakness of self-analysis; for he never dissociates himself from the accusations he piles on himself at the time of the events happening, and afterwards. In Wemmick's and Jaggers's character-formulations of people as either 'beaters or cringers' he remains a cringer, and unable to recognize himself in Herbert's genial view – 'a good fellow, with impetuosity and hesitation, boldness and diffidence, action and dreaming, curiously mixed in him' (p. 269). That positive evaluation, binary nonetheless in its terms, in the same way as the Panopticon system lends itself to an extreme form of binary division, is beyond him: his self-perception makes him oppressor, while, more accurately, he is victim. Foucault stresses how the healthy individual is defined in relation to that which has been labelled as delinquent, degenerate or perverse; and his studies of madness, of the birth of the clinic and of the prison all meet in this: 'when one wants to individualize the healthy normal and law-abiding adult, it is always by asking him how much of the child he has in him, what secret madness lies within him, what fundamental crime he has dreamed of committing' (*Discipline and Punish*, p. 193). On this basis, Pip might be said to be the creation of three discourses that intersect: he remains something of the child – his name, a diminutive, establishes that; he is never in a position, he feels, of equality with anyone else; his dreams of the file, of Miss Havisham hanging from the beam, of playing Hamlet without knowing more than five words of the play, his nightmarish sense of phantasmagoric shapes perceived in the rushlight in the Hummums, and his sense of being a brick in a house-wall, or part of a machine, 'wanting to have the engine stopped, and my part in it hammered off' (p. 472) – all proclaim his 'secret madness'. His sense of criminality is fed by virtually each act and its consequences that he undertakes.

A victim of the language system, only on one or two occasions does he reverse the role and become implicitly the accuser; one is where he prays over the head of the dead Magwitch: 'Lord be merciful to him a sinner' (p. 470) where commentators such as Moynahan have found something false. It is inappropriate, but it seems to belong to the Pip whose sense of himself is not free enough to allow himself to deconstruct the language system he is in. The odd thing is not that he fails to see himself as the sinner, as in the parable (*Luke* ch. 18), but that he should want to name Magwitch as such. But that fact of naming is a reflection of the way the dominated have no choice but to take over the language of their domination – to continue to beat, as they have been beaten, to continue to name disparagingly, as they have been named. That act in itself continues to name Pip – implicitly, as the Pharisee, of course. The question the novel asks is what else he might do: he seems caught. The self can only retreat from that dominant discourse through schizoid behaviour, as happens with Wemmick and his dual lifestyles, yet does not the 'Castle's' existence betray the prison's presence still in Wemmick's thinking? He, too, has not got away.

A second time when the language of Pip's oppression becomes one to oppress another is at the end of the book where he meets the younger Pip and suggests to Biddy that she should 'give Pip to him, one of these days, or lend him, at all events' (p. 490). To this Biddy responds 'gently' 'no', but her answer might well have been a horrified one in the light of what surrogate parents do to their children in the book: Pip is offering to play Magwitch to Biddy's child. He has learned nothing: is indeed a recidivist, unaware of how much he has been made himself a subject of other people's power and knowledge. Magwitch, similarly, 'owns' Pip (p. 339) as he says with pride: it is well-meaning as a statement, but with Foucault's aid it may be seen that Magwitch as a member of the class marginalized and set apart by the Panopticon society, has had to take on those dominant oppressive values, and talks the same language of property. His attitude is not inherently selfish, but it is a mark of his social formation which conditions him to speak as he does. In this most sociologically interactionist of novels, it is recognized that the self can use no other language than that given to it. What liberty there is is suggested by Orlick, who cringes after Joe beats him, beats Mrs Joe and secures her cringing – which, indeed, as 'a child towards a hard master' (p. 151) she seems to enjoy, as she continues to draw the sign of his power over her: such is the token of her self-oppression. (The contrast with Rosa Dartle, also the victim of a hammer-blow, is worth attention: Rosa's whole position as poor relation is self-oppressive.) Orlick, through a certain upward mobility, derived from his association with Compeyson, changes from the cringer himself (paid off by Jaggers from service at Satis House) to the accuser of Pip in the sluice-house. He perceives he has been marginalized, in some ways defined as delinquent, but it is an insight that could not be the source of social action or improvement, for it never extends beyond himself: as he says to Pip, 'you was favoured and he [Orlick] was bullied and beat' (p. 437). Out of that crazed imperception, he lashes out at Pip: the reverse action to Magwitch's, who almost equally arbitrarily identifies Pip with himself. (The novel wishes to close the gap between the convict and Pip, so Herbert says that Pip reminded Magwitch of the daughter he had lost.) Orlick and Magwitch go in opposite directions: what unites them (as it links them with Pip) is their sense that they are the watched, the ones under surveillance. Orlick's reactions to Pip look like Nietzsche's *ressentiment*,[15] that quality that Foucault has made much use of in discussing the origins of the impulse towards power. Dickens's 'cringer' is like Nietzsche's 'reactive personality': for Nietzsche, it is characteristically this type that, fired by resentment, tries to move into the legislative position. Orlick's rancour is born out of the inability that those watched in the Panopticon society have (since they have been put in individual cells, they cannot see each other) to read their situation as akin to that of other marginalized figures.

Thus the production, and reproduction, of oppression is what the book charts. Orlick attempts to move over to the other side in the Panopticon, and from the attempted assumption of that position, turns against Pip. Magwitch's acquisition of money is his attempt to move to the other side, to create a Pip, whom he surveys. In fact, he remains the criminal in the way he is named. Nor can Orlick change, and though he is in the county jail at the end, the replication of the book's past events seems safe with him when he is released: he really has no alternative, and as such he remains an apt commentary on the course an oppressed class must follow. Pip, in terms of status, moves over to the other side, in Panopticon terms, but his social formation is already firm, and basically he cannot change either: the events in the second part of his 'expectations' are an aberration from what he is in the first and third parts. Ironically, since he is cast there as guilty, what he is at those points is preferable to what he becomes in the second part.

As the recidivist, he wishes to be given Biddy's child, which would start again the whole cycle of oppression; and self-oppressive to the end, he writes out his autobiography – one that remains remarkably terse as to its intentions and its status as writing and which rolls out as though automatically, the product of a consciousness that remains fixed. Comparisons with the modes of David Copperfield's, or Esther Summerson's, or George Silverman's narratives would bear out this frozen, and at times almost perfunctory, manner. Miss Wade begins her account of herself sharply with the statement that she is 'not a fool'. Pip says nothing about himself as he is at the time of writing. He remains as someone who seems not to have gone beyond the emotional state documented in the writing, so that there is nothing cathartic about the confession, and no release is gained, just as Dickens's revised ending remains as ambivalent as the former, much more telegraphic one. For 'I saw no shadow of another parting from her' (p. 493) allows the ambiguity that they did or did not separate, and the narrator shows how his mind is closed now: what follows is not known. Writing about himself and his childhood experience, Dickens said 'I know how all these things have worked together to make me what I am'[16] in a confidence belonging to the *Copperfield* period and akin to that expressed so often in Wordsworth's *Prelude* of 1850. The distance from *Great Expectations* is pronounced: the very dryness of the narrative is an ironic comment on the book's title. The more buoyant, earlier statement may have its optimism unfounded as far as its belief in development goes, but the mode of writing in Pip's case may be seen as carceral: it belongs to the prison in its sense of giving an automatic, unstopping confession, which pauses not at all in its recounting of events and its self-accusation.

Foucault's 'birth of the prison', the concept of the individual, the privileging of the autobiographical mode – these related ideas are intrinsic to the novel, and while there is the creation of the human subject through a relaying of oppression and through a dominant discourse that he/she is within, there is also, in *Great Expectations*, implicit commentary about the mode of autobiography. Autobiography defines the subject confessionally; it puts upon it the onus of 'explanation', makes it prison-bound: a state that proves naturally acceptable to so much Romantic writing, where the tragic intensity of those who have to inhabit alienating spaces or constrictions can be defined as the source and inspiration of their reality. 'We think of the prison' – Eliot's reading of F. H. Bradley in *The Waste Land* proves comforting as it suggests that the essence of humanity is that it is confined, this is its common condition. In contrast, Foucault's analysis is precisely useful in its stress on the prison as the mode that gives the person the sense of uniqueness, the sense of difference from the others. In that sense, autobiography becomes a mode that assists in the reproduction of the discourse that the Panopticon society promotes. And in Pip's case, subjugated as he is by these discourses, the mode becomes a vehicle for 'self-reflection' – and for nothing else. Not, that is, the self thinking and moving from there into an area of thought where it can question the terms of its language, but the self continuing to reify its own status, to see it as an isolated thing. It continues a divisive trend. Not only is Pip's autobiography one that is markedly end-stopped in the sense that there is no feeling for a future, no way in which there can be a further development of the self, so that experience seems to avail nothing; but that cut-offness exists too in Pip's relations with others, in his inability to see others' complicity in the events surrounding him, save perhaps with Pumblechook, and there it is hardly difficult to see. It is inappropriate that Miss Havisham should say to him 'You made your own snares. *I* never made them' (p. 374). It is manifestly untrue as a statement; and especially as far as the second sentence goes, as Miss Havisham's own confession suggests, finishing as it does with her self-condemnatory immolation and her entreaty, 'take the pencil and write under my name, I forgive her' (p. 414) – Miss Havisham is the 'cringer' here, as so often. What is interesting is that Pip seems to receive this analysis and can't see that to individualize the issue in this way won't do. *Great Expectations* comes close to suggesting that in an understanding of a society, the concept of the individual is unhelpful, that what is important are the total manipulations of power and language by whatever group has the power of definition and control. Autobiography provides an inadequate paradigm.

Is that the final irony of *Great Expectations*, that it displays the bankruptcy of Pip's efforts to understand what has happened to him? That he speaks throughout in a language that has been given to him, and that includes the language of his perception of himself as a particular kind of being? If that is so, discussion might move at this point from what Pip might do with regard to his own inarticulateness in face of the dominant discourse, to what the text might do. The post-structuralist in Foucault displaces human consciousness for larger historical processes: Dickens as a 19th-century novelist is marked by more confidence in individual sentience. It might be possible to find in *Great Expectations* a modernity of attitude which means that its parabolic kind of narrative is open-ended; that the title hints at the space within it for the reader to construct his/her own sense of how to take it; that, unlike the warder at the heart of the Panopticon, the author is not felt to be directing and encouraging a labelling; that the text resists single meaning. The ambiguity of the ending, already discussed, is relevant here, and so too is the sense that the reader has only Pip's text to work upon, and that this is certainly not final or necessarily authoritative. At the same time, however, the bourgeois Dickens has been located often enough within the book: for example, what do we make of Herbert's reporting of his father's principle of belief that 'no man who ever was a true gentleman at heart ever was, since the world began, a true gentleman in manner . . . no varnish can hide the grain of the wood, and . . . the more varnish you put on, the more the grain will express itself' (p. 204)? Is not this like the voice of the conscious novelist, and if so does it not express a different, more essentialist view of humanity than the very relative one formed through the whole pattern of the book with its insistence on the social construction of identities? Herbert's decent liberalism of attitude, which is intended to cut through class distinctions, both in relation to the upwardly mobile and the aristocratic-snobbish, is tactfully put, but it represents a trans-historicalism, in its view of human nature 'since the world began', an 'essentialist' view of humanity.

I give this example as one of the many that might be cited to suggest that the novel resists the irony of its form – which, in its radicalness, is where Raymond Williams finds 'Dickens's morality, his social criticism';[17] and that it might allow for a basic human nature, which would stand against Foucault's account, since for the latter there can be no cutting through a statement which is not framed within the limits of a particular discourse. The passage quoted from the opening of chapter 32 has been similarly seen – as the authorial voice, as part of the classic realist text, as that where 'bourgeois norms are experienced as the evident laws of a natural order'.[18] But in response to this view that the novel does invest time and space in a 'decent' common-sense attitude, several points might be urged. The first would be that it was no more necessary to take the comment in chapter 32 as authorial than to assume that Herbert's views are purely normative. And even if they were, and Mr Pocket's views about what constituted a gentleman coincided with Dickens's, the statement might still be situation-specific, having to do with what a gentleman might be in a society that laid so much stress on this bourgeois title. But in any case, Mr Pocket's views themselves are not beyond criticism: chapter 23 where he appears presents him wittily as the liberal whose 'decent' attitudes are themselves subverted by his wife's tyrannies – he is nearly as helpless as Joe, and that ineffectuality itself invites criticism, is indeed even part of a self-oppression. Moreover, although the concept of a true gentleman may be a mirage pursued through the book (cp. Pip's uttering 'penitently' at the end about Joe – often seen as the ideal – 'God bless this gentle Christian man' (p. 472), as though here at last disinterested, decent qualities were being displayed), as a term it is itself not allowed to stand by the novel.

Joe drops out again of the London scene after Pip has recuperated: Pip's terms for him are part of the vocabulary he has learned to deploy from Satis House – and from exposure to Estella's power, which makes him tell Biddy that he wants to be a gentleman (p. 154). The term – even in Mr Pocket's oppositional formulation about it – is not one that fits Joe, even in Pip's modified way of putting it. Joe needs to be seen in another set of relations, and what Pip says about him is inappropriate because it bears more on Pip's sense of his own deficiency; Joe is what *he* is not; he has not succeeded in living up to the terms of his cultural formation that have been dictated to him, so he believes. What Joe is in rescuing Pip requires a set of terms that do not involve assimilation of him into the power relations and language of middle-class society, from which he is nearly totally excluded, save when he has to wear holiday clothes, and which are supremely irrelevant to him.

It is the cruellest irony for Pip that he must disparage himself and praise Joe so constantly in his narration. Joe does not require any setting down, but Pip has no means of assessing the forge and the village life independent of his own given language: under the influence of Satis House and its language he feels ashamed of home (p. 134). Nothing more is given of the forge in the novel apart from Pip's perception of it, and the absence of such a thing makes the torture for Pip, the prisoner in the Panopticon societal prison, the more refined. For it remains as a deceptive escape for him, although one that he cannot endorse (so that his intention to go back and marry Biddy has something masochistic and self-oppressive within it), and any step that he takes, either of accepting or rejoicing in it, remains a compromise. The split is caught finely in the scenes leading to his going to London in the first instance, and a compromise is dictated to him by the dividing nature of the society as prison. For Foucault argues that there is no 'knowledge that does not presuppose and constitute at the same time power relations' (*Discipline and Punish*, p. 27). That is, the birth of the prison – that most divisive of institutions – is an instrument not only to create Man as individual, to be known thus, but also ensures that there is no common language – no means of making a value-judgment which is outside the terms of a particular set of power-relations. Foucault is opposed to totalizing interpretations of society precisely because of the way they ignore the endless replication of modes of oppression, of imposition of languages. The methods of deployment of power are various, as are the social groupings; indeed *Great Expectations* displays something of that variousness. What Pip finds to be true of himself is the result of the way he has been set up; at the same time, he does not possess a set of terms to think about a different way of life – the forge – that are not themselves instrumental for control over that way of thinking. Difference is not allowed for. Pip is bought up completely. The illusion he is given is of seeing things whole, but to the very end he cannot see the forge way of life as something different from his, and one that his own language formation cannot accommodate, from the moment he got to Satis House.

The modernity of the novel lies in this area: Dickens commits himself to no view about Joe or Biddy, or Pip, but writes rather a *Bildungsroman* where the expectation that the hero will learn through experience is belied, and not only by the title. Readerly assumptions generated through the lure of the narrative are set aside, for the central figure can only proceed on the language assumptions given to him. *David Copperfield* was the standard kind of *éducation sentimentale; Great Expectations* questions the ideological assumptions inherent in the earlier book, by presenting (with the earlier novel consciously in mind, re-read just before embarking on it) a development that can be no development. If the hero learns at all, it is only within his terms of reference, so there is no breaking out from the obsession with the self. The mode of the novel is ironic (it is noticeable how Dickens emphasises what is 'comic' about it to Forster, as Forster relates in the *Life*:[19]): 'comic', in spite of the comedy within it, seems inappropriate, but perhaps it may draw attention to what is subversive about the book. And Dickens's absence of explanation about it only emphasises the extent to which he as author has receded: the novel stands alone, open-ended, marked out by the lack of 'closure' within it supplied by the moralist Dickens.

Whatever liberalism affects the book – as in the 'poor dreams' that nearly save Mr Jaggers in spite of himself, or in the way that Pip seems to enjoy a reasonable bourgeois existence in the Eastern Branch of Herbert's firm, or in its casualness about dates and historical positioning – is not central: the book has little faith in human nature considered as a Romantic, spontaneous and creative thing; no sense that the issues it addresses may be met by the middle-class values that commonly sustain the 19th-century novel. The interest in character here – which all so often forms the basis of Dickensian criticism – does not sanction itself in the individual as ultimately irrepressible. Rather, the idea of the Panopticon as the chief model for the formation of any individuality in 19th-century Britain makes for something much more complex and gives rise to the sense that the formation of individuality is itself delusory as a hope. It is itself the problem it seeks to solve – through its way of dividing a society and separating it. The prison is not the 'human condition' in a trans-historical sense, as Denmark was also a prison for Hamlet, but is the apt symbol for enforcing models of helplessness: the more aware the self is of its position, the more it confirms the prison, and thus cuts itself off further. To that diagnosis, which demands a consideration of power structures in society such as Foucault gives, and which draws attention to language as a way of making the person prison-bound, the autobiographical mode of *Great Expectations* bears witness. In itself the mode works to keep the narrator in the prison. Just as Wemmick's father and his pleasant and playful ways, and the possibility that Jaggers himself might one day want a pleasant home, also ensure that the prison's durability is not in question: these individual escapes, simply by staying within the limits of the individual idea, address, effectively, no problem at all.

Notes

1. F. R. and Q. D. LEAVIS, *Dickens the Novelist* (London: Chatto and Windus, 1970), p. 331.
2. BARRY SMART, *Foucault, Marxism and Critique* (London: Routledge and Kegan Paul, 1983), p. 90.
3. MICHEL FOUCAULT, *Discipline and Punish*, trans. Alan Sheridan (Harmondsworth: Penguin, 1979). All textual references are to this edition.
4. JEREMY BENTHAM, quoted in PHILIP COLLINS, *Dickens and Crime* (London: Macmillan, 1962), p. 18.
5. The theme is dealt with in MICHAEL IGNATIEFF, *A Just Measure of Pain: The Penitentiary in the Industrial Revolution, 1750–1850* (London: Macmillan, 1978).
6. JEREMY BENTHAM, quoted in PHILIP COLLINS, *Dickens and Crime*, p. 18.
7. See the *Pilgrim Edition of the Letters of Charles Dickens*, Vol. 3, 1842–3, ed. MADELINE HOUSE and GRAHAM STOREY (Oxford: Clarendon, 1974), pp. 105, 436, 110, for details on these prisons.
8. See MARK COUSINS and ATHAR HUSSAIN, *Michel Foucault* (London: Macmillan, 1984), pp. 183, 192, for further details about these prisons.
9. CHARLES DICKENS, *Great Expectations*, ed. ANGUS CALDER (Harmondsworth: Penguin, 1965), p. 280. All textual references are to this edition.
10. PHILIP COLLINS, *Dickens and Crime*, pp. 20–1.
11. LIONEL TRILLING, *Sincerity and Authenticity* (London: Oxford University Press, 1972), p. 24.
12. MICHEL FOUCAULT, *The History of Sexuality: Vol. 1. An Introduction*, trans. Robert Hurley (Harmondsworth: Penguin, 1981), p. 60.
13. F. R. and Q. D. LEAVIS, *Dickens the Novelist*, p. 288. Apart from this account of the novel, I am greatly in debt to JULIAN MOYNAHAN, 'The Hero's Guilt: The Case of *Great Expectations*', *Essays in Criticism*, 10 (1960), pp. 60–79, and A. L. FRENCH, 'Beating and Cringing: *Great Expectations*', *Essays in Criticism*, 24 (1974), pp. 147–68.
14. F. R. and Q. D. LEAVIS, *Dickens the Novelist*, p. 291.
15. 'Ressentiment' (translated as 'rancor') is discussed in detail in the first essay of *The Genealogy of Morals*, in FRIEDRICH NIETZSCHE, *The Birth of Tragedy and The Genealogy of Morals*, trans. Francis Golffing (Garden City, New York: Doubleday, 1956), pp. 158–87; see especially p. 170.
16. Quoted in JOHN FORSTER, *Life of Charles Dickens*, 2 vols. (London: Dent, 1969), Vol I, p. 32.
17. RAYMOND WILLIAMS, *The English Novel From Dickens to Lawrence* (London: Chatto and Windus, 1970), p. 48.
18. ROLAND BARTHES, *Mythologies*, trans. ANNETTE LAVERS (London: Grafton, 1989), p. 153.
19. JOHN FORSTER, *Life of Charles Dickens*, Vol. II, pp. 284–9.

8 Discipline in Different Voices: Bureaucracy, Police, Family and *Bleak House*

D. A. MILLER*

D. A. Miller is Professor of English at Harvard University, and the author of *Narrative and Its Discontents: Politics of Closure in the Traditional Novel* (Princeton: Princeton University Press, 1981), *The Novel and the Police* (Berkeley: University of California Press, 1988) and *Bringing Out Roland Barthes* (Berkeley: University of California Press, 1992). In the second of these books, from which the following extract is taken, Miller draws heavily on the work of Michel Foucault; readers may wish to compare his approach with that of Jeremy Tambling in Chapter 7. Miller's argument, conducted through studies of novels by Dickens, Wilkie Collins and Trollope, is that the characteristic forms and techniques of nineteenth-century novelistic fiction 'systematically participate in a general economy of policing power' (p. 2). Miller's particular emphasis in his chapter on *Bleak House*, from which this extract is taken, is on the relations which the novel establishes between the apparently opposed realms of public and institutional power and the inviolable privacy of home and family. This is not merely the theme of the novel, it is also a matter of the very experience of novel-reading itself, which enjoins what Miller sees as a closely regulated alternation between work and leisure, institution and domesticity. Miller goes on to explore the ways in which, for all its remorseless condemnation of bureaucracy and corruption, *Bleak House* mimics in its very form – even in its very unconscionable, Chancery-like length – the steadily deepening and diversifying powers of social discipline in the nineteenth century. Like J. Hillis Miller (Chapter 3), D. A. Miller sees *Bleak House* as a novel about the processes of interpretation itself. However, in a long note (see below, pp. 149–50 n. 9), he distinguishes his position from that of J. Hillis Miller, suggesting that the deconstructionist approach of the latter is too abstract, and fails to grasp the particular

*Reprinted from *The Novel and the Police* (Berkeley, Los Angeles and London: University of California Press, 1988), pp. 81–99, 105–6. The extract given here consists of sections IV, V, VI and VIII of chapter 3 of the book. These sections, along with their corresponding footnotes, have been renumbered accordingly.

historical ways in which the concern with interpretation orders nineteenth-century social life.

I

It would certainly appear as though the existence of that sheltered space which the novelistic representation labors to produce is unconditionally taken for granted in the novel form, whose unfolding or consumption has not ceased to occur in such a space all along. Since the novel counts among the conditions for this consumption the consumer's leisured withdrawal to the private, domestic sphere, then every novel-reading subject is constituted – willy-nilly and almost before he has read a word – within the categories of the individual, the inward, the domestic. There is no doubt that the shift in the dominant literary form from the drama to the novel at the end of the seventeenth century had to do with the latter's superior efficacy in producing and providing for privatized subjects. The only significant attempt to transcend the individualism projected by the novel took place precisely in Victorian England as the practice of the *family reading*, which may be understood as an effort to mitigate the possible excesses of the novel written for individuals by changing the locus of reading from the study – or worse, the boudoir – to the hearth, enlivened but also consolidated as a *foyer d'intrigue*. A Victorian novel such as *Bleak House* speaks not merely for the hearth, in its prudent care to avoid materials or levels of explicitness about them unsuitable for family entertainment, but from the hearth as well, implicitly grounding its critical perspective on the world within a domesticity that is more or less protected against mundane contamination.

Yet if only by virtue of the characteristic length that prevents it from being read in a single sitting, the novel inevitably enjoins not one, but several withdrawals to the private sphere. Poe, who first raised the issue of the effects of this length, considered the discontinuousness of novel reading to be one of the liabilities of the form, which thereby had to forego 'the immense benefit of *totality*'. In the novel state, Poe thought, the autonomy of 'literary concerns' was always being frustrated by the foreign intervention of 'worldly interests'.[1] If, however, novel reading presupposes so many disparate withdrawals to the private sphere, by the same token it equally presupposes so many matching returns to the public, institutional one. An important dimension of what reading a novel entails, then, would lie – outside the moment and situation of actual perusal – in the times and places that interrupt this perusal and render it in the plural, as a series. Just as we read the novel in the awareness that we must put it down before finishing it, so even when we are not reading it, we continue to 'live' the form in the mode of *having to get back to it*. Phenomenologically, the novel form includes the interruptions that fracture the process of reading it. And the technical equivalent of this phenomenological interpenetration of literary and worldly interests would be the practice of various realisms, which, despite their manifold differences, all ensure that the novel is always centrally about the world one has left behind to read it and that the world to which one will be recalled has been reduced to attesting the truth (or falsehood) of the novel. It is not quite true, therefore, that the novel is simply concerned to attach us to individuality and domesticity, to privacy and leisure. What the form really secures is a close *imbrication* of individual and social, domestic and institutional, private and public, leisure and work. A drill in the rhythms of bourgeois industrial culture, the novel generates a nostalgic desire to get home (where the novel can be resumed) in the same degree as it inures its readers to the necessity of periodically renouncing home (for the world where the novel finds its justification and its truth). In reading the novel, one is made to rehearse how to live a problematic – always surrendered, but then again always recovered – privacy.

II

The same opposition – or at least the question of one – between private-domestic and social-institutional domains that is produced in the representation and consumed as the form occurs again in the relationship between the representation and the form. For though the form projects itself as a kind of home, what is housed in this home, as its contents, is not merely or even mainly comfortable domestic quarters, but also the social-institutional world at large. If the novel is substantially to allege its otherness in relation to this world, and thus to vouch for its competence to survey, judge, and understand it, then far from seeking to be adequate or isomorphic to its contents (when these are carceral, disciplinary, institutional), it is instead obliged to defend itself against them by differentiating the practices of the world from the practices of representing it. The current critical fondness for assimilating form and content (via homologies, thematizations, *mises-en-abîme*) becomes no more than a facile sleight-of-hand if it does not face the complication it in fact encounters in the question of the difference between the two that the novel regularly raises.[2] Specifically, as I hope to show in a moment, *Bleak House* is involved in an effort to distinguish its own enormous length from the protractedness of the Chancery suit, and also its own closure from the closed case of the Detective Police. But even remaining at a general and fundamental level, we can see the difference in the fact that, for instance, while the world of *Bleak House* is dreary enough, yet were the novel itself ever to become as dreary, were it ever to cease *making itself desirable*, it would also by the same token cease to be read. Pleasurably, at our leisure and in our homes, we read the novel of suffering, the serious business of life, and the world out-of-doors. Moreover, the critical and often indignant attitude that *Bleak House*, by no means untypically, takes toward its social world reinforces this 'erotic' difference with a cognitive one: the novel views the world in better, more clear-sighted and disinterested ways than the world views itself.

The suit in *Bleak House* has only to be mentioned for its monstrous length to be observed and censured. 'Jarndyce and Jarndyce still drags its dreary length before the Court, perennially hopeless.'[3] The suit is not merely long, but – here lies the affront – excessively so, longer than it is felt it ought to be. Yet what Dickens calls the 'protracted misery' of the suit (54) – by which he means the misery of its protractedness as well as vice versa – cannot be explained merely as the consequence of gratuitous *additions* to a necessary and proper length, left intact, which they simply inordinately 'pad'. One of the ill effects of the length of the suit has been precisely to render unavailable the reality of a proper measure, of which the suit could be seen as an unwarranted expansion and to which it would be theoretically possible to restore it by some judicious abridgment. The further the length of the suit is elaborated, the more it abandons any responsibility to the telos or finality that originally called it forth, nominally continues to guide it even now, and would ultimately reabsorb it as the pathway leading to its own achievement. And along with the *formality* of an ending – the juridical act of decision – what would constitute the *substance* of one is put in jeopardy: namely, the establishment of the meaning of the original will. So nearly intertwined are ending and meaning that to adjourn the one seems to be to abjure the other: 'This scarecrow of a suit has, in course of time, become so complicated that no man alive knows what it means' (4).

The suit's effective suspension of teleology is, of course, scandalously exemplary of a whole social sphere that seems to run on the principle of a purposiveness without purpose. The principle is enunciated and enforced not only by the bureaucratic officials, who, when Jo is sick, 'must have been appointed for their skill in

evading their duties, instead of performing them' (432), but even by
the various policemen in the novel who enjoin Jo to 'move on' in his
perpetually maintained, displaced itinerary to nowhere.

Internalized, this lack of purpose emerges as character defects: the
long-windedness of Chadband, the aestheticism of Skimpole (who
begins sketches 'he never finished'), the flightiness of Richard. Such
instances, however, in which the sense of an ending seems entirely
given up, are no more symptomatic of the general social suspension
of finality than the abstract impatience and hopeful voluntarism
with which the sense of an ending is merely imposed on a state of
affairs that must thereby be misunderstood. Miss Flyte is mad to expect
a judgment 'shortly,' and Richard is certainly on the way to madness
when, logically, he argues that 'the longer [the suit] goes on, . . . the
nearer it must be to a settlement one way or other' (182). In
the progress of Hegelian Spirit, 'the length of this path has to be
endured because, for one thing, each moment is necessary' to the
emergence of the result;[4] whereas, the mere ongoingness of the un-
Hegelian suit brings madness to any attempt to make sense of this
length as a necessity, or in terms of the end-orientation that it
formally retains but from which it has substantially removed itself.
Finally, however, the length of the suit is devoid of necessity only
in terms of an eventual judgment. Just as the inefficiency of power in
Chancery showed up from another standpoint as the power of
inefficiency, so too what are in one perspective the superfluous, self-
subversive elongations of procedure become in another the
necessary developments of a power that – call it the English law –
has for its one great principle 'to make business for itself' (548).
Accordingly, the delays and remands that amount to an effective
suspension of its declared end should not be seen to debilitate
Chancery, but rather to allow one to take it seriously as – in Dickens's
facetious phrase from *The Old Curiosity Shop* (1841) – 'the long and
strong arm of the law'.[5]

In light of the fact that the novel about this long arm itself exercises
a considerable reach – that the representation *of* length goes on *at*
length too – we are invited to consider the extent to which the novel
runs the risk of resembling the Chancery suit that it holds in despite.
Certainly, the unfolding of the novel could be thought to parallel the
elaboration of the suit insofar as it threatens an analogous failure to
bring its ever more abundant materials to a proper or conceivably
adequate summation. We already noted how the long novel foregoes
'the immense benefit of *totality*' because it cannot be read at a single
sitting; but even if we were to export to the nineteenth century the
anachronism of a 'speed-reader,' Victorian practices of distributing
the novel-product would still render the interruptedness of reading

all but inevitable. Serial publication necessarily barred the reader from having full physical possession of the text he was reading until he was almost done with it; and even once the novel was published in volume form as a 'three-decker,' the ordinary subscription to the circulating libraries (which provided the majority of readers with their access to it) allowed to a borrower only one volume at a time. These determinations are of course merely external, but they are fully matched by the compositional principles of discontinuity and delay that organize the form from within its own structure: not only in the formal breaks of chapters, installments, volumes, but also in the substantive shifts from this plot-line to that, or from one point of view or narration to another; and generally in the shrewd administration of suspense that keeps the novel always tending toward a denouement that is continually being withheld. In Dickens, of course, the fissured and diffused character of novel form is far more marked than in the work of any of his contemporaries, extending from the extraordinary multitude of memorably disjunct characters, each psychologically sealed off from understanding any other, to the series of equally disparate and isolated spaces across which they collide. And, like the larger structures of suspense, even individual sentences will frequently derive their effects from the lengths to which they will go in withholding predication.[6] No doubt, both as a system of distribution and as a text, the Victorian novel establishes a little bureaucracy of its own, generating an immense amount of paperwork and sending its readers here, there, backward and forward, like the circumlocutory agencies that Dickens satirizes. On this basis, it could be argued that, despite or by means of its superficially hostile attitude toward bureaucracy, a novel like *Bleak House* is profoundly concerned to train us – as, at least since the eighteenth century, play usually trains us for work – in the sensibility for inhabiting the new bureaucratic, administrative structures.

To say this, of course, is to neglect what Roland Barthes has identified as the 'readerly' orientation of the traditional novel: the tendency of its organization to knit its discontinuities together by means of codes such as those ordering our perception of plot and suspense.[7] Although *Bleak House* baffles us in the first few hundred pages by featuring a profusion of characters who seem to have nothing to do with one another, a miscellany of events whose bearing on a possible plot is undecidable, and even two separate systems of narration that are unequal and unrelated, it simultaneously encourages us to anticipate the end of bafflement and the acquisition of various structures of coherence: in the revelation or development of relationships among characters; in the emergence of a plot whereby the mysteries of the text will be enlightened and its meanings fully named; and in the tendency of the two narrations to converge, as Esther's account comes to include characters and information that at first appeared exclusively in the anonymous one. In other words, the novel dramatizes the liabilities of fragmentation and postponement within the hopeful prospect that they will eventually be overcome. We consume the enormous length of a novel like *Bleak House* in the belief that it is eminently digestible – capable, that is, of being ultimately rendered in a readerly *digest:* a final abridgment of plot and character that stands for (and so dispenses with) all that came before it. From the standpoint of this promised end, the massive bulk of the novel will always have concealed the perfectly manageable and unmonstrous proportions of a much shorter, tauter form.

Yet however sustained, the mere promise of an ending, far from being sufficient to differentiate the novel from Chancery, would positively enlarge on the analogy between the novel's practices and those of the court, which also entices its subjects by means of promises, promises. We read the novel under the same assumption that Richard makes about the suit, that 'the longer it goes on, . . . the nearer it must be to a settlement'; and if the assumption is to be validated in the one case as it is discredited in the other, the novel is under obligation to make good its promise by issuing in judgments and resolutions. For even if we always know about the novel (as we do not about the suit) that its length is finite, involving only so many pages or installments, the vulgar evidence of an endpoint can never amount to the assurance of an *ending:* that is, the presence of a complex of narrative summations that would match or motivate the external termination of discourse with its internal closure. The suit, which attains an endpoint but no ending, embodies the distinction that the novel, to be different, will have to obliterate. Though the suit reaches a point at which it is correctly declared 'over for good' (865), this point is determined extrinsically by the lack of funds that prevents the protracted, complex cause from being pursued to a proper conclusion of its own. 'Thus the suit lapses and melts away' (867), instead of coming to the judgment that would have constituted a proper internal resolution. It is never known, for instance, whether the new will is a genuine document, and the project of finding out has been 'checked – brought up suddenly' upon what Conversation Kenge retains sufficient professional finesse to term the 'threshold' (866).

In a pointed and self-serving contrast, the novel brings its characters to judgment, its mysteries to solution, and its plots to issues that would make further narrative superfluous. Immediately following the end of the suit, as a sort of consequence and reversal of it, Richard's death illustrates the contrast. Insofar as this death is premature, of course, it may look as though Richard will merely reenact the abrupt check of the suit. Juridical discourse has ceased not because it has said what it wanted to say, but only for lack of funds to say it; and similarly, Richard's utterance is simply 'stopped by his mouth being full of blood' (868). But what is staged on the scene of Richard's deathbed is in fact his full recovery. In the paradoxical logic of nineteenth-century novelistic closure, whereby one sums up by subtracting, Richard is purged of unsteadiness and suspicion and so made whole. Whereas the suit ends as up in the air as ever it was, Richard's end achieves a fundamental clarification: 'the clouds have cleared away, and it is bright now' (869). His tearful recognition that John Jarndyce, whom he mistrusted, is 'a good man' renders him once more a good man himself. And his desire to be removed to the new Bleak House ('I feel as if I should get well there, sooner than anywhere') announces the redemptive turn from public institutional involvements to the domestic haven. As a result, even his death – no longer premature, but occurring only *after* the resolution of his character has been attained – bears witness to the seriousness of his conversion by making it permanent, the last word possible about him.

Unlike Chancery, then, the novel is willing to reward the patience that, like Chancery, it has required. The destiny of the long-suffering Esther is only the most obvious figure for the link the novel everywhere secures between the practice of patience and its payoff. In the reader's case, the link is affirmed each time he gets an answer to one of the questions or riddles he has endured; each time he enjoys the jubilation of recognizing a character who has appeared earlier; each time a new installment comes out to reward his month-long wait for it. It isn't Esther alone in *Bleak House* who is extraordinarily self-deprecating and diffident in the face of authority, be it the heavenly Father in whom 'it was so gracious . . . to have made my orphan way so smooth and easy,' or simply John Jarndyce, to whom she declares: 'I am quite sure that if there were anything I ought to know, or had any need to know, I should not have to ask you to tell it to me. If my whole reliance and confidence were not placed in you, I must have a hard heart indeed' (27, 99). The novel puts every reader in an equally subservient position of reliance upon the author, who, if one waits long enough (as, given the nature of the readerly text, one cannot but do), will delight us with the full revelation of his design, offering the supreme example of those happy surprises that Dickens's benevolent father-figures are fond of providing for those they patronize. Still less obviously, the novel develops our trust in the machinery of distribution itself, which can, for instance, be counted upon to provide the next installment at exactly the interval promised. In short, the novel encourages a series of deferential cathexes – all the more fundamental for being unconscious – onto various instances of authority. What is promoted in the process is a paternalism that, despite the dim view the novel takes of the power structures of the British state, can only be useful in maintaining such structures. To submit to the novel's duration is already to be installed within an up-beat ethic of endurance. If, as we speculated above, the novel trains us to abide in Chancery-like structures – by getting us to wait, as it were, in its very long lines – it does this only insofar as it is organized as a *reformed* Chancery, a Chancery that can moralize its procrastinations in a practice of delayed gratification. Recklessly, the court demanded an attendance so futile that it inspired dangerously anarchistic fantasies of destruction. More prudently, the novel, urging us to wait, also promises (to use the very formula of prudence) that we shall wait *and see*.

III

Though it goes to great lengths, *Bleak House* also goes to extremities to save these lengths from lapsing into mere unproductive extensions of the Chancery suit. Or rather, it saves them from such a fate *at* the extremities, or end-parts, in the production of a closure. Even so the novel cannot yet be considered to have won free of public, institutional attachments. For the very closure that secures a formal narrative difference between the novel and bureaucracy implicates the novel in a formal narrative resemblance to the institution that has played a sort of rival to the bureaucracy, the police. It is clear that the difference that obtains between Chancery and the novel applies equally in the relationship between Chancery and the police. In determining its own closure as revelation and fixed repose, the novel appears to have rejected the conception of termination proper to bureaucracy only to espouse the one proper to the police. The closural specimen that takes place, for example, at Richard's deathbed, even if it begins as though it will merely reflect the bureaucratic logic of lapse, achieves a permanent clarification of his character that rather subsumes the scene under the police model of closure as a double (cognitive and practical) apprehension. It can be further argued that, insofar as it arouses a desire for expeditious, conclusive solutions but only represents a single agency capable of providing them, the novel subtly identifies the reader's demand for closure with a general social need for the police, thus continuing

143

(with only a considerable increase of cunning) the apologetics for the new forces of order that Dickens began as an essayist in *Household Words*.

The novel, however, is just as little eager to appear an agency of the police as it was to resemble a relay of the Chancery system. The relatively friendly treatment that *Bleak House* accords to the Detective Police is qualified by a number of reservations about the nature and effects of its power. Most of these, like the other aspects of the police, are carried in the characterization of Inspector Bucket. His black clothes, linking him sartorially with Tulkinghorn and Vholes, darken his character as well with an association to the court; and like the undertaker to whose costume this dress also makes allusion, Bucket induces an ambivalence even in those he works for. Depending on the regularity of corruption, his profession has the doubly offensive aspect of a speculation on human weakness that happens also to be invariably justified. Yet the grief betokened by 'the great mourning ring on his little finger' (310) might as well take Bucket himself for its object as any of his clients. His nature subdued to what it works in, Bucket too may be counted among the victims of crime. 'Pour bien faire de la police,' Napoleon is supposed to have said, 'il faut être sans passion'. The moral horror of crime, which Dickens preserves (among other things) in his sensationalistic treatment of it, must be irrelevant – might even be counterproductive – to the professional dispassion required for the task of apprehending the criminal. This task may no doubt be considered itself a moral one. But the game function of detection thoroughly dominates whatever ethical ends it presumably serves; and, as Bucket himself can assure Sir Leicester, his profession has placed him utterly beyond the possibility of being scandalized: 'I know so much about so many characters, high and low, that a piece of information more or less, don't signify a straw. I don't suppose there's a move on the board that would surprise *me*; and as to this or that move having taken place, why my knowing it is no odds at all; any possible move whatever (provided it's in a wrong direction) being a probable move according to my experience' (726). The ethical perspective survives only in the faint melancholy with which Bucket, truly the 'modern prince' in this respect, appears to regret the necessity of his own pessimism; or in the personal ascesis that, when every consequence of desire proves criminal, is perhaps the only humane response remaining. Nonetheless, the melancholy is hardly sufficient to prevent him from eliciting the very weaknesses that are the object of its contemplation. The momentary collaboration between Skimpole and Bucket revealed at the end of the novel, an alliance of two species of moral indifference, throws no more discredit on the aesthete who delivers a dangerously ill child over to the police for no better reason than a bribe, than on the officer who extends the bribe for no better reason than to cover his client's prying. Even the ascesis surrenders its moral truth to the extent that it is the very evidence of Bucket's amoral professionalization. As Tulkinghorn's fate exemplifies, amateur detectives run amok because they are motivated by personal desires for possession. Renunciation is thus for the professional detective a positive qualification, much as what Bucket appears to lament as his barren marriage shows a clear profit as an amicable and highly efficient business partnership.

These reservations are most tellingly inscribed in the novel as a narrative difference, once again centering on the question of ending, between the novel and the detective story that it includes. According to what will later be codified as the 'classical' model, the detective story in *Bleak House* reaches its proper end when Bucket, having provided a complete and provable account of her guilt, arrests Mademoiselle Hortense for Tulkinghorn's murder. In the classical model, one may observe, though the security of its preferred decor, the locked room, is regularly breached, it is also invariably recovered in the detective's unassailable *reconstruction* of the crime. And similarly, in this not yet quite classical example, Bucket's ironclad case against Hortense may be understood as the reparation of Tulkinghorn's tragically vulnerable chambers. Yet if one tradition, the detective story, violates its closed rooms only to produce better defended versions of them in the detective's closed cases, another tradition, let us call it the Novel, violates even these cases. In this latter tradition, to which *Bleak House* ultimately bears allegiance, there is no police case so flawless that a loophole cannot be found through which its claims to closure may be challenged. Here our vision of the loophole is supplied by Mademoiselle Hortense:

'Listen then, my angel,' says she, after several sarcastic nods. 'You are very spiritual. But can you restore him back to life?'

Mr Bucket answers, 'Not exactly.'

'That is droll. Listen yet one time. You are very spiritual. Can you make an honourable lady of Her?'

'Don't be so malicious,' says Mr Bucket.

'Or a haughty gentleman of *Him*?' cries Mademoiselle, referring to Sir Leicester with ineffable disdain. 'Eh! O then regard him! The poor infant! Ha! ha! ha!'

'Come, come, why this is worse Parlaying than the other,' says Mr Bucket. 'Come along.'

'You cannot do these things? Then you can do as you please with

me. It is but the death, it is all the same. Let us go, my angel. Adieu
you old man, grey. I pity you, and I des-pise you!' (743)

Hortense enumerates the various existential problems that, outlasting
Bucket's solution, make it seem trivial and all but inconsequential.
Her purely verbal qualification is soon worked into the actual plot
when Bucket sets out in search of Lady Dedlock and finds her dead
body instead. However skillfully prosecuted, the work of detection
appears capable only of attaining a shell from which the vital
principle has departed. Other closural moments in *Bleak House*
similarly end by producing a corpse, as though the novel wanted
to attest, not just the finality, but also the failure of a closure that,
even as it was achieved, missed the essence of what it aspired to
grasp. In its ostentatious awareness of this failure, the novel defines
its relationship to the materials of police fiction that it has adopted.
On one side of this relationship there would be a detective story
whose shallow solution naively gratifies our appetite for closure; on
the other, there would be a novel that, insisting at the very moment
of solution on the insoluble, abiding mysteriousness of human and
literary experience, provides superior nourishment by keeping us
hungry.[8] Not to be identified with Chancery, the novel contrasts the
aimless suspension of the suit with the achievement of its own ending;
but not to be confused with the police either, it counters the tidy
conclusion of the case with a conspicuous recognition of all that must
elude any such achievement. If in the first instance, the novel
must affirm the possibility of closure, in the second it is driven to
admit the *inadequacy* of this closure.

In the end, then – precisely there – the novel's attempt to
differentiate its own narrative procedures from those of the
institutions it portrays falters, and the effort to disentangle itself from
one institution only implicates it in another. So the seemingly
perverse pattern continues wherein the novel is eager to produce a
sheltered space whose integrity it is equally willing to endanger. We
have seen how the novel establishes the opposition between the
private-domestic and the social-institutional (1) within the
representation, as the contrast between Esther's Bleak House and
Chancery, and between the former and the police; (2) as a formal
practice of consumption, in which the novel-reading subject shuttles
to and fro between the home in which the novel is read and the
world in which it is verified; and (3) at the intersection of the novel's
own representational practice with the represented practice of
institutions that it includes in its content. We have also seen how, in
every instance, the opposition is accompanied by the possibility that
it may be, or may have been, nullified. At the same time as the

existence of an 'outside' to institutional power is affirmed, that very affirmation is undercut with doubt.

Yet to describe the novel's rhetorical operation in this way, as the work of destructuration and subversion, is to identify it wholly with what is in fact only its negative moment.[9] We need to envision the positivity of this operation too, for what is put in question has also by the same token been put in place, and can be put to use as well. The ideological dividends paid in the difference between the 'inside' and the 'outside' of power are clear. The 'outside' gives the assurance of liberty that makes tolerable the increasingly total administration of the 'inside' and helps avoid a politicization of society as a whole. It also provides a critical space from which amendments and reforms useful to this administration can be effectively broached and imposed. As we began by observing, however, *Bleak House* troubles the straightforwardness of this difference, which it transforms into the question of a difference.

IV

Queen Victoria confided to her diaries: 'I never feel quite at ease or at home when reading a Novel.'[10] *Bleak House* makes itself as anxiogenic and incomplete as the home with which it identifies. For in an age in which productivity is valued at least as much as the product, the novel must claim no less the inadequacy than the necessity of closure. This inadequacy can now be understood – not in the old-fashioned way, as a failure of organic form, nor even in the new-fashioned way, as the success of a failure of organic form – but, in the broader context of institutional requirements and cultural needs, as the novel's own 'work ethic,' its imposing refusal of rest and enjoyment. Certainly, when reading this novel, though in the reasons of the hearth it finds its own reason for being, one never feels quite at home; perhaps, having finished it, one knows why one never *can* feel at home. For what now is home – not securely possessed in perpetuity, but only leased from day to day on payment of continual exertions – but a House? And what is this House – neither wholly blackened by the institutions that make use of its cover, nor wholly bleached of their stain – but (in the full etymological ambiguity of the word) irresolvably Bleak? 'Bleak House has an exposed sound' (68).

Notes

1. EDGAR ALLAN POE, 'Tale-Writing – Nathaniel Hawthorne,' in *The Complete Works of Edgar Allan Poe*, ed. JAMES A. HARRISON, 17 vols. (New York: George D. Sproul, 1902), 13: 153.
2. Even critics who propose an immediate identification of form and content in *Bleak House* are in practice compelled to acknowledge that the novel resists their enterprise. J. HILLIS MILLER's claim that *'Bleak House* has exactly the same structure as the society it exposes' has frequent recourse to concessive clauses that make allowance for 'Dickens's generous rage against injustice, selfishness and procrastination' or his 'sympathy for Gridley's indignant outrage' against the Chancery system ('Introduction' to *Bleak House* (Harmondsworth: Penguin, 1971) pp. 29, 27, reprinted in this present volume pp. 67–72.). And TERRY EAGLETON, for whom the novel is 'obliged to use as aesthetically unifying images the very social institutions . . . which are the object of [Dickens's] criticism,' is quite happy to register the 'contradictory' nature of the unity thus established (*Criticism and Ideology: A Study in Marxist Literary Theory* (London: Verso, 1976), p. 129, reprinted in this present volume, p. 156). Yet since both critics only recognize the difference between the novel and its world in the process of annulling it, they never permit themselves to consider seriously the *question* of the difference, and each is finally willing to pass off as a weakness of the text what is only a weakness in his account of it. In Miller's argument, in the absence of further treatment, evidence of the difference goes only to show that Dickens was curiously inconsistent. And in Eagleton's, such evidence would merely point to a text that is, to use his own expressive phrase about *Dombey and Son* (1846–48), 'twisted and self-divided by the very contradictions it vulnerably reproduces' (*Criticism and Ideology*, p. 127 and p. 155 of this present volume). Yet when, as it begins to appear, the difference between novel and world belongs to a series of analogous differences operating in the novel at several levels, then in dismissing the difference as an inconsequence or laying it to rest as a contradiction, we neglect a crucial aspect of the novel's own program, a central feature of its self-definition.
3. CHARLES DICKENS, *Bleak House* (Oxford: Oxford University Press, 1948), p. 4. For all further citations from the novel, page references to this edition will be given parenthetically in the text.
4. G. W. F. HEGEL, *Phenomenology of Spirit*, trans. A. V. Miller (Oxford: Oxford University Press, 1977), p. 17.
5. CHARLES DICKENS, *The Old Curiosity Shop* (Oxford: Oxford University Press, 1951), p. 553.
6. For example: 'Jostling against clerks going to post the day's letters, and against counsel and attorneys going home to dinner, and against plaintiffs and defendants, and suitors of all sorts, and against the general crowd, in whose way the forensic wisdom of ages has interposed a million of obstacles to the transaction of the commonest business of life – diving through law and equity, and through that kindred mystery, the street mud, which is made of nobody knows what, and collects about us nobody knows whence or how: we only knowing in general that when there is too much of it, we find it necessary to shovel it away – the lawyer and the law-stationer come to a Rag and Bottle shop' (135).
7. 'To end, to fill, to join, to unify – one might say that this is the basic requirement

of the *readerly*, as though it were prey to some obsessive fear: that of omitting a connection. Fear of forgetting engenders the appearance of a logic of actions; terms and the links between them are posited (invented) in such a way that they unite, duplicate each other, create an illusion of continuity. The plenum generates the drawing intended to "express" it, and the drawing evokes the complement, coloring: as if the *readerly* abhors a vacuum. What would be the narrative of a journey in which it was said that one stays somewhere without having arrived, that one travels without having departed – in which it was never said that, having departed, one arrives or fails to arrive? Such a narrative would be a scandal, the extenuation, by hemorrhage, of readerliness' (ROLAND BARTHES, *S/Z*, trans. RICHARD MILLER [New York: Hill and Wang, 1974], p. 105).

8. *Bleak House* is thus one of the first texts to adumbrate a position that with modernism becomes commonplace: namely, that a literature worthy of the name will respect mystery by keeping it inviolate. For a canonical allusion to the position, see Kafka's remarks on the detective story in GUSTAV JANOUCH, *Conversations with Kafka*, trans. GORONWY REES, 2d ed. rev. (New York: New Directions, 1971), p. 133; and among recent rehearsals, see DAVID I. GROSSVOGEL, *Mystery and Its Fictions: From Oedipus to Agatha Christie* (Baltimore: Johns Hopkins University Press, 1979). Yet insofar as the modernist cult of the irresolvable is perfectly consistent with the efficient working of the Court of Chancery, *Bleak House* is also one of the first texts to indicate the difficulties with this position, which advancing beyond cheap consolations, may only bind us more profoundly to a society that thrives on delayed and ever-incomplete satisfactions.

9 The moment exclusively occupies those two modes of literary criticism to which this essay may be thought to address itself: Marxism and deconstructionism. Contemporary Marxist criticism would construe the ambiguities we have noticed as the contradictions that inscribe the text's inevitable failure to make its domestic ideology cohere. By virtue of 'internal distanciation,' the literary text finds itself compelled to betray this ideology, if only in its hesitations, silences, discrepancies. Not altogether dissimilarly, deconstruction would take such ambiguities for the aporias in an allegory of the process and problems of signification itself. Intended meaning is always exceeded in the signifiers to which it commits its expression, since by their nature those signifiers defer meaning even as they differentiate it. The trace of such differentiation, furthermore, carrying over as a kind of residue from one signifier to another, undermines the integrity of each: so that, in the case of an opposition, one term will invariably prove to be contaminated with the term it is meant to oppose. Without insisting on the comparison, one might say that Marxist criticism, urgently putting under scrutiny the evidence of a text that thereby never fails to convict itself, proceeds rather like the Detective Police; whereas a deconstructive criticism, patiently willing to remain on the threshold of interpretation in the wisdom that every reading it might offer would be a misreading, behaves somewhat like the Court of Chancery. If only from *Bleak House*, however, we know that a practice claiming to resemble neither the bureaucracy nor the police merely uses this pretension to camouflage its alliances with both. For us, therefore, it cannot exactly be a matter of repudiating these critical modes, but rather of writing against them, as against a background. 'Against' Marxism, then, we stress the positivity of

contradiction, which, far from always marking the fissure of a social formation, may rather be one of the joints whereby such a formation is articulated. Contradiction may function not to expose, but to construct the ideology that has foreseen and contained it. And 'against' deconstruction, we should urge (rather as did Hegel in confronting the nothingness of skepticism) that undecidability must always be the undecidability of *something in particular*. The trouble with the deconstructionist allegory of signification is not that it is untrue, but that, despite the deceptive 'closeness' of the readings, it is abstract. Two things, I think, ought to remove the effects of undecidability and contradiction from the void in which deconstruction places them. For one, they have a history or genealogy that determines them and whose traces must be registered. It may be ultimately true, for instance, as J. HILLIS MILLER has said, that '*Bleak House* is a document about the interpretation of documents' (Introduction, p. 11 repr. p. 60, above), but the formulation elides the rivalrous differentiations among institutional practices through which the concern with interpretation comes to emerge (and then, not as a theme so much as the stakes in a contest). As a result, one misses seeing the extent of the novel's assumption that it is *not* a document like those it is about. For a second, these effects, once formed, are never left at large and on the loose to wreak havoc on discursive and institutional operations. On the contrary, the latter have always already drafted them into a service that takes its toll and whose toll, accordingly, needs to be assessed in turn. Thus, Miller's account keeps characteristic silence about what even *Bleak House* (for highly partisan reasons of its own, of course) is quite willing to publicize: that the hermeneutic problematic itself is an instrument in the legal establishment's will to power.

10 VISCOUNT ESHER, ed., *The Girlhood of Queen Victoria: A Selection from Her Diaries 1832–40*, 2 vols. (London: J. Murray, 1912), 2: 83. The citation comes from an entry for December 23, 1838.

9   Ideology and Literary Form: Charles Dickens

Terry Eagleton*

Terry Eagleton, who is Wharton Professor of English at the University of Oxford, is the most prolific and influential Marxist literary critic currently writing. In a steady flow of books and essays since the early 1970s, Eagleton has attempted to forge an 'emancipatory critical discourse' that would be responsive to the challenges and opportunities thrown up by the various bodies of theory that have emerged over the last twenty years or so – psychoanalysis, feminism, deconstruction, postmodernism – without losing the distinctively Marxist commitment to analysing the relations of literary texts and artistic works to conditions of material injustice and oppression. Eagleton became most widely known after his *Literary Theory: An Introduction* (Oxford: Basil Blackwell, 1983), which remains the most commonly used general introduction to different forms of literary theory. This text marks the beginnings of a conscious move on Eagleton's part from the rigorous, exacting style of analysis and exposition characteristic of his earlier work, to a more various, accessible and comic style of writing. But his work has maintained its sensitivity to duality and ambivalence, as well as its commitment to the idea of the public function and political responsibility of criticism. The short extract that appears below comes from *Criticism and Ideology* (London: Verso, 1976), a work in which Eagleton went further than he has subsequently been inclined to go along the path towards a 'scientific' criticism, which would map with exactitude and exhaustiveness the actions and effects of ideological contradictions and the place of literary texts in isolating and sustaining them. The remarks on Dickens form part of a longer chapter in *Criticism and Ideology* which examines the ideologies of 'organicism' in nineteenth- and early twentieth-century literature. By 'organicism', Eagleton means the ideal of spontaneously self-created and harmoniously unified social relations. Dickens's work is especially interesting for Eagleton because of its flagrant resistance to organic ideals and forms, whether in respect of the social relations his novels

---

*Reprinted from *Criticism and Ideology: A Study in Marxist Literary Theory* (London: Verso, 1976), pp. 102–3, 125–30.

represent or in terms of the characteristic structures and forms of the novels themselves. Disdainful of the organic principles of balance and the harmonious interpenetration of part and whole, Dickens's novels paradoxically centre around, and themselves derive a certain structural unity from, social institutions – such as Chancery or the Circumlocution Office – whose business is precisely to fragment or inhibit the achievement of social unity. Eagleton's work anticipates much contemporary criticism in its attention to the significance of the failure of Dickens's works to achieve 'coherence'.

Among Terry Eagleton's many other books are *Myths of Power: A Marxist Study of the Brontës* (1975; 2nd edn, Basingstoke: Macmillan, 1988); *Walter Benjamin: Or, Towards a Revolutionary Criticism* (London: New Left Books, 1981); *Literary Theory: An Introduction* (Oxford: Blackwell, 1983); *Against the Grain: Essays, 1975–1985* (London: Verso, 1986); *The Ideology of the Aesthetic* (Oxford: Blackwell, 1990) and *Ideology: An Introduction* (London: Verso, 1991).

Bourgeois ideology in nineteenth-century England confronted a severe problem. Nurtured in the sparse soil of Utilitarianism, it was unable to produce a set of potently affective mythologies which might permeate the texture of lived experience of English society. It needed, therefore, to have constant resort to the Romantic humanist heritage – to that nebulous compound of Burkean conservatism and German idealism, transmitted by the later Coleridge to Carlyle, Disraeli, Arnold and Ruskin, which has become known as the 'Culture and Society' tradition. It was a tradition which offered an idealist critique of bourgeois social relations, coupled with a consecration of the rights of capital. The peculiar complexity of English nineteenth-century ideology, founded on a complex conjuncture of bourgeois and aristocratic classes within the dominant bloc, lies in part in this contradictory unity between what Antonio Gramsci refers to as 'organic' and 'traditional' elements.[1] An impoverished empiricism, unable to rise to the level of an ideology proper, is driven to exploit the fertile symbolic resources of Romantic humanism, drawing on its metaphysical sanctions and quasi-feudalist social models to ratify bourgeois property relations. The 'Culture and Society' tradition is the literary record of this ideological conjuncture; John Stuart Mill, mechanistically harnessing Coleridge to Bentham in the late eighteen-thirties, provides one of its more palpable instances.[2]

Gramsci, indeed, has commented directly on this ideological formation in nineteenth-century England. 'There is a very extensive category of organic intellectuals – those, that is, who come into existence on the same industrial terrain as the economic group – but in the higher sphere we find that the old land-owning class preserves its position of virtual monopoly. It loses its economic supremacy and is assimilated as 'traditional intellectuals' and as directive (*dirigente*) group by the new group in power. The old land-owning aristocracy is joined to the industrialists by a kind of suture which is precisely that which in other countries unites the traditional intellectuals with the new dominant classes.'[3]

One aspect of this assimilation can be seen in bourgeois ideology's growing dependence on 'organicist' concepts of society.[4] As Victorian capitalism assumes increasingly corporate forms, it turns to the social and aesthetic organicism of the Romantic humanist tradition, discovering in art models of totality and affectivity relevant to its ideological requirements. During the second half of the century, the initially poetic notion of 'organic form' becomes progressively extended to the dominant literary mode of the time, fiction.

The major fiction of Victorian society was the product of the petty bourgeoisie. The Brontës, Dickens, Eliot, Hardy: it is with them, rather than with Thackeray, Trollope, Disraeli, Bulwer Lytton, that the finest achievements of nineteenth-century realism are to be found. Ambiguously placed within the social formation, the petty bourgeoisie was able on the whole to encompass a richer, more significant range of experience than those writers securely lodged within a single class. But it was also able to find epitomised in its own condition some of the most typical contradictions of bourgeois society as a whole. Indeed, 'conventional' bourgeois experience in England proved remarkably unpropitious for the production of major fiction.[5] Only writers with an ambivalent class-relation to the society could, it seemed, be open to the contradictions from which major literary art was produced. (This is true, earlier in the century, of Jane Austen, in whose work the situation of the minor gentry offers a peculiarly privileged focus for examining the conflicts and alliances between aristocracy and bourgeoisie.) As the petty-bourgeois realist tradition declines towards the end of the century into naturalism (Gissing, Wells, Bennett), its fraught, problematic relation to the society is, so to speak, confiscated by the *émigré* writers – James and Conrad, and later Eliot and Pound. A similarly ambiguous relationship occurs in twentieth-century Irish society, to produce the major art of Yeats and Joyce.

This is not to argue, however, that major nineteenth-century realism was the product of the 'class-ideology' of the petty bourgeoisie. For there is, strictly speaking, no such ideological sub-formation: 'petty-bourgeois ideology' exists as a strikingly pure and contradictory unity of elements drawn from the ideological realms of both dominant and dominated classes in the social formation. What is in question with all

of these texts is the peculiarly complex, over-determined character of
their mode of insertion into the hegemonic ideological forms – a
complexity which is in part the product of literary 'realism' itself. For
realism produces in one of its currents a 'democratic' ideology – one
progressively responsive to suppressed social experience and humbly
quotidian destinies. Yet its aesthetic ideology of 'type' and 'totality'
(and we should be in no doubt as to the *ideological* character of such
notions) insists on the integration of these elements into a unitary
'world view'. The ideology of the realist text resides not in this
dominant 'world view', but in the formal mutations and
displacements which signify its attempts to subordinate other modes
of discourse. In the case of the earlier Charles Dickens, for example,
each text is a veritable traffic-jam of competing fictional modes –
Gothic, Romance, moral fable, 'social problem' novel, popular
theatre, 'short story', journalism, episodic 'entertainment' – which
permits 'realism' no privileged status. The later 'realism' of Dickens
is thus of a notably impure kind – a question, often enough, of
'totalising' forms englobing non-realist 'contents', of dispersed,
conflictual discourses which ceaselessly offer to displace the securely
'over-viewing' eye of classical realism. If Dickens's movement
towards such realism produces a 'totalising' ideology, it is one
constantly deconstructed from within by the 'scattering' effect of
quite contrary literary devices. In the end, Dickens's novels present
symbols of contradictory unity (Chancery Court, Circumlocution
Office) which are the very principles of the novel's own construction.
Only these symbolic discourses can finally provide an 'over-view';
but precisely because their coherence is nothing less than one of
systematic contradiction, such an over-view is merely the absent
space within which disparate rhetorics are articulated.

The fact that Charles Dickens was an urban rather than rural petty
bourgeois marks a significant distinction between his fiction and that
of George Eliot. Of all the major English writers of the past century
and a half, Dickens is perhaps the least contaminated by organicist
ideologies. With him, the Romantic humanist critique of industrial
capitalism remains strikingly 'spontaneous', with none of the
elaborate ideological realisation it receives in the work of Carlyle or
D. H. Lawrence. Dickens treats the most available contemporary
forms of organicism – Young England, medievalism, the cult of
Nature, the Oxford movement – with the contempt of an *urban* petty-
bourgeois writer, one for whom there is no satisfactory withdrawal
into the mystifications of pastoral. The retreat to Nature in Dickens
is for the most part a negative gesture, associated with death and
regression to childhood, social disengagement rather than social
paradigm. If Nature for George Eliot suggests the socially structured

world of rural England, it is for Dickens a locus of sentimental moralism rather than of sociological law. Little Nell is a symbol of natural value expelled from the predatory city, but it is the archetypally urban Quilp who engages his author's imagination. The spontaneous, empiricist character of Dickens's Romantic humanism, evident in the 'Christmas spirit' and the vulgar vitalism of *Hard Times*, emerges as a significant aesthetic and ideological weakness. Yet in the mature work that very weakness productively deprives him of a ready-fashioned organicist ideology, *à la Daniel Deronda*, by which to mediate and 'resolve' the conflicts in question. In a transitional work like *Dombey and Son*, the absence of such an ideology results in a text twisted and self-divided by the very contradictions it vulnerably reproduces. The famous railways scene, for example, exhilaratedly affirms bourgeois industrial progress at the same time as it protests gloomily against it on behalf of the petty bourgeoisie it dooms to obsolescence. Yet although that protest is partly couched in natural imagery, Dickens has no organicist ideology like Eliot by which to aesthetically integrate his conflicting symbols, no ideological resources by which to secure a reconciliation of 'tradition' and 'progress'. The contradictions remain visibly inscribed in the text, to enrich and enliven its dramatically irregular development.

A central symbol of Dickens's Romantic humanism is childhood innocence, which the novels bring into a series of complex structural relations with adult experience. Since the child is isolated, victimised and unable to totalise his perceptually fragmented world, the positive value he incarnates figures effectively as a negation. Such negativity clearly reflects the theoretical limitations of Dickens's moralistic critique of bourgeois society: the child's passivity is a dramatic index of his oppression, but also removes him from the world into a realm of untaintable goodness. On the other hand, the child's very blankness brings into dramatic focus the social forces which dominate him; he becomes, in a Brechtian metaphor, the empty stage on which these historically typical forces contend. Oliver Twist is such a negative centre, whose effective absence from his own narrative allows him passively to focus the socially significant; yet his nullity is also determined by the novel's ideological inability to show him as social *product*. To do that, indeed, would be to undercut the very unhinging of Oliver from history which finally ensures his fabular triumph. The novel argues at once that Oliver is and is not the product of bourgeois oppression, just as the 'real' world of bourgeois social relations into which he is magically rescued is endorsed against the 'unreal' underworld of poverty and crime, while simultaneously being shown up by that underworld as illusory.

Dickens's fiction thus reveals a contradiction between the social reality mediated by childhood innocence, and the transcendental moral values which that innocence embodies. It is a contradiction intrinsic to petty-bourgeois consciousness, which needs to embrace conventional bourgeois ethics in an undermining awareness of the harsh social realities they suppress. One effect of this is a set of formal dissonances in the novels themselves. *Pickwick Papers*, for example, cannot really be a *novel* in the traditional sense, since Pickwick's complacent innocence renders him incapable of any significantly interconnected experience beyond the merely episodic. The book consequently needs a supplementary centre in Sam Weller, who, though officially subordinate (Pickwick's servant), is in fact the master. In a double displacement of the text's bourgeois blandness, the unpalatable experience it expels from its official narrative erupts elsewhere, in the grotesquely violent, death-obsessed tales by which that narrative is regularly interrupted. In a somewhat parallel way, Quilp in *The Old Curiosity Shop* symbolises the smouldering, anarchic vengeance which the novel wreaks on its own decorous, sentimental story-line.[6]

Dickens's fiction, like Eliot's, deploys literary devices to 'resolve' ideological conflict; but his novels are more remarkable than Eliot's for the clarity with which those conflicts inscribe themselves in the fissures and hiatuses of the texts, in their mixed structures and disjunct meanings. It is not that Eliot's work does not also reveal such formal dislocations, as I have suggested; it is rather that Eliot's writing, sustained by an aesthetic as well as social ideology of organic form, strives for such organic closure more consciously and consistently than does Dickens's. His novels, by contrast, offer their self-contradictory forms and internal inconsistencies as part of their historical meaning. Dickens's mature work certainly achieves aesthetic integration, but it is of a significantly different kind from Eliot's. Whereas Eliot's organicist ideology provides a structure for social totalisation, Dickens is forced in his later fiction to use as aesthetically unifying images the very social institutions (the Chancery Court of *Bleak House*, the Circumlocution Office of *Little Dorrit*) which are the object of his criticism. It is, ironically, these very systems of conflict, division and contradiction which provide Dickens with a principle of symbolic coherence. In this sense, the aesthetic unity of his mature work is founded, not on a mythology of 'organic community', but on exactly the opposite: on the historical self-divisions of bourgeois society. It is not that the early Dickens's perception of character as idiosyncratic and non-relational yields to a vision of social unity; it is rather that such non-relationship is now shown to be *systemic* – the function of decentred structures like Chancery, finance capitalism and the Circumlocution Office, elusive centres which seem all-pervasive yet everywhere absent.[7] Characters in later Dickens remain individually graphic and grotesque, but are now increasingly grasped as the bearers of these structures, which act as the true protagonists of the later fiction.

What Eliot's writing attempts to resolve *synchronically* – a conflict between two phases of bourgeois ideology, determined by certain mutations in the historical nature of English capitalism – Dickens's fiction moves through *diachronically*. The anarchic, decentred, fragmentary forms of the early novels correspond in general to an earlier, less organised phase of industrial capitalism; the unified structures of the mature fiction allude to a more intensively coordinated capitalism, with its complex networks of finance capitalism (Merdle in *Little Dorrit*), its progressively centralised state bureaucracy (the Circumlocution Office) and its increasingly monolithic ideological apparatuses (the educational system of *Hard Times*, the juridical structures of *Bleak House*).[8] (The railways of *Dombey and Son* mark a transitional stage in this development – a visibly unifying network which none the less, in the entrepreneurial 'spontaneity' of their creation and the heterogeneous quality of experience to which they give rise, recall the arbitrary, explosive energies of the early novels.) Yet this diachronic movement is not one from 'individualism' to 'community'. It is a movement from the novel of the absent centre (innocent child, blankly conventional adult) around which certain contradictions knot themselves, to the novel of the decentred totality – a novel which mimes, in its integrated symbolism, a set of conflicts and non-relations now grasped as systemic.

Notes

1. For Gramsci, 'organic' intellectuals are those who come into existence on the basis of an emergent social class, but who then confront – and need to vanquish and assimilate – those 'traditional' intellectual categories which survive from previous social conditions. Gramsci argues, significantly enough for the English tradition, that 'The popularised traditional type of intellectual is represented by the literary man, the philosopher, the artist', ANTONIO GRAMSCI, *Selections From the Prison Notebooks*, ed. and trans. QUENTIN HOARE and GEOFFREY NOWELL SMITH (London: Lawrence and Wishart, 1971), p. 9. It is important to distinguish Gramsci's use of the term 'organic' from the meaning I assign to it in this essay.
2. See JOHN STUART MILL, *Mill on Bentham and Coleridge*, ed. F. R. LEAVIS (London: Chatto and Windus, 1950). ERIC HOBSBAWM has noted the ideological limitations of 'pure' Utilitarianism – how its demystification of 'natural rights'

could seriously weaken the force of 'metaphysical' sanctions in the defence of property, substituting for them the considerably less powerful, politically more volatile category of 'utility'. See *The Age of Revolution: Europe 1789–1848* (London: Weidenfeld and Nicolson, 1962), p. 236.

3. Gramsci, *Selections From the Prison Notebooks*, p. 18.

4. I use 'organic' and 'organicism' to signify social and aesthetic formations with the supposedly spontaneous unity of natural life-forms, and more generally to denote symmetrically integrated systems characterised by the harmonious interdependence of their component elements.

5. This is one reason for the structural dissonances of some of Dickens's early fiction. Novels like *Nicholas Nickleby* and *Martin Chuzzlewit* present a blankly absent centre in the figure of the conventional, bourgeois-minded protagonist; the true life of the novels is to be found in the nooks and peripheries, swirling around this absent centre.

6. A point made by JOHN CAREY in *The Violent Effigy: A Study of Dickens's Imagination* (London: Faber and Faber, 1974), p. 26.

7. These complex totalities may be contrasted with the monistic industrial system represented by the sealed and static *Hard Times*, with its crude binary opposition between that system and 'life'. *Hard Times* can be seen in this sense as a false, premature over-totalisation.

8. It is not, naturally, a question of simple homology between literary and historical systems, as this formulation might seem to suggest. What is at issue, rather, is the difference between an earlier 'impure' articulation of discourses ideologically overdetermined by a relatively unsystematic Romantic humanism, and the *relatively* more coherent codes of the later fiction, overdetermined by the increasing predominance of corporatist ideological elements.

10 Writing as a Woman: Dickens, *Hard Times* and Feminine Discourses

JEAN FERGUSON CARR*

Jean Ferguson Carr is Professor of English at the University of Pittsburgh. She is the joint editor of *The Collected Works of Ralph Waldo Emerson*, 5 Vols (Cambridge, Mass.: Belknap Press, 1971–94), and, in addition to essays on Dickens, has published articles about Jane Austen and questions of literacy. In this essay, she first identifies a general tendency for Dickens's work to ally itself – and to be identified by others – with values of feeling and sympathy conventionally marked as female. She then undertakes a reading of *Hard Times* to investigate the nature and effects of Dickens's empathy with the position of women in his novels. Like Roger Fowler (Chapter 6) Jean Ferguson Carr uses Bakhtin to understand the political dynamics of the different voices in *Hard Times*. But, where Fowler emphasises the positive plurality of these voices, Carr's interest is in the process whereby the female voice is muted or silenced by the authoritative voice of Gradgrindery, a process which the novel both reproduces and resists. But this resistance can only ever be indirect, in the indication of the structural limit or incompleteness marked by female discourse, rather than the positive articulation of its discursive challenge. If Dickens's writing is powerfully identified with a female language and perspective that are seen as 'preposterous, impossible' (p. 172), it can also be seen as an authoritative appropriation of femininity, an appropriation which ironically cooperates with the muting of the actual historical voices of nineteenth-century women writers.

In his 1872 retrospective essay on Dickens, George Henry Lewes presents Dickens as an exemplary figure whose career has upset the balance between popular taste and critical judgement.[1] The essay depends on what seems initially an aesthetic opposition between show and Art, between 'fanciful flight' and Literature, but these critical terms also demark class and gender boundaries that preserve

---

*Reprinted from *Dickens Studies Annual*, 18 (1989), 161–78.

the dominant literary culture. Dickens becomes 'the showman beating on the drum,' who appeals to the 'savage' not the 'educated eye,' to 'readers to whom all the refinements of Art and Literature are as meaningless hieroglyphs'. He works in 'delf, not in porcelain,' mass producing inexpensive pleasure for the undiscerning reader, but is found wanting by the 'cultivated' reader of 'fastidious' taste. The essay attempts to contain Dickens' impact by identifying him as lower-class, uneducated, and aligned with feminine discourse, but it also suggests the difficulty of accounting for Dickens' influence and the importance of investigating the 'sources of that power'. Despite Lewes's isolation of Dickens as a 'novelty' or as a madman, he concedes that he 'impressed a new direction on popular writing, and modified the Literature of his age, in its spirit no less than in its form' (143).

Dickens' admirers, following John Forster, have responded to the essay as mistaken and insulting.[2] As John Gross wrote, the essay 'still has the power to irritate,' with its innuendo about hallucinations and lower-class vulgarity, and its casual anecdotes about the author's inadequate library.[3] Lewes's class bias and his narrow definition of education have undermined the influence of his critique of Dickens for modern readers, but his subtle positioning of Dickens in relation to women writers and his articulation of the categories by which novels will be judged has been more durable. When, for example, Gordon Haight concludes that 'Dickens was a man of emotion, sentimental throughout; Lewes was a man of intellect, philosophical and scientific' (167), he is echoing the gender-based oppositions of Lewes's argument.

The essay on Dickens is part of the broader attempt begun by Lewes in the 1840s to serve as arbiter of the emergent literary class and of its premier form, the novel. Like Lewes's 1852 essay 'The Lady Novelists,' it seeks to position those literary newcomers who threaten the status and boundaries of nineteenth-century literary territory, to control the impact of a broader-based literacy and of women's emergence into more public spheres.[4] The critique of Dickens depends on polarities that usually mark gender differences in nineteenth-century criticism, as, for example, the difference between feeling and thinking, between observing details and formulating generalizations. 'Dickens sees and feels,' Lewes intones,

> but the logic of feeling seems the only logic he can manage. Thought is strangely absent from his works . . . [K]eenly as he observes the objects before him, he never connects his observations into a general expression, never seems interested in general relations of things.
> (151)

Lewes makes still more explicit his identification of Dickens with this secondary realm of women's writing in this backhanded compliment:

> With a fine felicity of instinct he seized upon situations having an irresistible hold over the domestic affections and ordinary sympathies. He spoke in the mother-tongue of the heart, and was always sure of ready listeners.
>
> (146–47)

Dickens is thus identified with the feminine, as instinctual and fortunate, as seizing rather than analyzing, as interested in 'domestic affections and ordinary sympathies'. He 'painted nothing ideal, heroic,' Lewes explains. 'The world of thought and passion lay beyond his horizon' (147).

Lewes evokes many of the same oppositions when instructing Charlotte Brontë on the 'proper' realm for women writers, when cataloguing the 'lady novelists' of the day, or when marking the novel as the particular 'department' of women, the form that values '*finesse* of detail . . . pathos and sentiment'.[5] His acknowledgment that Dickens is 'always sure of ready listeners' rehearses a charge often made against nineteenth-century women writers, that the financial success and popularity of their work, its very attentiveness to audience concerns, marks it as 'anti– ' or 'sub-literary,' concerned with sales not posterity. Dickens thus joins the company of writers like Fanny Fern and Mary Elizabeth Braddon who, as one critic put it, discovered: 'a profitable market among the half-educated, . . . giving the undiscriminating what they wanted to read'.[6] The use of a category like the 'subliterary' works to regulate the effects of the novel as a newly-positioned literary discourse that challenges the cultural hegemony of upper-class men of letters.

In July 1845, Dickens described the aim and rhetorical stance of a proposed journal, *The Cricket*: 'I would at once sit down upon their very hobs; and take a personal and confidential position with them.'[7] In 1850, he finally established a periodical to fulfil the role of domestic comrade, that aspired 'to live in the Household affections, and to be numbered among the Household thoughts, of our readers'.[8] In establishing a journal to be 'familiar in their mouths as Household Words' (as the motto read), Dickens was making use of a feminine guise, privileging the intimate, private, and informal qualities usually associated with women over the social, public, and authoritative powers usually associated with men. But he was also disrupting the conventional wisdom that sharply divided the domestic and public spheres, for his journal insisted on the interpenetration of these realms.[9]

This gesture of cultural cross-dressing is part of a recurring exploration by Dickens in the 1850s of the discourses usually identified as feminine.[10] Michael Slater has argued that in the decade 1847 to 1857 Dickens was 'apparently preoccupied with women as the insulted and injured of mid-Victorian England,' and that the novels in this period feature more women characters in more prominent positions than do other of his novels. But he also sees Dickens as 'voicing no general condemnation of prevailing patriarchal beliefs and attitudes'.[11] I do not find it surprising that Dickens did not 'voice' a 'general condemnation' of the ideology within which he wrote. What I want to investigate is why his interest hovers at the edge of articulation, why it goes so far and then retreats, or goes so far and then is silent. Why is Dickens simultaneously empathetic with oppressed women and insistent on the constraints and stereotypes that restrict them? What does his practice suggest about how women are rendered silent in Victorian culture and novels, how their perspective is undermined or preempted? To use Pierre Macherey's terms, such issues become part of what is 'unvoiced,' 'unspoken' both in the novels and in Dickens' public postures.[12] The issue is not so much, then, whether Dickens crafted complex psychological women characters along the lines of George Eliot or Charlotte Brontë, but how women are positioned in the powerful discourses of the novels as in contemporary social practices. In Dickens' novels, the notion of 'writing as a woman' is problematic, as opposed to the confident assumptions Lewes makes of what it means 'to write as women,' of what the 'real office' is that women 'have to perform,' of the 'genuine female experience'.[13] Dickens' experimentation suggests that much is unknown, even to the women who 'experience' their lives and desires, that there is no ready language for what women wish to 'write'. Although Dickens himself certainly does not articulate a program of women's liberation, and indeed deploys many cultural tropes that restrict women as 'relative creatures,' his novels often make the 'commonsense' notions of Lewes untenable.[14]

The proliferation of child-wives in his novels and his portrait of Esther Summerson's strained narrative have often been cited by critics as signs of Dickens' preference for coy, idealized, and subservient women. His advocacy of the domestic values of hearth and home has similarly been dismissed as a sign of a peculiar weakness, a bourgeois sentimentality aimed at pleasing or appeasing his readers. Along with his taste for melodrama and Christmas morality, such quirks are explained away as a cultural disguise the master assumed to protect his more radical designs. The more critically acceptable Dickens provides cynical and witty analysis of cultural conventions and hypocrisies from a disengaged position. In other words, Dickens is valued as a prototype of the (male) modern artist as rebel and cultural critic; he is embarrassing in his assumption of what we label (female) 'Victorian' values. Like Lewes, then, we perpetuate the stigma of writing as a woman, associating feminine discourse with a lack of analysis and rigor, with pandering to 'cheap' tastes. And we resist identifying Dickens with either its problems or its effects.

When Dickens' experimentation with 'writing as a woman' is examined within this contest for literary territory and power, it involves more than merely being a woman writer or adopting a feminine persona.[15] By aligning himself with terms and oppositions usually associated with women (for example, fancy vs. reason or fact, the personal vs. the institutional), Dickens, in effect, explores how his own position as a writer of fiction is marked off as suspect or inferior.[16] He experiments with writing that traverses opposed realms and deploys narrative tropes that mark breaks in discursive power – stuttering, deception, metaphor, eccentricity, strain of voice or prose, interruptions. In this context, for example, Dickens' insistence on a linkage between 'romance' and familiar things is more than a personal credo or a rehearsal of a romantic ethos.[17] The preference in *Hard Times* of the devalued term 'fancy' over the more culturally respectable term 'imagination' locates his argument in a contemporary ideological contest, rather than as a repetition of an earlier aesthetic debate. The problematic position of women characters and writers functions as a figure of Dickens' own position in a culture suspicious of fancy and wary of claims to 'domestic' power. Deflecting the unease of his position onto women as an oppressed class allows Dickens to be more extreme and critical than he could if he were evaluating his own position directly.[18]

I would like to focus on what has usually been cited as a negative portrait of women, the failure to create a strong, likable heroine or a credible mother figure in *Hard Times* (1854). The novel itself is an instance of the conditions of feminine discourse, written not in any expansive artistic mode, but under the urgency of periodical publishing, as a project his printers hoped would attract readers to *Household Words*. Dickens disliked the conditions of weekly publication and deplored as 'CRUSHING' the consequent lack of 'elbow-room' and 'open places in perspective'.[19] But the process must have underscored the constraints embedded in the social and material production of discourse. Indeed much of the novel explores what cannot be said or explained, what cannot be portrayed. The women of this fictional world in particular are restricted by and to their social positions, defined within narrow ideological bounds that afford little relief. The characters do not operate primarily in personal relationships to each other, nor do they 'forget' their social positioning, or the polarities that operate in Coketown. They are constructed in oppositions, as women and men, mothers and daughters, middle-class thinkers and lower-class workers. The usual cultural positions for women remain curiously unpopulated, incomplete, present but not functioning as they ought. This schematic underdevelopment need not be explained away as a technological effect of the novel's weekly form, or as a style of abstraction.[20] The ideological and technical constraints also create the possibility for Dickens to write as if from within the realm that Lewes marks off for women writers – a realm of fancy, romance, ordinary events, and mass production; a realm that remains apart from what fastidious or learned readers will value.

The novel is constrained from the beginning by the powerful social discourse of the Gradgrind system, which exists in the novel as what Bakhtin called 'the word of the fathers'. Bakhtin argues that such a word need not be repeated or reinforced or even made persuasive, but has 'its authority already fused to it':

> The authoritative word demands that we acknowledge it, that we make it our own; it binds us, quite independent of any power it might have to persuade us internally; we encounter it with its authority already fused to it . . . It is, so to speak, the word of the fathers. Its authority was already *acknowledged* in the past. It is a *prior* discourse. It is therefore not a question of choosing it from among other possible discourses that are its equal.[21]

Against such a word, opposition or argument is already preempted, made secondary or unhearable. Unlike the opposing terms of 'wonder' and 'fancy,' which require constant justification in the novel, the simplest reference to 'fact' evokes the authority of learning and scientific knowledge. The effect of such an authority is to make all private exchanges in the book dependent on arguments that cannot be imagined within the novel's authorized categories, so that the characters speak a kind of shadow dialogue.

The effect of this social construction is especially destructive to the transparent figure who serves as the heroine's mother. In a more self-consciously 'feminist' novel, Mrs Gradgrind might be expected to suggest the alternative to patriarchal discourses. In *Hard Times*, the mother is comically ineffectual and trivial, represented not as a person but as an object, as a 'feminine dormouse' (102), and a 'bundle of shawls' (59). Yet she is not even a particularly satisfactory object. Her central representation, repeated three times, is as a 'faint transparency' that is 'presented' to its audience in various unimpressive attitudes:[22]

> Mrs Gradgrind, weakly smiling and giving no other sign of vitality, looked (as she always did) like an indifferently executed transparency of a small female figure, without enough light behind it.
>
> (60)

A transparency is an art form popularized by the dioramas in which a translucent image painted on cloth is made visible by backlighting.[23] Its fragility and potential for varying production make the transparency a felicitous medium to suggest Mrs Gradgrind's ambivalent positioning. The failure of the transparency renders her almost invisible in the novel, making her neither a pleasing image nor one that is easily readable. But the particularity of the image insists on a producer as well as a product, raising the issue of what painter 'executes' her so indifferently, what producer withholds the light that might have made her more substantial, in other words, why she has been neglected as a cultural formation. Vaguely discernible through the translucent object, the producer remains a shadowy, unnamed, prior force, whom we know by traces and effects. At Mrs Gradgrind's death, for example, we are told of an effect, but not of a cause – 'the light that had always been feeble and dim behind the weak transparency, went out' (226). And the physical depiction of her as recumbent, 'stunned by some weighty piece of fact tumbling on her' (59; see also 60, 62, 137) leaves unnamed the force that stuns her with its weight and carelessness. We are left with an authorless piece of evidence, a 'piece of fact'; but in *Hard Times* 'fact' is easily traced back to the Gradgrind system. When we are told that finding herself alone with Gradgrind and Mr Bounderby is 'sufficient to stun this admirable lady again, without collision between herself and any other fact' (62), we know what constitutes her as an object of its gaze. It is under her husband's 'wintry' eye that Mrs Gradgrind becomes 'torpid again' (102); under Sissy Jupe's care or even in Louisa's presence, she can be 'rendered almost energetic' (94). Both fact and its proponents are equally capable of rendering Mrs Gradgrind nonexistent, a product of a careless fancy: 'So, she once more died away, and nobody minded her' (62).

Mrs Gradgrind has been so slighted as a 'subject' that she is surprised when Louisa asks about her: 'You want to hear of me, my dear? That's something new, I am sure, when anybody wants to hear of me' (224). And the outcome of such a lifetime of being constituted by others is that she cannot even claim to feel her own pain; when Louisa asks after her health, she answers with what the narrator calls 'this strange speech': 'I think there's a pain somewhere in the room . . . but I couldn't positively say that I have got it' (224). She is certainly slighted by Dickens, appearing in only five of the novel's thirty-seven chapters, and then usually in the final pages or paragraphs. Even her introduction seems almost an afterthought, located not in the chapter with Mr Gradgrind, the children, or even the house (ch. 3), but in parenthetical position as audience for Mr Bounderby (ch. 4).[24] But if Dickens is cavalier about her presence, he strongly marks her absence from that nineteenth-century site for Mother, as idealized figure in her children's memories or in their imaginative dreams of virtue.[25] Mrs Gradgrind's expected place as her children's earliest memory has been usurped by the father who appears as a 'dry Ogre chalking ghastly white figures' on a 'large black board' (54). Louisa's return 'home' for her mother's death evokes none of the 'dreams of childhood – its airy fables' and 'impossible adornments' that Dickens describes as 'the best influences of old home'; such dreams are only evoked as a lengthy litany of what her mother has *not* provided for her child (223).

Mrs Gradgrind does not offer a counter position – covert or otherwise – to the world of fact and ashes. She cannot overtly defy her husband, nor can she save herself from her daughter's scorn. Her advice to Louisa reflects this helplessness, and its incomprehension of the accepted referents makes her ridiculous in her child's eyes: 'Go and be somethingological directly,' she says (61), and 'turn all your ological studies to good account' (137). When she is dying, Mrs Gradgrind tries to express her loss – of something and of words with which to articulate it – to her daughter:

> But there is something – not an Ology at all – that your father has missed, or forgotten, Louisa. I don't know what it is . . . I shall never get its name now. But your father may. It makes me restless. I want to write to him, to find out for God's sake, what it is. Give me a pen, give me a pen.
>
> (225)

To the transparent Mrs Gradgrind, all authoritative knowledge must come from the father, yet she worries that he has missed or forgotten something. She does not imagine herself finding or naming it, but remembers it as unsaid. The outcome of this 'insight' is invisible to the patriarchal eye; it disappears as 'figures of wonderful no-meaning she began to trace upon her wrappers' (225–26). When Louisa tries to fashion a meaning of her mother's words, her aim is to 'link such faint and broken sounds into any chain of connexion' (225), in other words, to translate her mother into the Gradgrind discourse. Mrs Gradgrind emerges 'from the shadow' and takes 'upon her the dread solemnity of the sages and patriarchs' (226) – she 'hears the last of it' – only by dying, not as a living speaker addressing her daughter knowingly and directly. She remains stubbornly unincorporated by the novel's powerful discourses, a no-meaning that can be neither heard nor reformed.

But the mother is ridiculous, rather than tragic, only within the father's terms of judgment – terms which a society divided into opposites cannot unimagine or unspeak, and against which the lower-class opposition of fancy and heart will have little impact. The mother's very imprecision undercuts the authority of the father's discourses, making them a lesson imperfectly learned and badly recited. The novel cannot construct an imagined alternate culture, in which Mrs Gradgrind would 'discover' the language to define the 'something missing,' in which 'ological' would not be required as an ending that validates an object's existence. Instead it unfolds the boundaries and effects of such a system. Louisa learns painfully that Mrs Gradgrind's point-of-view has been confined to its position of 'no-meaning' (225) by concerted efforts by her father and his system of definition. Towards the end of the novel, Louisa reverses the charge of 'no-meaning' and demands that her father justify instead what his 'meaning' has produced: 'Where are the graces of my soul? Where are the sentiments of my heart? What have you done. O father, what have you, with the garden that should have bloomed once, in this great wilderness here!' (239). In this confrontation, Louisa recognizes the contest her father has suppressed and her mother has barely suggested, a contest for how to determine the shape and value of the social realms:

> I have grown up, battling every inch of my way . . . What I have learned has left me doubting, misbelieving, despising, regretting, what I have not learned; and my dismal resource has been to think that life would soon go by, and that nothing in it could be worth the pain and trouble of a contest.
>
> (240–41)

The novel presents several scenes between Louisa and her father in which this authority is examined and questioned, scenes which pointedly exclude Mrs Gradgrind, as someone whose objections or interests are irrelevant. The chapter 'Father and Daughter' opens with an oblique questioning of the absolute value of such authority (131–32), but only once the 'business' is resolved does Gradgrind

167

suggest, 'now, let us go and find your mother' (137). Yet the exploration of Gradgrind's power makes an obscure and unacknowledged connection between his power and her mother's 'death' from the novel. By what seems a frivolous word-game on the part of the narrator, Gradgrind's governmental blue books (the emblem of his power) are associated with an infamous wife-killer: 'Although Mr Gradgrind did not take after Blue Beard, his room was quite a blue chamber in its abundance of blue books' (131). The narrator denies that this 'error' has any meaning, thus resisting the implication that Gradgrind's intellectual system of power has something to do with the oppressed status of his wife. The blue books are accorded the power of fact, which is to prove 'usually anything you like,' but the narrator's flight of fancy is not to prove anything. It refers, not to the authoritative realms of statistics and science, but to fairy-tales; it is not a 'fact' derived from texts, but is 'something missing,' an association produced by the unconscious. It remains, at best, as a kind of insider's joke, in which readers can remember that its 'power' derives from texts with which Dickens was aligned, both in general (fiction and fairy tale), and explicitly (Blue Beard is the basis for Dickens' Captain Murderer, whose tale he published in 1860 as one of his 'Nurse's Stories').[26]

The reference to the wife-killer, Blue Beard, who charms all with his show of courtesy and devotion before devouring his wives in the privacy of their home, is an 'error' that suggests the gap between public and private, between acknowledged power and covert violence. Like the marginalized tensions created by Mrs Gradgrind throughout the novel, this slip of the pen provokes despite its claim to marginality. The error is allowed to stand, thereby suggesting what would otherwise be too bizarre to consider. It reminds us that Gradgrind has been a social 'wife-killer,' obliterating his wife's role as mother to her daughter and keeping her from fuller participation in the daughter's narrative. He has 'formed his daughter on his own model' (168), and she is known to all as 'Tom Gradgrind's daughter' (143). He has isolated Louisa in his masculine realm, depriving her of any of the usual female resources with which to oppose his power; as Tom mentions with devastating casualness, Louisa 'used to complain to me that she had nothing to fall back upon, that girls usually fall back upon' (168). The reference to Blue Beard reminds us that Gradgrind's realm is *not* absolute except by force and mystification, that his 'charmed apartment' depends on the exclusion of a more powerful, more resistant 'other'. The rest of the chapter teases out the possibilities that his power can be questioned. Through a series of fanciful images – that make the narrator not an unworthy companion of Mrs Gradgrind – the absolute value of his authority is obliquely undermined. Gradgrind is presented as needing to enforce his positions with military might, relying on his books as an 'army constantly strengthening by the arrival of new recruits'. His solutions persist because they are isolated within a necromancer's circle, protected from critique or even outside knowledge. From his enclosed, abstracted fortress, he orders the world as if 'the astronomer within should arrange the starry universe solely by pen, ink and paper, . . . could settle all their destines on a slate, and wipe out all their tears with one dirty little bit of sponge' (131–32). All these questions about Gradgrind's power are delivered as amusing details, as arguments the novelist is not able to give serious articulation. Yet the details attack not the effect of Gradgrind's power, as Louisa does with hopeless inertia, but the claim to power, its genealogy and maintenance.

It is not surprising that Louisa and her mother, and even Dickens, cannot find words for what is missing from their lives, words having been usurped as the tools of the Gradgrind system, defined and delimited by male authority. Mrs Gradgrind does not articulate an opposition, nor does the novel openly pursue the traces of her petulant complaints. *She* remains unaware that her headaches and worries are symptoms of a cultural dissatisfaction, although she knows that her head began 'to split' as soon as she was married (137). She complains to Louisa about the trouble that comes from speaking – 'You must remember, my dear, that whenever I have said anything, on any subject, I have never heard the last of it; and consequently, that I have long left off saying anything' (225), but the ideological implications of these remarks are shortcircuited by the personal contexts in which she declines to speak. These scenes do not transform Mrs Gradgrind into a covert rebel, but represent her as willful and self-absorbed, betraying Sissy and Louisa by her silence and diverting attention from their more pressing needs.

In fact, Mrs Gradgrind seems to exist primarily as the cautionary exemplum of the Gradgrind system, having been married for the 'purity' of being as free from nonsense 'as any human being not arrived at the perfection of an absolute idiot, ever was' (62). She proves her usefulness to the system, admirably serving as the negative against which the father seems more caring, more responsive than he seems in isolation. Her mother seems unsympathetic to Louisa's discontent, worrying over it as 'one of those subjects I shall never hear the last of' (138). And she serves as the agent who reinscribes the ideological positions of the Gradgrind system, who insists on reality being defined as what is kept 'in cabinets' or about which one can 'attend lectures' (61). Louisa is scolded for running off to look at the forbidden circus by her mother, not by the father whose prohibition it is and who has caught her in the crime. The hapless Mrs Gradgrind 'whimpers' to her daughter; 'I wonder at you. I declare you're enough to make one regret ever having had a family at all. I have a great mind to say I wish I hadn't. *Then* what would you have done, I should like to know' (61). Yet in this pathetic effort to enforce her husband's laws, Mrs Gradgrind has unknowingly allied herself with her child's rebellion. Her words give her away: she has 'wondered' (a crime against reason), she has 'regretted' (a crime against fact), and she has 'wished' (a crime against her husband). Dickens notes that 'Mr Gradgrind did not seem favourably impressed by these cogent remarks'. Yet what seems initially a silly, self-indulgent speech has deflected the father's wrath from his daughter and has suggested the terms for opposition – wonder, regret, desire.

Hard Times appears to authorize an oppositional discourse of fancy, which is lisped by the circus-master Sleary and represented in Sissy Jupe, the substitute mother whom Gradgrind praises as the 'good fairy in his house' who can 'effect' what 10,000 pounds cannot (294). Gradgrind's approval, and the conventionality of Sissy's depiction as a house fairy, devalues her status as an opposition figure. Indeed Sissy rarely speaks in opposition, or at all. Her power is cited by men like Harthouse and Gradgrind, and by the narrator. Unlike Mrs Gradgrind, Sissy cannot be mocked for 'cogent remarks,' but simply *looks* at Louisa 'in wonder, in pity, in sorrow, in doubt, in a multitude of emotions' (138). Her effect is largely due to the novelty of her discourse, a novelty produced by her status as an outsider who does not understand the conventions of the system. 'Possessed of no facts' (49), girl number twenty does not recognize that 'fancy' is a significant term, but uses it unthinkingly. She silences the cynical Harthouse by presenting 'something in which he was so inexperienced, and against which he knew any of his usual weapons would fall so powerless; that not a word could he rally to his relief'. Sissy insists on her words to Harthouse remaining a 'secret' and relies on a 'child-like ingenuousness' to sway her listener. And what Harthouse notices is her 'most confiding eyes' and her 'most earnest (though so quiet)' voice (252–57). Sissy's 'wonder' is powerful only as long as she does not 'speak' it in her own right, but presents it in her disengaged role as go-between. Her 'power' depends on 'her entire forgetfulness of herself in her earnest quiet holding to the object' (253) – depends, in other words, on a strenuous denial of herself as a contestant for power. The narrator comments that 'if she had shown, or felt the slightest trace of any sensitiveness to his ridicule or astonishment, or any remonstrance he might offer; he would have carried it against her at this point' (255).

Sissy's discourse derives its power, not from any essential woman's knowledge that Louisa and her mother could share, but from her experience as a working-class child who knows counter examples and a different word than 'fact'. Louisa acquires from Sissy not the power to be 'a mother – lovingly watchful of her children' but to be 'learned in childish lore; thinking no innocent and pretty fancy ever to be despised' (313). The opposition Sissy seems to represent – of imagination, emotion, questioning of patriarchal discourses – stands like the circus-master's fancy, a fantastic dream that amuses children but does not displace Gradgrindian fact. It has no ability to construct a shared feminine discourse that can alter the rigid polarities of fact and fancy, meaning and no-meaning. When Louisa tries to inquire about such forbidden topics as love, she is on her own, pursuing a 'strong, wild, wandering interest peculiar to her, an interest gone astray like a banished creature, and hiding in solitary places' (98).

In her dramatic confrontation with her father (238–42), Louisa tries to construct a realm outside the powerful sway of reason and logic. Yet she can imagine this realm only as the 'immaterial part of my life,' marking it as that which has no material existence or is irrelevant. She thereby perpetuates the construction of her world as absolute in its polarities – as a world that is either material or immaterial, fact or fancy, reason or nonsense.[27] To use Bakhtin's terms, she remains 'bound' to 'the authoritative word' in its totality; she cannot 'divide it up,' or 'play with the context framing it' or 'play with its borders' (Bakhtin, 343). She suggests she might have come closer to a desired end 'if I had been stone blind; if I had groped my way by my sense of touch, and had been free, while I knew the shapes and surfaces of things, to exercise my fancy somewhat, in regard to them' (240). Passionate as this scene is, Louisa's specific argument shows the difficulty of evading the power of patriarchal discourse; she can only 'prove' the worth of an oppositional realm by the tools she has learned from her father. Her vision remains defined as 'no-meaning,' as existing only in opposition to what persists as 'meaning', Louisa tries to imagine a realm 'defying all the calculations ever made by man, and no more known to his arithmetic than his Creator is,' but ends up describing herself as 'a million times wiser, happier'. Like her mother, her power lies in speaking the father's word imperfectly, making her father's statistical practices meaningless by her exaggerated application. Like her mother, Louisa's complaints refer only to 'something' missing; there are no words for what might be gained. The Gradgrind system is too powerful to allow Louisa or her mother to break away or to communicate very well with each other. All they can do, in their separate ways and unbeknownst to each other, is to disrupt the functioning of the father's word, and to indicate a lack, an incompleteness.

The schematic quality of *Hard Times* indicates a broader lack or incompleteness in the authoritative discourses of Dickens' social and literary world. Like Louisa and Mrs Gradgrind, Dickens must articulate his valuing of 'fancy' and his concern about crossing proscribed boundaries in language devalued by the patriarchal discourses of reason and fact. That Lewes sees him as hallucinating a world no wise man would recognize indicates the disturbing effect of this crossing of boundaries. Both Lewes and Dickens identify the disturbance as somehow connected with women, seeing women as touched by issues that more successfully acculturated males do not notice. Lewes saw much of Dickens' power – and what made him a disturbing novelist – as the ability to represent something that could not otherwise be acknowledged. 'What seems preposterous, impossible to us,' he wrote in 1872, 'seemed to him simple fact of observation' (Lewes, 145). Writing as a woman places Dickens in a position to observe what seems 'preposterous, impossible'.

At the same time, of course, for a powerful male novelist like Dickens, the position of outsider is exaggerated. Dickens can be seen as exploiting the exclusion and material oppression of women and the poor when they serve as analogies for his own more temperate marginality as a lower-middle class writer of fiction in a literary culture that preferred educated reason over experienced fancy. For male writers like Dickens and Trollope, writing 'as a woman' brought literary respect and considerable financial return, whereas a writer like Charlotte Brontë was censured for her unwomanly productions and underpaid by her publisher.[28] Unlike women who transgress the boundaries of the literary establishment, Dickens could signal his difference as significant rather than ridiculous. Unlike the poor with whom he was so closely identified, Dickens had access to the means of publication; he had the influence and position to pressure contemporary methods of production and dissemination of literary and social discourse. Such was his influence as spokesman of social discontent, that women writers of the nineteenth century, in both England and America, had to come to terms with his boundaries and codes, with his literary conventions for observing the social world and its institutions. Writers like Mary Elizabeth Braddon, Elizabeth Gaskell, Elizabeth Stuart Phelps, and Rebecca Harding Davis both quote and revise his portrayal of women's writing and social position. Their attempts to write as women are circumscribed within Dickens' example and within the audience that he so powerfully swayed.

This assessment of Dickens' sympathetic identification with

feminine discourses in the 1850s returns to the intertwined, ideological interests involved in any attempt to write 'as a woman,' in any project that *assumes* the position of an outsider, of an other. Dickens' experimentation with excluded positions of women and the poor provided him with a way of disrupting the status quo of the literary establishment. But, ironically, his experimentation also helped him capitalize on his status as an outsider in that literary realm. The inarticulate masses became, in effect, his constituency and his subject matter, supporting his powerful position within the literary and social establishment as arbiter of how to write about cultural exclusion. Dickens' growing influence as an editor and public spokesman for the literary world makes his representations of women's writing dominate the literary scene. His example carves out a possible space for women writers in his culture, but it also takes over that space as its own. His assumed position as outsider complicates assumptions about gender difference in writing and problematizes what Lewes so confidently called 'genuine female experience'. It disrupts and forces out into the open the literary establishment's defensive cultural narratives, and, in the process, constructs its own protective practices and standards. In writing as a woman, in speaking for a silenced group, Dickens both makes possible and makes complicated a challenge to 'the father's word' by those who use 'the mother-tongue'.

Notes

1. 'Dickens in Relation to Criticism,' *Fortnightly Review* 17 (1872): 141–54. Lewes had written in *The Leader* in 1852 about *Bleak House* and had engaged with Dickens in a debate about the scientific basis for spontaneous combustion. For an early summary of the relationship between the two, see GORDON S. HAIGHT, 'Dickens and Lewes,' *PMLA*, 71 (1956): 166–79.
2. See Forster's rebuttal of Lewes's essay in *The Life of Charles Dickens* (1872–1874), ed. A. J. HOPPÉ, 2 vols (1927; London: Dent, 1966), II. 267–79. Forster argued: 'When the characters in a play are puppets, and the audiences of the theatre fools or children, no wise man forfeits his wisdom by proceeding to admit that . . . through his puppets, he spoke "in the mother-tongue of the heart" ' (2.270). See also the excellent discussion of Lewes's essay by GEORGE H. FORD, in *Dickens and His Readers: Aspects of Novel-Criticism Since 1836* (1955; repr. New York: W. W. Norton, 1965), pp. 149–54, which focuses on Lewes's concern about 'realism' and his derogation of Dickens' imagination. Ford describes the essay as 'an extremely sophisticated piece of irony' (151) and as 'the most effective attack on Dickens ever written' (154). 'Like the walrus and the carpenter,' he concludes, 'Lewes weeps over the oysters he is

consuming, and he assures his victim and his audience that it is all for the best' (154).

3. *The Rise and Fall of the Man of Letters* (London: Macmillan, 1969) 73. Gross discusses Lewes's career as writer and editor of periodicals but does not mention his influence on any women writers except George Eliot. For other discussions of Lewes's influence as a critic, see MONIKA BROWN, 'George Henry Lewes,' *DLB 55: Victorian Prose Writers before 1867*, ed. WILLIAM B. THESING (Detroit, Mich.: Gale Research, 1987), 128–41; HAROLD OREL, *Victorian Literary Critics* (New York: St. Martin's Press, 1984), pp. 5–30; EDGAR W. HIRSHBERG, *George Henry Lewes* (New York: Twayne, 1970); ALICE R. KAMINSKY, 'George Eliot, George Henry Lewis, and the Novel,' *PMLA*, 70 (1955): 997–1013; MORRIS GREENHUT, 'George Henry Lewes as a Critic of the Novel,' *Studies in Philology* 45 (1948): 491–511.

4. In 'The Principles of Success in Literature,' a six-part essay appearing 'by the editor' of the new *Fortnightly Review* in 1865, Lewes discussed the 'profession' of literature, and the necessity to protect it from the 'incompetent aspirants, without seriousness of aim, without the faculties demanded by their work,' those who 'follow Literature simply because they see no other opening for their incompetence; just as forlorn widows and ignorant old maids thrown suddenly on their own resources open a school' (1 [1865]: 86). As he did of his letters and reviews of Brontë, Lewes saw this essay as furnishing 'nothing more than help and encouragement' (86). Lewes's defense of literature is generous in comparison to the vituperative review of *A Tale of Two Cities* by JAMES FITZJAMES STEPHEN, who blamed Dickens for 'infect[ing] the literature of his country with a disease' and promoting instead an 'incurable vulgarity of mind and of taste, and intolerable arrogance of temper.' He charged him with a 'complete disregard of the rules of literary composition' and a lack of 'intellectual excellence' or concern for 'the higher pleasures' of fiction (*Saturday Review* 8, 17 December 1859: 741–43).

5. 'The Lady Novelists,' *Westminster Review* 58 (1852): 72. See also 'The Principles of Success in Literature,' and his reviews of Brontë's *Jane Eyre, Shirley,* and *Villette*. Only Brontë's side of their correspondence seems to have survived, but her letters to Lewes and to her friend W. S. Williams discuss what Lewes wrote to her; see CLEMENT SHORTER, *The Brontës: Life and Letters*, 2 vols. (1908: reprinted New York: Haskell House, 1969). In a letter to her 'mentor' (Nov. 6, 1847). Brontë recites the terms of Lewes's advice, his warning to 'beware of melodrama,' his exhortation to 'adhere to the real,' and describes her early adherence to such 'principles': 'I restrained imagination, eschewed romance, repressed excitement . . . sought to produce something which should be soft, grave, and true.' But she also questions the authority of his views: 'when [imagination] is eloquent, and speaks rapidly and urgently in our ear, are we not to write to her dictation?' (1. 365–66). In her letter of Jan. 12, 1848, following Lewes's review of *Jane Eyre*, Brontë writes, 'If I ever *do* write another book, I think I will have nothing of what you call "melodrama"; I *think* so, but I am not sure' (1. 386). Brontë was furious at Lewes's published 'discovery' that she was a woman, especially after she had requested that he avoid the issue. She wrote to him on Jan. 19, 1850: 'after I had said earnestly that I wished critics would judge me as an *author*, not as a woman, you so roughly – I even thought so cruelly – handled the question of sex' (2. 106). I am indebted to MARGARET L. SHAW's discussion of Lewes's effect on Charlotte Brontë and

his efforts to consolidate the emerging category of the 'man of letters' (PhD dissertation, University of Pittsburgh, 1988). See also FRANKLIN GARY, 'Charlotte Brontë and George Henry Lewes,' *PMLA*, 51 (1936): 518–42.

6. JAY B. HUBBELL, *Who Are the Major American Writers?* (University of North Carolina P, 1972) p. 79. Hubbell was specifically discussing the 'decline' of literature in the 1870s in America. In the 1872 essay Lewes argued that unknowledgeable readers 'were at once laid hold of by the reproduction of their own feelings, their own experiences, their own prejudices' (151).

7. Letter to John Forster, *The Letters of Charles Dickens*, ed. MADELINE HOUSE and GRAHAM STOREY, The Pilgrim Edition, Vol. 4 (Oxford: Clarendon Press, 1965–88): 328.

8. CHARLES DICKENS, 'Preliminary Word,' *Household Words* 1 (March 1850): 1.

9. For the details of Dickens' periodical experimentation, see ANNE LOHRLI, ed., *Household Words* (Toronto: University of Toronto Press, 1973), and HARRY STONE, ed. *Charles Dickens' Uncollected Writings from Household Words*, 2 vols. (Bloomington: Indiana University Press, 1968).

10. In 'Critical Cross-Dressing: Male Feminists and the Woman of the Year,' *Raritan* 3(1983): 130–49, ELAINE SHOWALTER considers whether the fashion in the 1980s to address the 'woman question' is a disguised form of 'power play': 'Is male feminism a form of critical cross-dressing, . . . or is it the result of a genuine shift in critical, cultural, and sexual paradigms . . .?' (131, 134).

11. *Dickens and Women* (Stanford, Calif.: Stanford University Press, 1983), pp. 243–44. In her essay, 'Writing in a "Womanly" Way and the Double Vision of *Bleak House*,' *Dickens Quarterly*, IV, 1 (1987): 3–15, SUZANNE GRAVER makes a compelling argument for Dickens' 'masculine stake' in discerning contemporary gender relations, in representing the value and authority of women's knowledge. Although she argues for Dickens' 'remarkably insightful portrait of a woman experiencing her knowing self as not-knowing' (10), she also charges him with using 'Esther's obliqueness not to subvert Victorian womanly ideals but to celebrate a dutifully willed acceptance of them' (4).

12. *A Theory of Literature Production*, trans. GEOFFREY WALL (1966; London: Routledge & Kegan Paul, 1978); see especially pp. 82–9.

13. 'The Lady Novelists' (1852), p. 72.

14. The phrase 'relative creatures' is from SARAH STICKNEY ELLIS's influential advice book, *The Women of England* (London, 1838; reprinted Philadelphia: Herman Hooker, 1841) p. 100. See DIANNE SADOFF's discussions of women characters in *Monsters of Affection: Dickens, Eliot and Brontë on Fatherhood* (Baltimore, Md.: Johns Hopkins University Press, 1982), pp. 58–64. See also ANNE ROBINSON TAYLOR's discussion of Esther, 'The Author as Female Child,' in *Male Novelists and Their Female Voices: Literary Masquerades* (Troy, NY: Whitson Publishing Co., 1981), pp. 121–56.

15. See PEGGY KAMUF, 'Writing like a Woman,' in *Women and Language in Literature and Society*, ed. SALLY MCCONNELL-GINET, RUTH BORKER, and NELLY FURMAN (New York: Praeger, 1980), pp. 284–99, for an argument against an essentialist 'female writing' (as proposed in PATRICIA SPACKS, *The Female Imagination*, 1972) and her warning about seeing literature as 'expressions, simple and direct, of individual experience' (286).

16. In 'Patriarchy Against Itself – The Young Manhood of Wallace Stevens,' *Critical Inquiry* 13 (Summer 1987): 742–86, FRANK LENTRICCHIA discusses Stevens's

sense of poetry as a 'lady-like' habit, his 'feminization of the literary life' and his 'struggle to overcome this feminization' which his culture equated with 'the trivialization of literature and the literary impulse' (751). He argues for 'the cultural powerlessness of poetry in a society that masculinized the economic while it feminized the literary' (766).

17. In *Bleak House* (1852), for example, his preface proposes to explore 'the romantic side of familiar things,' and the opening number of *Household Words* insists 'that in all familiar things, even in those which are repellent on the surface, there is Romance enough, if we will find it out' (1 [1850]: 1).

18. For an analysis of Dickens' habit of deflecting self-critique. see JEAN FERGUSON CARR, 'Dickens and Autobiography: A Wild Beast and his Keeper,' *ELH* 52 (1985): 447–69. See also Carr, 'The Polemics of Incomprehension: Mother and Daughter in *Pride and Prejudice*,' in *Traditions and the Talents of Women*, ed. FLORENCE HOWE (Champaign, Ill.: University of Illinois Press, 1989).

19. Letter to John Forster, [February 1854], *The Letters of Charles Dickens*, ed. WALTER DEXTER, vol. 2 (London: Nonesuch Press, 1937–38): 543. To Mrs Richard Watson, Nov. 1, 1854, he wrote that he felt ' "used up" after Hard Times' and that 'the compression and close condensation necessary for that disjointed form of publication gave me perpetual trouble' (2. 602). See his letter to Miss Coutts, Jan. 23, 1854 (2. 537) for a description of his printers' urging to write the novel. In *Dickens' Working Notes for his Novels* (Chicago, Ill.: University of Chicago Press, 1987), HARRY STONE discusses Dickens' efforts to accommodate his working procedures to the constraints of weekly serialization (p. 249), and the plans show his calculations for the unfamiliar size of a weekly part (pp. 251–53).

20. See, for example, DAVID CRAIG's discussion of the novel's 'simplifying mode,' in his introduction to *Hard Times: For These Times* (New York: Penguin, 1969), p. 28. All following page references are to the Penguin edition.

21. M. M. BAKHTIN, *The Dialogic Imagination*, ed. MICHAEL HOLQUIST, trans. CARYL EMERSON and MICHAEL HOLQUIST (Austin and London: University of Texas Press, 1981), p. 342.

22. See also 137, 224. This passage is one of the few references to Mrs Gradgrind in Dickens's working plans for the novel (Stone, 253): 'Mrs Gradgrind – badly done transparency, without enough light behind.'

23. In *The Shows of London* (Cambridge, Mass.: Harvard University Press, 1978). RICHARD D. ALTICK defines transparencies as 'pictures made with translucent paints on materials like calico, linen, or oiled paper and lighted from behind in the manner of stained glass' (p. 95) and discusses their popularity in the Chinese shadow and magic-lantern shows of the 1770s (p. 119) and in the dioramas of the 1820s on (pp. 169–70). In Daguerre's 'double-effect' technique, transparencies were painted on both sides, their appearance transformed by the amount and angle of light shown through the image (pp. 169–70). Transparencies, or lithophanes as they were sometimes called, could also be small porcelain figures held against a light.

24. Dickens changed his mind about its positioning, marking in his working plans its postponement from ch. 3 (*'No not yet'*) to ch. 4 (*'Now, Mrs Gradgrind'*) (Stone, p. 253).

25. His working plans indicate an early decision about whether to make it 'Mrs Gradgrind – or Miss? Wife or sister? *Wife*' (Stone, p. 253). In *Dickens at Work* (London: Methuen, 1957), JOHN BUTT and KATHLEEN TILLOTSON argue that the

choice of 'wife' over 'sister' emphasizes 'more powerfully' the absolute influence of Gradgrind over his children. (p. 206).

26. Reprinted in *Charles Dickens: Selected Short Fiction*, ed. DEBORAH A. THOMAS (New York: Penguin, 1976), pp. 218–29. The naive narrator of the tale assumes Captain Murderer 'must have been an offshoot of the Blue Beard family, but I had no suspicion of the consanguinity in those times.' Like Gradgrind, Captain Murderer's 'warning name would seem to have awakened no general prejudice against him, for he was admitted into the best society and possessed immense wealth' (p. 221). And, like Gradgrind, much of his power comes from being the determiner of meanings and names.

27. Several of Dickens' initial titles in his working plans for the novel reflect this insistence on polarity: 'Hard heads and soft hearts,' 'Heads and Tales,' and 'Black and White' (Stone, p. 251).

28. See MARGOT PETERS's discussion of the inequity of publishers' payments, in *Unquiet Soul: A Biography of Charlotte Brontë* (1975; reprinted New York: Atheneum, 1986), p. 355–56. Brontë received the same unsatisfying sum of £500 for her third novel *Villette* as she had for the first two, as compared to Thackeray's £4200 for *The Virginians* or the £1000 Dickens could command for a short story. Peters quotes George Gissing's telling comment about author-publisher relations:

> A big, blusterous, genial brute of a Trollope could very fairly hold his own, and exact at all events an acceptable share in the profits of his work. A shrewd and vigorous man of business such as Dickens . . . could do even better . . . But pray, what of Charlotte Brontë? Think of that grey, pinched life, . . . which would have been so brightened had [she] received but . . . one-third of what in the same space of time, the publisher gained by her books.
>
> (355–56)

11 Homophobia, Misogyny, and Capital: The Example of *Our Mutual Friend*

EVE KOSOFSKY SEDGWICK*

Eve Kosofsky Sedgwick is Professor of English at Duke University, and the author of a number of works which explore the relations between power, gender and sexuality, and compel particular attention to the importance of same-sex desire in maintaining conventional sexual orderings. Among her works are *The Coherence of Gothic Conventions* (New York: Methuen, 1976); *Between Men: English Literature and Male Homosocial Desire* (New York: Columbia Press, 1985); *Epistemology of the Closet* (Berkeley: University of California Press, 1990); *Tendencies* (Durham: Duke University Press, 1993); *Fat Art, Thin Art* (Durham: Duke University Press, 1994); *Performativity and Performance* (London: Routledge, 1995) and *Shame and Its Sisters: A Silvan Tomkins Reader* (Durham: Duke University Press, 1995). In this extract from *Between Men*, Sedgwick shows the impact on *Our Mutual Friend* of a complex mapping of sexual conflicts and affiliations on to conflicts and affiliations of class in the nineteenth century. She identifies in the novel a series of homosocial mirrorings and rivalries between men. These are expressed in a series of triangles which enact patriarchal transactions that are played out over women, but never, as she puts it, end in them. The culmination of this argument is her analysis of the class and erotic struggle between Bradley Headstone and Eugene Wrayburn. Sedgwick's essay presents *Our Mutual Friend* as a narrative of male socialisation, in which the powerful, but infantile lure of homosociality is steadily eschewed in favour of heterosexual and homophobic patterns of desire.

By the time of *Great Expectations, Our Mutual Friend*, and *Edwin Drood*, Dickens' writing had incorporated the concerns and thematics of the paranoid Gothic as a central preoccupation. Specifically, each of these novels sites an important plot in triangular, heterosexual romance – in the Romance tradition – and then changes its focus as

---

*Reprinted from *Between Men: English Literature and Male Homosocial Desire* (New York: Columbia Press, 1985), pp. 163–79.

if by compulsion from the heterosexual bonds of the triangle to the male-homosocial one, here called 'erotic rivalry'. In these male homosocial bonds are concentrated the fantasy energies of compulsion, prohibition, and explosive violence; all are fully structured by the logic of paranoia. At the same time, however, these fantasy energies are mapped along the axes of social and political power; so that the revelation of intrapsychic structures is inextricable from the revelation of the mechanisms of class domination.

In the half-century or so between the classic Gothic and Dickens, the terms of engagement between homophobia and class structure had become ever more differentiated. The normative status of the rural gentry in Hogg had to a large extent devolved onto (some version of) the English middle class – mediated by genealogical narratives like *Henry Esmond* and *The Princess*. And an anxious self-definition of that class, in male-homosocial terms, as against those both above and below on the social ladder, was effected, as well as critiqued, by neo-Gothic writers such as Dickens.

Our Mutual Friend is *the* English novel that everyone knows is about anality. The inheritance at the center of the plot is immensely valuable real estate that contains a cluster of what Dickens calls 'dust heaps'. Layers of scholarly controversy have been devoted to the contents of Victorian dust heaps; and, led by Humphry House's *The Dickens World*, many critics have agreed that human excrement was an important (and financially valuable) component of the mounds. Such critics as Earle Davis, Monroe Engel, J. Hillis Miller, and Sylvia Bank Manning have given this thematic element a good deal of play, often, as F. S. Schwarzbach says, 'with the intention of establishing whether Dickens did or did not understand Freud's later formulation of the psychic relation between human waste and money'.[1] But although many of those who write about Dickens' conjunction of excrement and money refer to Freud, sometimes by way of Norman O. Brown, most of the substance of Freud's (and Brown's) argument is missing from their accounts. Their point is most often far simpler and essentially moralistic: that money and excrement are alike because (more or less) they are worthless, *bad*. Thus Earle Davis writes:

> Economically speaking, [Dickens'] world could see no difference between unearned increment and diffused excrement . . . [I]n every part of London he saw mankind straining and struggling over a dung heap . . . His pen became an excretory organ spouting out a sizzling cover for all the organic corruption which lay festering in the values that money set, the awful offal of Victorian standards.

Davis concludes his 'post-Freudian' reading with the ancient favorite text of Chaucer's Pardoner:

> At the bottom of all is money, the love of money at the cost of everything else. It is the overwhelming desire for money which lands most people in the filth of Hell.[2]

Perhaps it would be more precise, then, to say that *Our Mutual Friend* is the only English novel that everyone *says* is about excrement in order that they may *forget* that it is about anality. For the Freudian insights, elided in the critics' moralistic yoking of filth and lucre, are erotic ones. They are insights into the pleasures, desires, bonds, and forms of eros that have to do with the anus. And it is precisely the repression of these pleasures and desires that, in Freud, turns feces into filth and filth into gold. A novel about the whole issue of anal eroticism, and not merely a sanitized invective against money or 'filthy lucre' or what critics have come to call 'the dust-money equation,' would have to concern itself with other elements in the chain Freud describes: love between man and man, for instance; the sphincter, its control, and the relation of these to sadism; the relations among bodily images, material accumulation, and economic status. It would also offer some intimations, at least, of adult genital desire, and repression, in relation to the anus. Furthermore a novel that treated these issues would necessarily cast them in the mold of a particular, historical vision of society, class, power, money, and gender.

One curious thematic marker in *Our Mutual Friend* that has gone critically unnoticed, and that the novel itself tends to muffle, is a name. An important character in the novel chooses to call herself Jenny Wren, but we are told – just once – that that is not the name she was born with. Her real name is Fanny Cleaver. Unlike the later, funny, almost childishly deflationary name, Fanny Assingham, in *The Golden Bowl*, Fanny Cleaver is a name that hints at aggression – specifically, at rape, and perhaps at homosexual rape.[3] The pun would seem a trivial accident, were it not a small pointer to something much more striking: that there are two scenes in *Our Mutual Friend* whose language does indeed strongly suggest male rape.[4] These are Bradley Headstone's attack on Rogue Riderhood (discussed below), and the attack on John Harmon in chapter 13. Another thematic 'clue' functions at a different level to solicit the twentieth-century reader's attention to the male homosocial components in the book. One of the male protagonists lives in domestic happiness with another man, and at moments of particular intensity he says things like, 'I love you, Mortimer.'[5]

In some simple sense, therefore, this must be a novel that delineates something close to the whole extent of the male homosocial spectrum, including elements of homosexual genitality. Just what version of male homosociality most concerns it, however? The sweet avowal, 'I love you, Mortimer,' almost promises the sunny, Pickwickian innocence of encompassing homosocial love rendered in the absence of homophobia. At the same time, to give a *woman* a name like Fanny Cleaver may suggest something almost opposite: homophobia, in the absence of homosexuality. And those golden dust heaps are the emblem of a wholly abstracted anality: they do not refer us to any individual or sentient anus. To understand the very excess, the supervisibility of the homosocial/homophobic/ homosexual thematics in this novel requires us to see that for Dickens the erotic fate of every female or male is also cast in the terms and propelled by the forces of class and economic accumulation.

Let me begin by tracing a chain of Girardian triangles within one of the novel's plots, a chain reaching from the lowest class up to the professional class. It begins with the three members of the Hexam family: Gaffer Hexam, the father, an illiterate scavenger who makes his living by fishing corpses from the Thames and robbing them; Lizzie Hexam, his beautiful, good, and loyal daughter; and Charley Hexam, his son, whom Lizzie protects from their father's violent resentment until Charley is old enough to run away and go to school. These three comprise the first triangle.

Charley is determined and industrious enough to go from a Ragged School to a National School, where he becomes a pupil-teacher under the sponsorship of a young schoolmaster, Bradley Headstone, Bradley, like Charley, began as a pauper, and Dickens says, 'regarding that origin of his, he was proud, moody, and sullen, desiring it to be forgotten'. Yet an intense bond soon develops between the schoolmaster and young Charley. After the father's death, Bradley advises Charley to have no more to do with his impoverished, illiterate sister. Charley begs Bradley to come meet Lizzie first, however, and Bradley finds himself, as if by compulsion, violently in love with her.

The triangles of the Hexam family and of Charley, Lizzie, and Bradley are complicated by another triangle. Eugene Wrayburn, a young barrister and one of the heroes of the novel, also falls in love with Lizzie. He, like Bradley, has an intense encounter with Charley before meeting Lizzie, although in this case the intensity takes the form of instant, almost allergic dislike on both sides. And Eugene has another, apparently non-triangular, love relationship – it is he who says, 'I love you, Mortimer'. Mortimer Lightwood is an old friend and protégé of Eugene's from public school, and the two, while making languid efforts to succeed in the law, make a household together.

Already contrasts of class are appearing under the guise of contrasts of personality and sexuality. One great evidence of class and control divides this little world in two as absolutely as gender does, though less permanently: the division of the literate from the illiterate. And after Gaffer's early death, only one of these people – Lizzie, the desired woman – remains illiterate. The quarrel between the schoolmaster and Eugene is over who will teach her to read. But even within the masculine world of literacy, the gradations of class are unforgiving. Charley's and Bradley's relation to knowledge is always marked by the anxious, compulsive circumstances of its acquisition. Dickens says of the schoolmaster,

> From the early childhood up, his mind had been a place of mechanical stowage . . . There was a kind of settled trouble in the face. It was the face belonging to a normally slow or inattentive intellect that had toiled hard to get what it had won, and that had to hold it now that it was gotten. (II,1)

Bradley seems always to be in pain, 'like . . . one who was being physically hurt, and was unwilling to cry out' (II,1); his infliction of pain on others seems to come from even greater spasms of it within himself; talking to Lizzie about his desire to teach her to read, for example, he seems to be hemorrhaging internally:

> He looked at Lizzie again, and held the look. And his face turned from burning red to white, and from white back to burning red, and so for the time to lasting deadly white. (II,11)

In fact, to borrow an image from a patient of Freud's, the schoolmaster behaves socially like a man with a hungry rat in his bowels. And for him, the rat represents not money but more specifically his small private capital of knowledge. Or rather it represents the alienation from himself of the profit of his knowledge. For the knowledge never makes *him* wiser; it is quite worthless outside the schoolroom; it merely places him, more decisively even than illiteracy would, in a particular, low position in the line of production of labour for a capitalism whose needs now included a literate, rather than merely a massive, workforce. Bradley's one effort to invest his nest egg for his own profit – to teach Lizzie to read, as part of that triangular transaction with Charley – is imperiously overruled by Eugene, who wants to pay for his own person to do the teaching. 'Are you her schoolmaster as well as her brother's?' asks Eugene scornfully, and instead of using his name, will only call him, 'Schoolmaster'. Bradley, as usual, loses control of his composure and complexion – for he is merely 'used to the little audience of a school, and unused to the larger ways of men' (II,6).

Eugene, on the other hand, though not wealthy, is a gentleman and a public-school boy. His relation to his own store of knowledge is the confident one of inconspicuous consumption: he can afford to be funny and silly. He likes to say things like 'But then I mean so much that I – that I don't mean' (II,6). Or

> 'You know that when I became enough of a man to find myself an embodied conundrum, I bored myself to the last degree by trying to find out what I meant. You know that at length I gave it up, and declined to guess any more.' (II,6)

Mortimer sees him affectionately as 'this utterly careless Eugene'. He has no consciousness of knowledge, or even of power, as something to be struggled for, although his unconscious wielding of them makes him not only more loveable and relaxed than Bradley but also much more destructive. The moral ugliness of Eugene's taunts against the schoolmaster is always less striking, in the novel's presentation, than the unloveliness of the schoolmaster's anxiety and frustration. Bradley the pauper, thinking to make himself independent by his learning, finds that he has struggled himself into a powerless, alienating position in an impervious hierarchical economy. Eugene Wrayburn, like Yorick imagining himself as marginal, passive, and unempowered in his relation to the economy, nevertheless speaks with the full-throated authority of a man near its very center.

Bradley's relation with Charley and Eugene's with Mortimer differ on the basis of class, and the position of Lizzie in each relationship is accordingly different. Charley's offer of Lizzie to his schoolmaster represents the purest form of the male traffic in women. Charley explains it to Lizzie this way:

> 'Then *I* come in. Mr Headstone has always got me on, and he has a good deal in his power, and of course if he was my brother-in-law he wouldn't get me on less, but would get me on more. Mr Headstone comes and confides in me, in a very delicate way, and says, "I hope my marrying your sister would be agreeable to you, Hexam, and useful to you?" I say, "There's nothing in the world, Mr Headstone, that I could be better pleased with." Mr Headstone says, "Then I may rely upon your intimate knowledge of me for your good word with your sister, Hexam?" And I say, "Certainly,

Mr Headstone, and naturally I have a good deal of influence with her." So I have, haven't I, Liz?'

'Yes, Charley.'

'Well said! Now you see, we begin to get on, the moment we begin to be really talking it over, like brother and sister.' (II,15)

To Bradley, his triangle with Charley and Lizzie represents not access to power within the society but a dire sliding away from it; and this is true whether one takes his desire for Lizzie or for Charley to represent the main erotic bond. No wonder he says to Lizzie, in an example of his resentful style of courtship:

'You are the ruin – the ruin – the ruin – of me . . . I have never been quit of you since I first saw you. Oh, that was a wretched day for me! That was a wretched, miserable day!' (II,15)

No; the closest relation to patriarchal power for Bradley in this tangle comes in the link of rivalry between himself and Eugene Wrayburn. And it soon emerges that this is, indeed, for him, the focus of the whole affair. In the painful scene with Lizzie I have been quoting, Bradley makes a threat against Eugene, and when she responds, indignantly, 'He is nothing to you, I think,' he insists, 'Oh yes he is. There you mistake. He is much to me.' What? she asks.

'He can be a rival to me *among other things* . . . I knew all this about Mr Eugene Wrayburn, all the while you were drawing me to you . . . With Mr Eugene Wrayburn in my mind, I went on. With Mr Eugene Wrayburn in my mind, I spoke to you just now. With Mr Eugene Wrayburn in my mind, I have been set aside and I have been cast out.' (II, 15; emphasis added)

After Lizzie has refused Bradley and left London, the desiring relation between Bradley and Eugene, far from dissipating, becomes hotter and more reciprocal. The schoolmaster decides – wrongly – that he can find Lizzie by following Eugene everywhere he goes, and, Eugene says,

'I goad the schoolmaster to madness . . . I tempt him on, all over London . . . Sometimes, I walk; sometimes, I proceed in cabs, draining the pocket of the schoolmaster, who then follows in cabs. I study and get up abstruse No Thoroughfares in the course of the day [while Bradley is teaching]. With Venetian mystery I seek those No Thoroughfares at night, glide into them by means of dark courts, tempt the schoolmaster to follow, turn suddenly, and catch him before he can retreat. Then we face one another, and I pass him as unaware of his existence, and he undergoes grinding torments . . . Thus I enjoy the pleasures of the chase . . . just now I am a little excited by the glorious fact that a southerly wind and a cloudy sky proclaim a hunting evening.' (III,10)

In Surtees's *Handley Cross*, Mr Jorrocks declaims that "Unting' is 'the image of war without its guilt, and only five-and-twenty per cent of its danger,' but it is less lucky than that for the men who are caught up in this chase. One day on a towpath Bradley attacks Eugene from behind; the two men struggle in an embrace, and Eugene, both arms broken, nearly drowns. Soon after that, another man, a lockkeeper with the sinister and important name Rogue Riderhood, who has been dogging and blackmailing Bradley Headstone, finds himself, too, attacked from behind. This is one of the scenes whose language is that of male rape:

Bradley had caught him round the body. He seemed to be girdled with an iron ring . . . Bradley got him round, with his back to the Lock, and still worked him backward . . . 'I'll hold you living, and I'll hold you dead! Come down!'
  Riderhood went over into the smooth pit, backward, and Bradley Headstone upon him. When the two were found, lying under the ooze and scum behind one of the rotting gates, Riderhood's hold had relaxed, probably in falling, and his eyes were staring upward. But, he was girdled still with Bradley's iron ring, and the rivets of the iron ring held tight. (IV, 15)

Sphincter domination is Bradley Headstone's only mode of grappling for the power that is continually flowing away from him. Unfortunately for him, sphincter control can't give him any leverage at all with women – with Lizzie, who simply never engages with him, who eludes him from the start. It only succeeds in grappling more closely to him men who have already been drawn into a fascinated mirroring relation to him – Eugene, with whom he has been engaged in that reversible hunt, and Rogue Riderhood, in whose clothing he had disguised himself for the assault on Eugene. His initial, hating terror of Lizzie was a terror of, as he kept putting it, being 'drawn' from himself, having his accumulated value sucked from him down the great void of her illiteracy and powerlessness. But, classically, he is the Pinchwife-like man who, fearing to entrust his relations with patriarchy to a powerless counter, a woman, can himself only be used as a woman, and valued as a woman, by the men with whom he comes into narcissistic relation.

In the novel's social mapping of the body, Bradley, like some other figures at the lower end of the respectable classes, powerfully represents the repressive divorce of the private thematics of the anus from the social forces of desire and pleasure. Dickens does precede Freud, Ferenczi, Norman O. Brown, and Deleuze/Guattari, among others, in seeing digestion and the control of the anus as the crucial images for the illusion of economic individualism: cross-culturally, Brown remarks, 'the category of "possession," and power based on possession, is apparently indigenous to the magic-dirt complex'.[6] One thematic portrayal of this exclusion is a splitting of the body between twin images of a distended gut and a distended disembodied head. Bradley Headstone (and note his name), the most wrackingly anal of the characters, also appears repeatedly as a floating 'haggard head in the air' (III,10; III,11); Mr Venus, a taxidermist and articulator of skeletons, with his shop full of hydrocephalic babies in jars, is himself given to 'floating his powerful mind in tea' (III,7); illiterate 'Noddy' Boffin dandles the head of his walking stick at his ear like the head of a floating 'familiar spirit' or baby, and himself seems to turn into a great heavyheaded puppet at the end of the novel (IV,3; IV,13); and so on. The unanxious version of *homo digestivus* is the 'hideous solidity' that the firmly bourgeois Podsnaps and their circle share with their 'corpulent straddling' tableware:

> Everything said boastfully, 'Here you have as much of me in my ugliness as if I were only lead; but I am so many ounces of precious metal worth so much an ounce; wouldn't you like to melt me down?' . . . All the big silver spoons and forks widened the mouths of the company expressly for the purpose of thrusting the sentiment down their throats with every morsel they ate. The majority of the guests were like the plate . . . (I,11)

This strain of imagery, of course, culminates in the monstrous dust-heaps themselves. In short, one thing that goes on when the human body is taken as a capitalist emblem is that the relation of parts to wholes becomes problematic; there is no intelligible form of circulation; the parts swell up with accumulated value, they take on an autonomous life of their own, and eventually power comes to be expressed as power over reified doubles fashioned in one's own image from the waste of one's own body. Power is over dolls, puppets, and articulated skeletons, over the narcissistic, singular, non-desiring phantoms of individuality.

For Bradley Headstone, dissociation, anxiety, toil, and a crippling somatic self-consciousness mark the transition into respectability, and make heavy and humiliating work of his heterosexual involvement. How differently they manage these things in the upper classes. While Bradley's intentions toward Lizzie, however uneasy, had been strictly honorable, Eugene Wrayburn has no intentions toward her at all. Mortimer asks him,

> 'Eugene, do you design to capture and desert this girl?'
> 'My dear fellow, no.'
> 'Do you design to marry her?'
> 'My dear fellow, no.'
> 'Do you design to pursue her?'
> 'My dear fellow, I don't design anything. I have no design whatso-ever. I am incapable of designs. If I conceived a design, I should speedily abandon it, exhausted by the operation.' (II,6)

This is the opposite of Bradley's compulsive, grasping relation to power. Eugene sees himself as a little leaf borne upon a stream; and an image that is often associated with him is the pretty river that supplies power to the papermill where Lizzie finally gets work. But Eugene's lack of will is enormously more potent than Bradley's clenched, entrapping will, simply because the powerful, 'natural' trajectory of this stream is eternally toward swelling the exploitive power of ruling-class men over working-class women. Resolute and independent as Lizzie is, weak and passive as *he* is, Eugene barely has to make a decision, much less form a design, in order to ruin her.

> The rippling of the river seemed to cause a correspondent stir in his uneasy reflections. He would have laid them asleep if he could, but they were in movement, like the stream, and all tending one way with a strong current . . . 'Out of the question to marry her,' said Eugene, 'and out of the question to leave her.' (IV,6)

It is traditional, in criticism of *Our Mutual Friend*, to distinguish two groups of thematic imagery, that surrounding the river and that surrounding the dust-heaps. If, as I have suggested, the dust-heaps can be said to represent an anthropomorphization of capital that is most closely responsive to the anxieties of the petit-bourgeoisie, then the river, in a sense, offers a critique of that in terms of a more collectively scaled capitalism, organized around alienation and the flow of currency. Its gender implications are pointed and odd: all the men in this waterside novel are strikingly incompetent about the water; there are seven drownings or near-drownings, all of males; men are always dragging each other into the river; and only one person, Lizzie, has the skill to navigate a rescue. At the same time, women are in control only in correctly understanding the current of power as always flowing away from themselves. Gazing into the river, both Lizzie and Eugene read in it the image of Lizzie's inability to resist ruin.

Just as Eugene's higher status enables his heterosexual relationship to be at once more exploitive and less guilty than Bradley's, so his desiring relationship with a man can be at once much more open and much less embroiled in repressive conflict than any of Bradley's. Interestingly, though it is more open, it also seems much less tinged with the sexual. Imagery of the sphincter, the girdle, the embrace, the 'iron ring' of the male grasp, was salient in those murderous attacks on men by Bradley Headstone. By contrast it is utterly absent from the tenderer love between Eugene and Mortimer. They live together like Bert and Ernie on Sesame Street – and who ever wonders what Muppets do in bed? This thematic reticence, if it is reticence, in contrast to the hypersaturation with anal thematics of Bradley's part of the story, can perhaps best be accounted for not by some vague invocation of 'Victorian prudery,' but by thinking about how the libidinal careers of Victorian gentlemen were distinguished, in fiction and in ideology at any rate, from those of males of higher and lower class.

The obstacles to mapping this territory have been suggested before. The historical research on primary sources that would add texture and specificity to generalizations is only beginning to be done, or at any rate published; at the same time, the paradigms available for understanding the history of sexuality are in rapid and productive flux. The best that I can attempt here is perhaps to lay out in a useful codified form what the 'common sense' or 'common knowledge' of the (essentially middle-class) Victorian reader of novels might be likely to have been, buttressed by some evidence from biographies. I wish to make clear how tentative and how thoroughly filtered through the ideological lens of middle-class literature these generalizations are, but still to make them available *for* revision by other scholars.

With respect to homosocial/homosexual style, it seems to be possible to divide Victorian men among three rough categories according to class. The first includes aristocratic men and small groups of their friends and dependents, including bohemians and prostitutes; for these people, by 1865, a distinct homosexual role and culture seem already to have been in existence in England for several centuries. This seems to have been a milieu, at once courtly and in touch with the criminal, related to those in which the usages of the term 'gay' recorded by John Boswell occurred.[7] It seems to have constituted a genuine subculture, facilitated in the face of an ideologically hostile dominant culture by money, privilege, internationalism, and, for the most part, the ability to command secrecy. Pope's lines on Sporus in 'Epistle to Dr Arbuthnot' do, however, presuppose his audience's knowledge that such a role and culture exist. This role is closely related to – is in fact, through Oscar Wilde, the antecedent of – the particular stereotype that at least until recently has characterized American middle-class gay homosexuality; its strongest associations, as we have noted, are with effeminacy, transvestitism, promiscuity, prostitution, continental European culture, and the arts.

For classes below the nobility, however, there seems in the nineteenth century not to have been an association of a particular personal style with the genital activities now thought of as 'homosexual'. The class of men about which we know most – the educated middle class, the men who produced the novels and journalism and are the subjects of the biographies – operated sexually in what seems to have been startlingly close to a cognitive vacuum. A gentleman (I will use the word 'gentleman' to distinguish the educated bourgeois from the aristocrat as well as from the working-class man – a usage that accords, not with Victorian ideology, but with Victorian practice) had a good deal of objective sexual freedom, especially if he were single, having managed to evade the great cult of the family and, with it, much of the enforcing machinery of his class and time. At the same time, he seems not to have had easy access to the alternative subculture, the stylized discourse, or the sense of immunity of the aristocratic/bohemian sexual minority. So perhaps it is not surprising that the sexual histories of English gentlemen, unlike those of men above and below them socially, are so marked by a resourceful, makeshift, *sui generis* quality, in their denials, their rationalizations, their fears and guilts, their sublimations, and their quite various genital outlets alike. Biographies of English gentlemen of the nineteenth and early twentieth centuries are full of oddities, surprises, and apparent false starts; they seem to have no predetermined sexual trajectory. Good examples include Lewis Carroll, Charles Kingsley, John Ruskin, and a little later, T. E. Lawrence, James M. Barrie, T. H. White, Havelock Ellis, and J. R. Ackerley, who describes in an autobiography how he moved from a furtive promiscuous homosexualiy to a fifteen-year-long affair of the heart with a female dog.[8] The sexuality of a single gentleman was silent, tentative, protean, and relatively divorced from expectations of genre, though not of gender.

In fiction, a thematically tamer but structurally interesting and emotionally – very often – turbid and preoccupying relationship was common between single gentlemen: Pendennis and Warrington,

Clive Newcome and J. J. Ridley, the two Armadales of Collins'
Armadale, the gentlemen of the Pickwick Club, resemble Eugene and
Mortimer in the lack of remark surrounding their union and in the
shadowy presence of a mysterious imperative (physical debility,
hereditary curse, secret unhappy prior marriage, or simply extreme
disinclination) that bars at least one of the partners in each union
forever from marriage.

Of the sexuality of English people below the middle class, reliable
accounts are difficult to assemble. Both aristocratic and (early
twentieth-century) middle-class English male homosexuality seem to
have been organized to a striking degree around the objectification
of proletarian men, as we read in accounts by or of Forster, Isherwood,
Ackerley, Edward Carpenter, Tom Driberg, and others; at the same
time, there is no evidence (from these middle-class-oriented accounts)
of a homosexual role or subculture indigenous to men of the
working class, apart from their sexual value to more privileged men.
It is possible that for the great balance of the non-public-school-
educated classes, overt homosexual acts may have been recognized
mainly as instances of violence: English law before the Labouchère
amendment of 1885 did not codify or criminalize most of the spectrum
of male bodily contacts, so that homosexual acts would more often
have become *legally* visible for the violence that may have
accompanied them than for their distinctively sexual content. In
middle-class accounts of the working class, at any rate, and possibly
within the working class itself, there seems to have been an association
between male homosexual genitality and violence, as in Dickens'
treatment of Bradley Headstone's anal eroticism in terms exclusively
of murder and mutilation.

Since most Victorians neither named nor recognized a syndrome of
male homosexuality as our society thinks of it, the various classes
probably grouped this range of sexual activities under various moral
and psychological headings. I have suggested that the working class
may have grouped it with violence. In aristocrats – or, again, in
aristocrats as perceived by the middle class – it came under the
heading of dissolution, at the very time when dissolution was itself
becoming the (wishful?) bourgeois-ideological name for aristocracy
itself. Profligate young lords in Victorian novels almost *all* share the
traits of the Sporus-like aristocratic homosexual 'type,' and it is
impossible to predict from their feckless, 'effeminate' behavior
whether their final ruin will be the work of male favorites, female
favorites, the racecourse, or the bottle; waste and wastage is the
presiding category of scandal. Fictional examples of this ambiguous
style include Lord Frederick Verisopht (with his more 'masculine,'
less aristocratic sidekick, Sir Mulberry Hawk), in *Nicholas Nickleby*;

Count Fosco (with his more 'masculine,' less aristocratic sidekick, Sir Percival Glyde) in *The Woman in White*; Lord Porlock, in *The Small House at Allington* and *Doctor Thorne*; in a more admiring version, Patrick, Earl of Desmond (with his more 'masculine,' less aristocratic sidekick, Owen Fitzgerald) in Trollope's *Castle Richmond*; and Lord Nidderdale (with Dolly Longstaffe) in *The Way We Live Now*. In each case there is explicit mention of only female erotic objects, if any; but in each case the allegedly vicious or dissolute drive seems more visibly to be directed at a man in more immediate proximity. Perhaps the most overtly sympathetic – at any rate the least grotesque, the closest to 'normal'-seeming – of the men in this category is also one who is without a title, although within the context of the novel he represents the vitiated line of a rural aristocracy. That is Harold Transome, in *Felix Holt*. To his sexual history we receive three clues, each tantalizing in its own way: we hear – mentioned once, without elaboration – that the woman he had married in his Eastern travels was one whom he had bought as a slave;[9] we hear – mentioned once, without elaboration – that he has brought a (different) woman back with him from the East;[10] but the person of whom we hear incessantly in connection with Harold is his plangent, ubiquitous manservant-companion:

> 'I don't know whether he's most of a Jew, a Greek, an Italian, or a Spaniard. He speaks five or six languages, one as well as another. He's cook, valet, major-domo, and secretary all in one; and what's more, he's an affectionate fellow ... That's a sort of human specimen that doesn't grow here in England, I fancy. I should have been badly off if I could not have brought Dominic.'[11]

Throughout a plot elaboration that depends heavily on the tergiversations of a slippery group of servants-who-are-not-quite-servants, who have unexplained bonds from the past with Dominic, one waits for the omniscient, serviceable, ingratiating character of Dominic to emerge into its full sinisterness or glamor or sexual insistence – in vain, since the exploitive 'oriental' luxuries of his master can be perceived only in a sexually irresolute blur of 'decadence'. Perhaps similarly, the lurid dissipations of the characters in *The Picture of Dorian Gray* are presented in heterosexual terms when detailed at all, even though (biographical hindsight aside) the triangular relationship of Basil, Dorian, and Lord Henry makes sense only in homosexual terms.

Between the extremes of upper-class male homosocial desire, grouped with dissipation, and working-class male homosocial desire, grouped perhaps with violence, the view of the gentleman, the public-school product, was different again. School itself was, of course, a crucial link in ruling-class male homosocial formation. Disraeli (who was not himself an Etonian) offers the flattering ideological version of Eton friendships in *Coningsby*:

> At school, friendship is a passion. It entrances the being, it tears the soul. All loves of after life can never bring its rapture, or its wretchedness; no bliss so absorbing, no pangs of jealousy or despair so crushing and so keen! What tenderness and what devotion; what illimitable confidence; what infinite revelations of inmost thoughts; what ecstatic present and romantic future; what bitter estrangements and what melting reconciliations; what scenes of wild recrimination, agitating explanations, passionate correspondence; what insane sensitiveness, and what frantic sensibility; what earthquakes of the heart, and whirlwinds of the soul, are confined in that simple phrase – a school-boy's friendship![12]

Candid accounts agree that in most of the public schools, the whirlwinds of the soul were often acted out in the flesh. Like the young aristocrat, the young gentleman at those same public schools would have seen or engaged in a variety of sexual activities among males; but unlike the aristocrat, most gentlemen found neither a community nor a shared, distinctive sexual identity ready for adults who wanted more of the same. A twentieth-century writer, Michael Nelson, reports asking a school friend, 'Have you ever had any homosexual inclinations since leaving Eton?' 'I say, steady on,' his friend replied. 'It's all right for fellows to mess one another about a bit at school. But when we grow up we put aside childish things, don't we?'[13]

David Copperfield, among other books, makes the same point. David's infatuation with his friend Steerforth, who calls him 'Daisy' and treats him like a girl, is simply part of David's education – though another, later part is the painful learning of how to triangulate from Steerforth onto women, and finally, although incompletely, to hate Steerforth and grow at the expense of his death. In short, a gentleman will associate the erotic end of the homosocial spectrum, not with dissipation, not with viciousness or violence, but with childishness, as an infantile need, a mark of powerlessness, which, while it may be viewed with shame or scorn or denial, is unlikely to provoke the virulent, accusatory projection that characterizes twentieth-century homophobia.

This slow, distinctive two-stage progression from schoolboy desire to adult homophobia seems to take its structure from the distinctive anxieties that came with being educated for the relatively new class of middle-class 'gentlemen'. Unlike title, wealth, or land, the terms that defined the gentleman were not clearly and simply hereditary but had somehow to be earned by being a particular kind of person who spent time and money in particular ways. But the early prerequisites for membership in this powerful but nebulous class – to speak with a certain accent, to spend years translating Latin and Greek, to leave family and the society of women – all made one unfit for any other form of work, long before they entitled one to chance one's fortune actively in the ruling class.

The action of *Our Mutual Friend* brings to a close that long abeyance in Eugene's life between, so to speak, being *called* and being *chosen* for the professional work of empire. (For instance, he has been called to the Bar, but no one has yet chosen to employ him.) His position is awash with patriarchal authority, the authority of the law itself, but none of it belongs to him yet. In just the same way, having been removed from his family as a child, he will soon be required to return – and in the enforcing position of *paterfamilias*, a position that will lend a retroactive meaning and heterosexual trajectory to his improvised, provisional relationship with Mortimer and his apparently aimless courtship of Lizzie. In the violence at the end of the novel, we see the implacability with which this heterosexual, homophobic meaning is impressed on Eugene's narrative: Bradley, his rival, nearly kills him by drowning; Lizzie saves him; while he seems to be dying, Mortimer interprets his last wishes as being that he might marry Lizzie; and when he comes back to life, he is already a married man. 'But would you believe,' Lizzie asks afterwards, 'that on our wedding day he told me he almost thought the best thing he could do, was to die?' (IV,16)

There is one character to whom this homophobic reinscription of the bourgeois family is even more crippling than it is to Eugene, who already, by the end of the novel, looks almost 'as though he had never been mutilated' (IV, 16). That person is, of course, Lizzie. The formal, ideological requirements for a fairytale 'happy ending' for her are satisfied by the fact that she is not 'ruined' by Eugene, not cast into the urban underclass of prostitution, but raised up into whatever class the wife of a Victorian barrister belongs to. Eugene is determined to fight for his right to have her regarded as a lady. But with all that good news, Dickens makes no attempt to disguise the terrible diminution in her personal stature as she moves from being the resentful, veiled, muscular, illiterate figure rowing a scavenger boat on the Thames, to being a factory worker in love, to being Mrs Eugene Wrayburn *tout court*. Admittedly, Lizzie has been a reactionary all along. But she has been a blazing, courageous reactionary: she has defended and defied her violent father; she has sacrificed everything for her beastly brother; she gave up a chance to form an alliance with an older woman, a tavern-keeper, just because the woman would not accept her father; she took off for the countryside to save her honor from the man she loved; and she unhesitatingly risked her life to save his life. But all her reactionary courage meets with a stiflingly reactionary reward. Lizzie stops being Lizzie, once she is Mrs Eugene Wrayburn.

As we see how unrelentingly Lizzie is diminished by her increasingly distinct gender assignment, it becomes clearer why 'childishness,' rather than femininity, should at that moment have been the ideological way the ruling class categorized its own male homosexuality. As Jean Baker Miller points out in *Toward a New Psychology of Women*, an attribution of gender difference marks a structure of *permanent* inequality, while the relation between adult and child is the prototype of the *temporary* inequality that in principle – or in ideology – exists only in order to be overcome: children are supposed to grow up into parents, but wives are not supposed to grow up into husbands.[14] Now, the newly significant class of 'gentlemen,' the flagship class of English high capitalism, was to include a very wide range of status and economic position, from plutocrats down to impoverished functionaries. In order to maintain the illusion of equality, or at any rate of meritocratic pseudoequality, *within* the class of gentlemen, and at the same time justify the magnification of distinctions within the class, it clearly made sense to envision a long, complicated period of individual psychic testing and preparation, full of fallings-away, redefinitions, and crossings and recrossings of lines of identification. This protracted, baffling narrative of the self, a direct forerunner of the twentieth-century Oedipal narrative, enabled the process of social and vocational sorting to occur under the less invidious shape of different rates of individual maturation.

Not until this psychologistic, 'developmental' way of thinking had been firmly established was the *aristocratic* link between male homosexuality and *femininity* allowed to become an article of wide public consumption – a change that was crystallized in the Wilde affair and that coincided (in the 1890s) with the beginnings of a dissemination across classes of language about male homosexuality (e.g. the word 'homosexual'), and with the medicalization of homosexuality through an array of scientific 'third sex' and 'intersex' theories.

But during all this time, for women, the immutability of gender inequality was being inscribed more and more firmly, moralistically, and descriptively in the structure of bourgeois institutions. As the contrasting bodily images in *Our Mutual Friend* suggest, woman's deepening understanding, as she saw the current flowing away under her own image, came for the most part at the cost of renouncing individual ownership and accumulation. The division of cognitive labor that emerged with the bourgeois family was not a means of power for women, but another part of the edifice of master-slave subordination to men. Sentient middle-class women of this time perceive the triangular path of circulation that enforces patriarchal power as being routed through them, but never ending in them – while capitalist man, with his prehensile, precapitalist image of the body, is always deluded about what it is that he pursues, and in whose service. His delusion is, however, often indistinguishable from real empowerment; and indeed it is blindest, and closer to real empowerment, in his triangular transactions through women with other men.

Notes

1. F. S. Schwarzbach, *Dickens and the City* (London: Athlone Press, 1970), pp. 198–9.
2. Earle Davis, *The Flint and the Flame: The Artistry of Charles Dickens* (Columbia, Mo.: University of Missouri Press, 1963), pp. 266, 271.
3. This is not a necessary inference from the pun, because of the gender ambiguity of the word 'fanny': it apparently referred to female genitals throughout the nineteenth century in England, but cf. for example, Pope's portrayal of the homosexual Lord Hervey as 'Lord Fanny' in the eighteenth century ('pure white curd of asses' milk'); and Fanny Assingham.
4. On the whole I consider the term 'male rape', where the meaning is clear in context, preferable to 'homosexual rape', since men who rape men are often not homosexual either by self-attribution or by habitual sexual practice; the violent and often the specifically *homophobic* content of this crime is more relevant to our concerns here than its apparently *homosexual* orientation.
5. Charles Dickens, *Our Mutual Friend*, ed. Stephen Gill (Harmondsworth: Penguin, 1971), Bk. IV, ch. 10, p. 812. Further citations will be incorporated in the text and designated by book and chapter number.
6. Norman O. Brown, *Life Against Death: The Psychoanalytic Meaning of History* (Middletown, Conn.: Wesleyan University Press, 1970), p. 300. The association between possession and the control of the anus must have something to do with an odd feature of the male 'rape' discussed in this essay: it is the participant who would ordinarily be termed passive – the one associated with the 'iron ring' of the sphincter – who is presented as the *aggressor*; the phallus itself barely figures in this 'rape'.
7. John Boswell, *Christianity, Social Tolerance, and Homosexuality: Gay People in Western Europe from the Beginning of the Christian Era to the Fourteenth Century* (Chicago: University of Chicago Press, 1980), p. 43.
8. J. R. Ackerley, *My Father and Myself* (London: Bodley Head, 1968).

9. GEORGE ELIOT, *Felix Holt, The Radical,* Illustrated Cabinet Edition, 2 Vols. (Boston: Dana Estes, n.d.), Bk. III, ch. 10.

10. Ibid., Bk. III, ch. 3.

11. Ibid., Bk. I, ch. 2.

12. BENJAMIN DISRAELI, *Coningsby, or The New Generation* (London: Longmans Green, 1881), ch. 9.

13. MICHAEL NELSON, *Nobs and Snobs* (London: Gordon and Cremonesi, 1976), p. 147.

14. JEAN BAKER MILLER, *Toward a New Psychology of Women* (Boston: Beacon Press, 1976), ch. 1.

12 Repression and Representation: Dickens's General Economy (*Our Mutual Friend*)

JOHN KUCICH*

John Kucich is Professor of English at the University of Michigan, and the author of *Excess and Restraint in the Novels of Charles Dickens* (Athens: University of Georgia Press, 1981), *Repression in Victorian Fiction: Charlotte Brontë, George Eliot, and Charles Dickens* (Berkeley: University of California Press, 1987) and *The Power of Lies: Transgression in Victorian Fiction* (Ithaca: Cornell University Press, 1994), a body of work which investigates the social and psychological dynamics in which nineteenth-century literature participates. In this essay, he sets out to reexamine the critical commonplace that Dickens's work is divided between the forces of repression and of violent excess. Like Christopher Morris (Chapter 4), Kucich suggests that the self must be seen as figural or linguistic in nature. For Kucich, the self is formed and sustained out of a linguistic interchange or 'economy' of the principles of repression and violence, an economy which works not to disrupt, but to reinforce individual identity. But, in the provocative further move, Kucich draws on the work of the surrealist writer and philosopher Georges Bataille, to suggest that Dickens's work also reaches after another, paradoxical economy, in which rupture and excess are valued for their own sake and beyond any possibility of recuperation in the service of self-identity. In contrast to Eve Kosofsky Sedgwick (Chapter 11), who reads *Our Mutual Friend* as a narrative of containment, Kucich's reading of the same novel aims to show that characters such as Bradley Headstone and Eugene Wrayburn are riven and driven by desire that exceeds rather than confirming the integration of the self. For Kucich, such unmasterable excess is associated with a 'general economy' of collective life, which goes beyond every attempt to close or contain it in actual social forms.

Modern criticism has largely accepted the idea that Dickens is a novelist of divided sensibilities. Any number of writers have defined

---

*Reprinted from *Nineteenth-Century Fiction*, 38 (1984), 62–77. A number of contextualising end notes have been omitted.

this rift along similar lines; irrepressibly drawn to the rebellious, the unlawful, the murderous, Dickens also seems to circumscribe human experience within inflexible moral and ideological boundaries. Humphry House's classic remarks on the murder of Nancy in *Oliver Twist* pinpoint the now familiar conundrum: 'How utterly remote are these scenes and this state of mind from the earnest moralities of the Preface! To understand the conjunction of such different moods and qualities in a single man is the beginning of serious criticism of Dickens.'[1] But however it has been understood, the contradiction between Dickens's delighted identification with his violent characters and his careful repression of violent tendencies in his heroes and heroines, has created for most readers a central, insuperable dilemma. Variously accounted for, it is never resolved. This opposition has even come to seem a commonplace nineteenth-century phenomenon; it now seems to us emblematic not only of Dickens but of Victorian culture as a whole that the creator of Daniel Quilp, Jonas Chuzzlewit, and Bradley Headstone should also have been the champion of Little Nell, David Copperfield, and Esther Summerson. It may also seem a mark of Dickens's frustration with stark self-conflict of this kind that violence and aggression should embody so completely the force of his characters' repressed desires.

But the very obviousness of this stalemate between violent and repressive energies should be suspect. After all, to perceive such an opposition as an irreducible one is immediately to distance and to define it, in one way or another, as a dilemma whose force of contradiction no longer exerts its power over us. As Edmund Wilson stigmatized it over forty years ago, this opposition appears to be the sign of some deep and curious failure – at bottom, a symptom of both Dickens's and the Victorians' inability to reconcile human energies with the needs of culture and conscience, to reconcile desire with moral limits.[2] While judgments of this kind might on the surface seem forgiving, as Wilson's certainly means to be, they also serve the interests of a cultural mythology all our own. That is, they celebrate our own adjustment of desire and repression as a sign of general progress toward personal authenticity and psychological maturity. Modern political demystifications expose this mythology most clearly: as Herbert Marcuse and others have argued for some time, late capitalism encourages the stigmatizing of repression as an enemy of the self in order to increase the general circulation of (and knowledge about) personal desire in institutionalized channels – a process Marcuse calls 'repressive de-sublimation'.[3] To internalize this shift as a movement toward 'self-realization' is to succumb to dangerous, even tyrannical illusions about personal autonomy that are, in fact, state-generated. Michel Foucault has taken this argument a step further, claiming that nineteenth-century 'discipline' itself marks the institutional creation of exploitable psychic self-enclosures: self-conflict, whatever else its effects, sustains a politically vulnerable but still cherished illusion of self-sufficiency.[4] Such political analyses are at best a roundabout way of approaching Dickens's opposition of violent desire and repression, though they do encourage us to question both the seeming naturalness of that opposition and our spontaneous – but slightly contradictory – tendency to read such opposition as an incomplete stage of development in the Victorian self.

From a similarly motivated but more literary point of view, Dickens's apparent dualism, rather than being a symptom of unresolved conflict, can be recognized as a coherent strategy of representation. It is possible, that is, to understand a certain use of repression in Dickens not as a psychological mechanism – which we have come to think of as a simultaneous concealment and displacement of dangerous primary energies, a falsification – but as a rhetorical figure. Far from concealing its operation – as a classically Freudian mechanism of repression would – repression in Dickens actually names itself as repression and details its function, assigning itself a specific set of meanings and values. To define repression in this sense as a tropological code suggests, among other things, that psychic states in Dickens are themselves only the product of linguistic manipulations, which belie the unmediated, monadlike structure of the self usually associated with ego psychology and its depth/surface model of desire and repression. As Hillis Miller and others have insisted, characters in Dickens are constituted on purely linguistic foundations.[5] And these linguistic foundations shape their psychic structures in ways that are obscured by essential notions of the self, which view repression in particular as the shell over an unconscious, naturalized kernel of truth about identity rather than as one diacritical figure in a more fluid linguistic system.

Dickens's figural opposition of violence to repression actually undermines the depth/surface model of psychological autonomy as well as reshaping our understanding of violence and repression as necessarily oppositional psychic forces. For Dickens's novels stress the hidden similarities of meaning latent in these two terms and then work to promote one as the recognizable sign of the other. That is to say, his superficial polarization of violence and repression is only the first step in Dickens's attempt to overcome the very difference encoded in these oppositional semantic categories. Freed from the essentialist convention of Western thought that represents human psychic energy in this rigidly binary way, Dickensian repression actually helps articulate and even idealize a certain kind of violence, rather than simply denying or sublimating it. To reexamine the use of repression in Dickens as part of a linguistic system, then, is to see it eventually as a complex representation of its opposite – of the very violence it seems to reject – rather than simply as the trace of latent fears and cultural taboos against violence. The psyche modeled on such a trope may be a viable kind of nineteenth-century exemplary personality, as we will see, but it is a psyche subject to the discontinuities and the slippage of language rather than a psyche grounded in the surface/depth relation we employ too readily in understanding Victorian identity crises. Dickens's novels thus reveal a tension between essentialist and linguistic representations of the self that any nonfigural conception of repression alone tends to obscure.

The figural quality of the Dickensian psyche becomes more apparent when one considers, first, how Dickens unveils the identity underlying more conventional representations of violence and repression. In the novels what repression comes to share with violence is a fundamental law of psychological economy. Both violence and repression are presented initially as attempts to collapse the limits of the self as it is conceived in subject-centered terms. Yet both are condemned to exchange these self-transcending energies for self-interested ones, an exchange that prevents any such escape. Dickens recognizes that within the system of psychic representation conventionally available to him any pursuit of a liberating self-negation – whether in passion or in constraint – is inevitably reabsorbed in an economy of self-coherence. For Dickens, this is in fact his characters' great dilemma. Consistently he presents violent and repressed characters as fundamentally alike in their obedience to his economic law, their apparent differences dissolving in an identity basic to subject-centered conceptions of the psyche.[6] Hence the many torturous self-examinations Dickens's later heroes and heroines undergo, their convoluted attempts to purge self-interest from their acts of generosity – attempts to escape the self that only discover how subtle the economy of self-gain can be. Mark Tapley, who looks to gain 'some credit' for himself by staging the greatest possible self-sacrifice, helps begin this series in a whimsical way; Esther Summerson renders the problem more enigmatic and perplexing; Arthur Clennam and Eugene Wrayburn nearly despair of finding a way out of the labyrinthine economy of self and selflessness. Thus, too, the more readily apparent identity of violence and selfishness that typifies Dickensian villains from Bill Sikes onwards. Bradley Headstone is perhaps the most forceful example of a man for whom murder brings no release from the agony of personal boundaries. But the obsessiveness of Dickens's murderers is always rooted in their circular, claustrophobic economy of passion and guilty self-recognition.

Dickens's instincts as a writer did not verge toward tragic impasse, however. For at the same time that Dickens was at pains to make the circularity of this psychic economy evident, he was also bent on pushing toward an apparent impossibility: that is, toward the inclusion of a disruptive freedom within the imprisoning economy of human identity. By abandoning an essentialist, subject-centered economy of violence and repression for one based in a more transpersonal symbolic order. Dickens's novels try to do exactly what they seem to despair of doing; they try to reconcile whatever rupture of psychic coherence might lie beyond violence and beyond repression with a stable representation of identity, which ought logically to be destroyed by such rupture. Borrowing a set of terms from Georges Bataille, who spent a lifetime thinking these problems through, we might say that Dickens replaces what Bataille would call a restricted economy – one in which all self-negation is reappropriated as some form of self-coherence – with a general economy – an open, indefinite, paradoxical kind of economy in which psychological rupture is valued for its own sake as a kind of transient violence done to identity.[7] Bataille imagined that such rupture might be represented as a propensity of the subject without being convertible to identity, consciousness, or knowledge. In other words, in a general economy energies destructive to identity would be assigned a place of their own within identity without ever being recuperated as its justification or its ground. The psyche might contain its own negation, but it could never know or absorb that negation. For Bataille, this kind of synthetic or general economy could only be conceived on highly self-reflexive levels of representation – primarily, in ritual, in sacrifice, and in art – because outside of these symbolic orders it must appear to human consciousness only as an image of self-contradiction, the apparently insuperable opposition of life and death itself.[8] But in self-consciously manipulated forms of representation such a general economy might become a more fruitful model of psychic structures than essentialist conceptions, based as they are in a restrictively economic opposition of violence to repression, and psychic rupture to psychic conservation, within a homogeneous order of the self.

Dickens seeks to represent a general psychic economy of this kind primarily by organizing violence and repression in his heroes in a nonoppositional way. To employ an overworked but still useful vocabulary: on the level of representation Dickens find a metonymic role for violence within the heroes' version of moral constraint – that is, he creates a complementary echoing from one term to the other along a single chain of meaning. Violence and repression enter into a linguistic relationship of similarity, rather than opposition, but their similarity is of a special, metonymic type. Neither violence nor repression becomes the ground for the other, in the way that metaphor grounds one term in another; rather, they border each other as congruent parts of the same psychic system. They become associational, not substitutive, terms – parts of a larger order, not comprehensive images of that order as a whole.[9] In this way Dickens is able to end the identity of violence and repression as undifferentiated forms of a restricted economy and to create out of their very recombination a new, unexpected, and paradoxical system. In effect, Dickens is able to differentiate between the two terms in a modified way: the novels ultimately designate violence as a purely noneconomic rending of identity, and repression as the framework of coherence that borders this rupture, pointing toward rupture metonymically – as a slightly displaced, equivalent state that, nevertheless, is not explained or circumscribed by repression and that is not reduced to anything other than a rupture. Repression thus enters into an efficient cooperation with violence, a kind of continuity of meaning, without being named as violence itself and without profiting from violence. Thus, the restrictive economy of either violence or repression taken alone is overcome. Through this impossible, general economy, organized through a metonymic relation between terms usually seen as oppositional, Dickens hoped to abolish what could otherwise be only a tragic economy of the mind.

This abstract formulation needs to be fleshed out with textual examples. It is worth noting first, though, that Dickens's concern with repression as the metonymic sign for psychic violence developed gradually over the course of his career. The abrupt, melodramatic separation of violent and virtuous factions in his early novels gives way slowly – never completely – to a concern with the writing of violence directly into virtue. Minor characters – Bucket, Pancks, Jaggers, Jenny Wren – become increasingly ambiguous: all these late figures make explicitly violent designs compatible with a framework of self-repression. And, at the same time, central characters are absorbed in a gradual, ambiguous conversion to virtue, in which hard-won strategies for achieving self-effacement are paralleled by symbolic initiations into violence. The static virtue of Mr Pickwick and Oliver Twist is replaced not only by a narrative of conversion but also by a familiar series of dark doublings: Pip shadowed by the violent Orlick, Clennam by Blandois, Wrayburn by Headstone. Since in his last finished work, *Our Mutual Friend*, Dickens makes his equation of repression and violence most clear, it seems appropriate

at this point to describe the figural relationships in that novel as a
way of making this representational strategy more apparent.

In *Our Mutual Friend* public society is initially presented as the
realm of a restricted economic violence. The various geographic and
social compartments of London are all saturated with death, cruelty,
waste; and at the center of the double plot lie two strange 'murders'
– the Harmon mystery and the protracted stalking of Wrayburn. Yet
for society in *Our Mutual Friend*, the truth about violence and death
is that they are claustrophobically inscribed within a circle of utility.
The recycling of death as a mere financial event defines this process
grimly enough – Gaffer Hexam converts corpses into capital, as does
Mr Venus. Gaffer even counters Lizzie's revulsion from death in the
first chapter by growling: 'As if it wasn't your living! As if it wasn't
meat and drink to you!'[10] And the novel's central metaphor – the
source of Harmon's fortune in dust – suggests both that human waste
is marketable and that human markets spring from waste – a kind of
forthrightness about the social economy of death that is suppressed
by the class pretensions of characters like the Veneerings to 'bran'-
new'-ness. But even in more indirect, psychological terms, characters
always confuse acts of violence with economic motives. One thinks
of the Lammles, whose quest for vengeance coincides with
profiteering, or of Jenny Wren, whose peculiar form of voodoo
doubles as her trade. Most importantly, perhaps, Bradley Headstone's
violence – both inward and outward – has its roots in economic
constraint and class antagonism. In these characters violence becomes
implicated in both fiscal and psychic economies, which together insure
the survival of self-coherent identity.

This economic reappropriation of violence ultimately blurs both
poles of the exchange. Violence and utility become mutually
convertible, as part of a general theme of nondifferentiation that
suffuses the book. And this nondifferentiation seems to contaminate
them both, draining violence of its transcendent potential, and
draining utility of the innocence and dignity middle-class society
seeks to give it. The novel's panoramic views of London all stress
this bleak nondifferentiation, this economic equivalence of death
and gain. The landscape is hybrid, neither dead nor alive but trapped
in diminished versions of both states at once. Signs on warehouses
become 'inscriptions over the graves of dead businesses' (I, 14), and
litter becomes a claustrophobic sign of waste within prosperity: 'that
mysterious paper currency which circulates in London when the wind
blows, gyrated here and there and everywhere. Whence can it come,
whither can it go?' (I, 12). Anonymous crowds complete this dreary,
restricted economy: Headstone at one point watches while
'melancholy waifs and strays of housekeepers and porter sweep

melancholy waifs and strays of papers and pins into the kennels, and other more melancholy waifs and strays explore them, searching and stooping and poking for anything to sell' (II, 15). And characters like Wegg, Riderhood, and the Lammles remind us how impure violence can be when it is conscripted as the means to a publicly legitimate selfhood. This kind of nondifferentiated exchange between violence, death, and waste on the one hand and survival on the other – psychic as well as physical – generates much of the frustration and solipsism felt by characters caught up in the quagmires of the novel's social logic.

At the same time, the novel makes it very clear that self-sacrifice and generosity are caught in a similar straitjacket. What does Eugene hope to gain, for example, by helping Lizzie? Pressed by Lightwood, he cannot say. For Bradley Headstone, the selfish motive in his parallel offer to educate Lizzie is unmistakable. Sardonically calling him 'a disinterested person' (II, 11), Jenny Wren turns her doll Mrs Truth to the wall while Headstone pleads his case. And generations of readers, along with the Inexhaustible Baby, have felt some discomfort when John Harmon's scheme to reeducate Bella, which seems generous on the surface, ultimately imprisons her as a kind of possession in Harmon's own private dollhouse.

For Dickens, violence always has the greater potential to shatter this kind of psychic economy, to evoke an energy that transcends the subject. And in *Our Mutual Friend*, as in other novels, Dickens establishes some slight connection to raw, unrecuperated violence for his favored characters. Very tentatively, he allows his heroes to share in the novel's gratuitous violence against various scapegoats: Jenny Wren dashes pepper into Fledgeby's vinegar plaster, Sloppy deposits Wegg in a scavenger's cart. But if Dickens was sensitive to the dilemma of restricted psychic economies, he was also aware that any successful disruption of these psychic economies by violence alone must make violence absolute and uncontrollable – as it is finally in Headstone's suicide. Faced with this grim double bind, Dickens solves the problem of restrictively economic violence by incorporating violence metonymically within a subtle and complex configuration of themes that are loosely associated with repression: self-sacrifice, self-control, disinterest. This process involves several figural equations between violence and instances of such repression, as well as a precarious partitioning of these terms, which keeps violence separate from the explicitly moral, self-repressive signs of personal identity Dickens leaves us with in his heroes and heroines.

We should notice, first of all, that a repression very similar to Headstone's dominates the lives of the two male heroes, Wrayburn and Harmon. At the Veneerings, Wrayburn is said to be 'buried alive'

(I, 2) by social and paternal pressures. Harmon, playing Rokesmith, is frequently described as repressed and diffident in Bella's presence. And yet both men – like Headstone again – are dominated either by desires for violence or by frustrations that are constantly associated with violence. Wrayburn is often ready to strangle that parody of romantic release, Lady Tippins: at one point he 'trifles quite ferociously with his dessert-knife' (I, 2); at another, he 'appears to be contemplating all the wrong he would like to do – particularly to the present company) (I, 10). And Harmon is mastered by an attraction to Bella that, frustrated, parallels the volatile disappointments of Headstone and Venus. On first witnessing Harmon's confusion, Bella tells her father, 'Pa . . . we have got a Murderer for a tenant' (I, 4).

What distinguishes the latter two characters from Headstone, in fact, is not that they are immune to self-conflict but that their doubleness represents a general psychic economy in which both the radical violence of desire and the self-denial of moral coherence are exercised at the same time rather than suffered as an opposition. For one thing, Dickens associates their general self-repression with violent death, an association that is not completely explicable through a subject-oriented logic of psychic refusal, or reducible to it. Both men, of course, undergo a ritual death by water, and the importance of this ritual violence is crucial to the way we view Wrayburn and Headstone. But such violence is hardly presented as a consequence of the two heroes' intentions or consciousness. More importantly, though, both characters willingly do violence to their old identities. They destroy their pasts much more completely, in fact, than Headstone can destroy his – Harmon through a succession of assumed roles and through his readiness to leave London, which would abolish both his hereditary claims and his proximity to Bella, Wrayburn through his morbidly self-destructive refusal to accept the terms of his father's world. But though crucial in the reader's eyes, these willful and extravagant self-negations are only tangentially related to the actions that finally define these characters to themselves and to others – especially to their future wives – as morally valuable because self-denying: the Secretary's chivalric self-restraint and respect for Bella; Wrayburn's strict promise to Lizzie that he will make something of himself and his final refusal to exploit her. Self-violence and self-integrity seem consistent in these two characters without being strictly interdependent as signs of identity.

The psychological gap here between self-violence and moral action is emphasized by the interventions of other characters who must arrange the two heroes' psychological resolution from without. Harmon and Wrayburn are saved from the finality of their self-negations only through external agencies – through Mrs Boffin's recognition of Harmon and Mr Boffin's plot for reclaiming Bella; through Lizzie's rescue of Wrayburn from the river; and through Jenny Wren's symbolic contribution of the word 'wife' to Wrayburn's deathbed incoherence. Without the interventions of others, the violent self-obliterations of Harmon and Wrayburn would come to nothing. We are meant to feel their passivity at the end of the novel, their refusal to convert psychological suicide to some interpersonal coin. In this way the continuity of such self-violence with the more conservative, economic badges of each character's identity is accomplished through the transpersonal and associational logic of representation, not through an essentialist psychological integration. Through a purely narrative association with the finality of death and self-negation, Harmon's and Wrayburn's self-repressions – and consequent rewards – are able to signify an absolute dissolution of psychic boundaries, while such dissolution signifies moral restraint in return. The two states, apparently mutually exclusive, refer to each other metonymically without either one seeming either a more primary or an oppositional category. Instead, they articulate each other as congruent elements of a general economy of character. And in this context the emotional blandness of Harmon, Lizzie, Wrayburn, and Bella at the end of the novel may be a claim to moral order, but it is also the sign of a deeply hidden violence done internally and without calculation to identity. Without the characters' awareness or design, violence is allowed to stand for repression, and vice versa, in a symbolic organization that absorbs both into the novel's eventual resolution.

We should remember, too, that the exercise of violence in these characters is far from simply internal. In oddly tangential ways the heroes share in a more aggressive but still noneconomic kind of violence. Wrayburn, cloaked in his refusal to compromise Lizzie, gains an enormous advantage in indifference with which to torture Headstone – a sadistic enterprise that in its very gratuitousness springs from and helps confirm his own psychological freedom. And Harmon, disguised as the friend of George Radfoot, is able to intimidate and coerce Riderhood with the threat of latent violence – the knife and club that dangle from his belt, the threatening tone of his voice. A similar pattern emerges in Mr Boffin, who after suppressing his familiar, genial identity enters a world of class violence. All these characters, in their disguises and displaced identities, share the potential for violence in self-performance that Dickens underlines through characters like the Lammles and that he dramatized in various ways throughout his career. But what differentiates the violence of Dickens's heroes from the violence of other characters is its freedom from any restrictive, subjective economy – at least, from any subjective economy defined by the narrative. Expressly designed to serve the interest of others – or, in Wrayburn's case, to be gratuitous – and carried out in various guises as displaced, disjunctive psychic potentials, such violence is partitioned off from stable moral identity. The very presence of a moral economy of self-denial – which is the explicit means by which these characters recognize their own and others' personal value – is what ultimately ensures that this violence will have no economic return for them. In essence, a seemingly inconsistent potential for violence is associated with Dickens's good characters, as a contiguous mark of their effective virtue, without being simply translatable into the self-denying dimension of their public selves.

The crucial point is that such associations are represented by the text without being assimilated to a classic model of psychological coherence. Suicidal or aggressive violence never becomes a dimension of identity through which these characters understand themselves; rather, it is represented by the text as a kind of displacement along the chain of a character's attributes that only the reader can recognize and assimilate. Wrayburn, for instance, cannot achieve such integration himself but can only say to Lizzie at the end: 'There is a sharp misgiving in my conscience that if I were to live, I should disappoint your good opinion and my own – and that I ought to die, my dear!' (IV, 11). Harmon, somewhat fantastically, is able to win Bella's love twice – once as the morally upright Rokesmith and later as the self-displacing, psychologically suicidal heir – without this doubleness somehow changing the nature of Bella's loving recognition. In order for Dickens's virtuous characters to be redeemed and rewarded, their repressions must be incorporated in a social – and a narrative – economy rather than a merely self-enclosed and subjective one. To preserve the tangential nature of psychic violence, the 'worthiness' of the repressed character must be recognized by others, and by the text – in *Our Mutual Friend* through the novel's providential arrangement of marriages and fortunes. Through this metonymic relationship, rather than an essentialist one that would place violence and repression in a more direct confrontation, repression's new economy is not at all private, though it is nevertheless efficient. The model of the psyche it suggests is a discontinuous one mediated by language and by the novel's system of character representation rather than designated as an image of autonomous self-integration. And only through such representation can the opposition between violence and repression be reconstituted as an image of the cooperative, expansive general economy in which Dickens imagined his characters and readers might participate.

One of the ironies here is that by representing self-transcending violence as contiguous with self-repression Dickens ultimately emphasizes the gap between emotional experience and public life, the inability of individuals to put themselves in an active relation to some shared social order. As sociologists like Richard Sennet have argued, the cult of voluntary repression in Victorian culture is finally an enemy of public life rather than a guarantee of it.[11] To inscribe the general economy of violence and repression within a linguistic relationship centered on, if not fully resolvable within, the emotional range of the self – and not to represent it as a singular image of public action – is to prevent any collective experience of psychological rupture. Bataille has characterized the capitalist period on the whole as a movement inward of any general economies and an abandonment of the public world to restrictive economies.[12] The gap between public society and personal quest in *Our Mutual Friend* fulfills this pattern, and the relation between individual refusal and public recognition I have described in Dickens thus takes place on the level of a mythologized, textual wish, not in the realm of an actual or achievable social order.

But there is a larger problem. Dickensian repression, whatever its mythological qualities, constitutes in its symbolic freedom a claim to cultural status, a claim that asserts the privileges of a certain personality type over those of money or blood. In the final chapter of *Our Mutual Friend* Lightwood's search for 'the voice of society' and its authoritative response to Wrayburn's marriage finally turns up an odd formula, which is articulated by the marginal aristocrat Twemlow, of all people – namely, that the feelings of a gentleman are sacred and above exposure, or, to put this inversely, that suppression of one's feelings is a code by which 'gentlemen' might be recognized. The final victory of one cluster of characters in the novel over the illegitimate society of the Veneerings and Podsnaps hinges not so much on the virtue of the heroes' self-sacrifice as on a certain precise analogy between repression and radically liberating passion – that is, on an affirmation of the transcending freedom implicit in the general economy, a freedom signified by an ostentatious refusal of self. To put it simply, Dickens's heroes exemplify the passion of repression, not the repression of passion. What we need to recognize, then, is the way in which Dickensian repression, once represented as a general economy, becomes a tool of mastery. That is to say, the economy of repression that Dickens's heroes discover is in fact a way of asserting the privileged place of those who can generate this representation of themselves, who can make others read the claim to dignity and freedom implied by a certain code of histrionic self-repression. In effect, a metonymical relationship has become a metaphorical one.

The metonymic role of repression and violence in Dickens deserves much further study. Among other things, though, this relationship clearly suggests that much of the self-constraint readers often scorn in Dickens's heroes – and in Victorian fiction generally – is not at all an attempt to deny human needs for emotional extension. Instead, it is designed as a representational strategy for conceiving what such fulfillment might be like. What often appears to the modern sensibility as a neurotic deviation from psychic norms is actually a method of representing and recovering, in a general, nonrestrictive economy, the self-transcending consummation we have come to associate conventionally with violent passion. Seen as a trope, repression in Victorian fiction is not so very different from the modern myths of psychic liberation to which we usually oppose it. To say that there is a general economy of violence and repression in Dickens is in fact to restore to Dickensian repression some of the active force it lacks when stigmatized as part of a psychic refusal.

Notes

1. *All in Due Time: The Collected Essays and Broadcast Talks of Humphry House* (London: Hart-Davis, 1955), pp. 195–6.
2. See Wilson's seminal essay, 'Dickens: The Two Scrooges,' *The Wound and the Bow* (New York: Oxford University Press, 1941), pp. 1–104.
3. *Eros and Civilization: A Philosophical Inquiry into Freud* (New York: Beacon Press, 1955), p. ix: 'the advanced industrial society democratizes release from repression – a compensation which serves to strengthen the government which allows it, and the institutions which administer the compensation.' See also MICHEL FOUCAULT, *The History of Sexuality*, Vol. I, trans. ROBERT HURLEY (New York: Pantheon Books, 1978), and *Discipline and Punish: The Birth of the Prison*, trans. Alan Sheridan (New York: Pantheon Books, 1978), for an account of how modern discourse about sexuality and passion is inscribed within the domain of political power. Similar political critiques of the unmediated 'naturalness' of the desire/repression duality have become commonplace even in more politically moderate writers. See, for example, DANIEL BELL, *The Cultural Contradictions of Capitalism* (New York: Basic Books, 1976); or CHRISTOPHER LASCH, *The Culture of Narcissism: American Life in an Age of Diminishing Expectations* (New York: Norton, 1979). Much as I respect the general direction of thought about repression in these writers, I hope to show that any full understanding of repression in nineteenth-century literary texts must be less conspiratorial and more complex in terms of self-representation.
4. See especially 'Part III: Discipline,' in FOUCAULT, *Discipline and Punish*, pp. 135–69.

5. See, in particular, J. HILLIS MILLER, *The Form of Victorian Fiction* (Notre Dame: University of Notre Dame Press, 1968).

6. In my book *Excess and Restraint in the Novels of Charles Dickens* (Athens: University of Georgia Press, 1981), I use this formulation of both psychological and representational claustrophobia as the basis for various thematic discussions. Missing from those discussions is some sense of how Dickens's rhetoric in and of itself overcomes that claustrophobia by redefining psychic categories – as I will argue below.

7. The relevant text here is *La Part maudite*, introd. de JEAN PIEL (Paris: Éditions de Minuit, 1967). For an excellent discussion of 'general' and 'restrictive' economies in Bataille, see MICHELE H. RICHMAN, *Reading Georges Bataille: Beyond the Gift* (Baltimore: Johns Hopkins University Press, 1982).

8. See 'Hegel, la mort, et le sacrifice,' *Deucalion*, No. 5 (1955). pp. 21–43.

9. I am using Lacanian definitions of metaphor and metonymy. For a fuller explanation of these terms, see 'The agency of the letter in the unconscious or reason since Freud,' in JACQUES LACAN, *Écrits: A Selection*, trans. Alan Sheridan (New York: Norton, 1977), pp. 146–78, or ANIKA LEMAIRE's excellent discussion in *Jacques Lacan*, trans. David Macey (Boston: Routledge, 1977), pp. 30–64. To cite one example from Lemaire (p. 33), we might say that the chain 'thatch-straw poverty' is a metaphoric one, because it locates a substitute meaning or condensation, 'poverty,' for the term 'thatch' that grounds it in a different, more determined level of the signified. But the chain 'cabin-hovel-palace-den-burrow' is metonymic because it traces a continuity or displacement of meaning along a single chain of complementarity, with no single term representing a 'whole' or transcendent category of signification that includes the others.

10. CHARLES DICKENS, *Our Mutual Friend*, ed. STEPHEN GILL (Baltimore: Penguin, 1971), Vol. I, ch. 1. Further references are to volume and chapter numbers in this edition.

11. See RICHARD SENNETT, *The Fall of Public Man: On the Social Psychology of Capitalism* (New York: Vintage Books, 1978), esp. pp. 161–74.

12. BATAILLE, *La Part maudite*, pp. 179–94.

13 Space, Place and the Body of Riot in *Barnaby Rudge*

STEVEN CONNOR*

Steven Connor is Professor of Modern Literature and Theory at Birkbeck College, London. His first book, *Charles Dickens* (Oxford: Blackwell, 1985), looked at the work of Dickens through a number of different critical-theoretical lenses, including structuralism, deconstruction, psychoanalysis and Marxism. In subsequent books, he has turned to more contemporary literary and cultural topics, with his study of Beckett, *Samuel Beckett: Repetition, Theory and Text* (Oxford: Blackwell, 1988) his investigation of theories of the post-modern, in his *Postmodernist Culture: An Introduction to Theories of the Contemporary* (Oxford: Blackwell, 1989) and his meditation on the problem of value in contemporary cultural theory, *Theory and Cultural Value* (Oxford: Blackwell, 1992). More recent publications include *The English Novel in History from 1950 to 1995* (London: Routledge, 1995) and *James Joyce* (Bristol: Northcote House, 1996). In this essay he draws on theories of the constructed nature of social space developed in anthropology and cultural studies to analyse the representation of the disturbances of space in *Barnaby Rudge*. His argument is that the novel bears the impress of mid-nineteenth-century attempts to pattern and regulate the spaces of the city, even as it testifies to political anxieties that this patterning fails to quell. In *Barnaby Rudge*, the imagination of riot causes paradoxical forms of riot in the imagination of space itself.

It is perhaps no surprise that Dickens's congenitally riotous imagination should have been drawn to the imagining of actual riot, in his treatment of social and political upheaval in *Barnaby Rudge* (1841). The imagination of riot in this novel is bound up in a particularly intense way with the imagination of space and place. The particular fascination of the Gordon Riots for Dickens was that they took place in the streets of London, in locations that could still be seen, recognised and named. The novel is energised by the *frisson* of

---

*Written for this volume and previously unpublished.

representing familiar places torn apart by conflict, with houses destroyed, streets and squares turned into battlefields, and the very anatomy of the city transformed by riot. Others have documented exhaustively the particularity of Dickens's evocation of London and its places and spaces. The sense which his novels give of the palpability of place, and especially of the palpability of the city of London, remains intense and captivating for contemporary readers. His novels display a kind of kinetic memory of the streets and territories of London, appropriately enough, one might think, when one remembers what an inveterate walker of those streets Dickens was. But there is a contradiction here; Dickens needed to surrender his writing to the crammed, dissolving energy of the streets, to their characteristically modern scene of traffic and tumult. But he also needed to take possession of those streets, pacing them out and imaginatively introjecting them; in abandoning himself to the disorientations of the street, Dickens strives to make them his own.

The dynamics of space and place in Dickens's most openly political novel, *Barnaby Rudge*, respond to the more general politicisation of the space of the city which took place in the middle years of the nineteenth century, as the extraordinary growth of London brought about a heightened sense of the social and political meanings of the city's topography. This manifested itself most pressingly in the increasing need to create and sustain physical and spatial separations, in the face of influences, social, political and economic, which threatened to dissolve them. Increasingly, the tendency of city design in the nineteenth century was to map out patterns of distinction in the actual physical disposition of the city, distinctions between working and living environments (with the growth of the suburb from about mid-century and the Wemmick-like distinction between the office and the hearth), distinctions between urban and rural areas, distinctions between classes and ethnic groups, and distinctions between the so-called 'separate spheres' of male and female life. Increasingly, the city became a living diagram of these patterns of social distinction, along with all their irresistible possibilities of transgression and collapse. There were more maps of London, and more different kinds of map, produced in the first fifty years of the nineteenth century than there had been for the previous two and a half centuries, this urgent cartographic activity responding to the multiple patterns of discrimination and itinerary according to which the city of London was administered, experienced and imagined. The first half of the nineteenth century saw maps and guides produced for pedestrians, maps to show coach and cab fares, the routes of canals, omnibuses and railways, guide books showing the location of places of entertainment, legitimate and risqué, and sights of interest, even a 'puzzle map' called the 'Labyrinthus Londiniensis, or the Equestrian Perplexed', which was suggested by the number of 'Stoppages occasioned by repairing the Streets'.[1]

The importance of mapping is also to be found in other forms of representation of the city, and especially the tradition of 'topographic' townscape, which had been stimulated by the visits of the Italian painter Canaletto to London in 1746–55. Topography in painting and graphic representations of the city meant the depiction, often with great architectural fidelity, of the principal public buildings of a city, usually gathered together in such a way as to suggest a picturesque 'prospect' and a pleasing coordination of elements. Caroline Arscott and Griselda Pollock discuss a particular innovation in the early nineteenth-century visual representation of the city, in the form of the panorama. This was a huge circular view of London from some high point (often Greenwich Hill), which enabled the eye to take in at once not only the detail of the major landmarks of the city, but also its rural setting, in the pastoral scene of Greenwich park in the foreground; one of the most influential of these urban panoramas was Turner's *London* (1809).[2] The most important structural feature of these visual representations of the city is their coordination of wholeness and particularity. A sense of integrated totality is given in the coordination of patterns of distinction, between town and country, mercantile and domestic, rich and poor, work and leisure, respectable and criminal.

Such mappings of places become increasingly, and intensely political through the nineteenth century. In particular the mapping of the city established a complex series of anxieties and problems regarding health and sickness, order and disorder. Indeed, one of the most vigorous cartographic enterprises of the century came about as a direct result of a concern with hygiene. Following a number of disturbing cholera outbreaks during the 1830s and 1840s, Edwin Chadwick produced his *Report on the Sanitary Condition of the Labouring Population of Great Britain* in 1842 and, as a result of the recommendations of this report, the Metropolitan Commission for Sewers was set up in 1847 to rework and unify the piecemeal arrangements for the channelling and disposal of sewage from London. This plan necessitated a completely new and comprehensive map of London showing the levels of every area of land to be drained, a map that had been completed by 1849. Henceforth, the mapping of the city would need to take much more account of flows, rhythms and processes – would need to include the element of time in its calculations.

The general concern with health and disease, coupled with the growing interest in and understanding of the processes by which

disease was transmitted, simultaneously intensified the desire for
clear distinctions between the different regions of the city and
heightened the concern that such distinctions could break down or
be blurred. This complex series of worries about place and disease is
enacted and explored in particular in Dickens's *Bleak House* (1853), in
which the threat of contagion seems to symbolise and engender the
collapse of categoriality as such.[3] But such misgivings are already in
evidence in *Barnaby Rudge*. When, in chapter 75, Gabriel Varden
comes to Sir John Chester in his chambers to inform him of his
suspicions about his identity, Chester remains unruffled until he
learns exactly where Varden has just come from:

> 'Good Gad!' cried Sir John, hastily sitting up in bed; 'from Newgate,
> Mr Varden! How could you be so very imprudent as to come from
> Newgate! Newgate, where there are jail-fevers, and ragged people,
> and bare-footed men and women, and a thousand horrors! Peak,
> bring the camphor, quick! Heaven and earth, Mr Varden, my dear,
> good soul, how *could* you come from Newgate?'
>
> Gabriel returned no answer, but looked on in silence while Peak
> (who had entered with the hot chocolate) ran to a drawer, and
> returning with a bottle, sprinkled his master's dressing-gown and
> the bedding; and besides moistening the locksmith himself, plenti-
> fully, described a circle about him on the carpet.[4]

This strikingly recapitulates another scene from much earlier in the
novel in which Chester is visited by Sim Tappertit. ' "Pray, Mr
Tappertit," ' Chester asks, observing the lock that Tappertit is carrying,
' "has that complicated piece of ironmongery which you have done
me the favour to bring with you, any immediate connection with the
business we are to discuss?" ' When he discovers that it is merely
on its way to be fitted to a warehouse door in Thames Street, Chester
continues ' "Perhaps, as that is the case . . . and as it has a stronger
flavour of oil than I usually refresh my bedroom with, you will oblige
me so far as to put it outside the door?" ' (24: 245–6). In both scenes,
there is the threat of the violation of boundaries, between health and
sickness, the rich and the poor, the legitimate and the criminal. In
both cases too, there is a dependence on spatiality and physical
distance to maintain distinctions – making a circle of disinfectant,
putting the lock outside the door (and thus, bizarrely, as it were,
locking out the lock) – even as there is an uneasiness about the
manner of the infection that may cross those boundaries. In both
cases, the abhorred object may transmit itself by smell, thus
breaching the fundamental distinction between the body and its
exterior; the strong 'flavour of oil' given off by Tappertit's lock runs

together smell and taste, while oiliness in Dickens often seems to sicken because it lies indefinitely between solidity and liquidity.

The fear of infection emerges from a general metaphorical equivalence between the city and the human body that was already well established by the mid-nineteenth century. As Peter Stallybrass and Allon White have shown,[5] the topography of the city came increasingly to be modelled on an idea of the upright body, with its fixing of the distance between the head or reasoning faculty and the lower portions of the body, the genitals and the anus. The distinction between sight and smell which is exemplified in the two episodes just discussed, and which is itself best grasped perhaps as a distinction between distinctness and the breakdown of distinctness, correlates with this vertical mapping of the city-body. If in some versions of this model the city/body is conceived of as a single organism made up of cooperating parts, in others, the integrity of the body is guaranteed by a phantasmal expulsion of what is seen as its waste or effluvia, in the poverty, disease and suffering of the city. The drainage movement represents one enactment of this hygienic psychotopography, in the desire to enforce an absolute separation of the integral body from what it expels.

But there is a variant of this vertical model of the body which has much more interesting consequences and effects in Dickens's writing and in the mid-century representation of the city in general. For what is expelled from below in the human body is also what comes from inside it. Equivalent to the upper-lower topography of the city/body, therefore, is an economy of inner and outer, in which the body's own interior is conceived as alien and threatening. A directional paradox arises here, in that the maintaining of clear distinctions must depend, not merely upon the separation of the body from its effluvia, the purgative bringing of what is inside into the outside, but also on the reverse of that process, in an ideal of continence, or the keeping of what is inside out of sight. This brings about in its turn an intensified sense of liminal or borderline states, since, as Mary Douglas observes: 'The body is a model which can stand for any bounded system. Its boundaries can represent any boundaries which are threatened or precarious.'[6]

The drainage movement of the 1840s seems to have effected a shift away from the model of continence to that of purgation in the political and physiological imagination of the space of the city. Robert Southey, writing in 1829 about the political dangers of urbanisation, in his *Sir Thomas More: or, Colloquies on the Progress and Prospects of Society*, refers explicitly to the Gordon riots which are Dickens's theme in *Barnaby Rudge* as an example of the kind of violent political convulsion which might again take place in London:

Look at the populace of London, and ask yourself what security there is that the same blind fury which broke out in your childhood against the Roman Catholics may not be excited against the government, in one of those opportunities which accident is perpetually offering . . . Think for a moment what London, nay, what the whole kingdom would be, were your Catilines to succeed in exciting as general an insurrection as that which was raised by one madman in your childhood! Imagine the infatuated and infuriated wretches, whom not Spitalfields, St. Giles's and Pimlico alone, but all the lanes and alleys and cellars of the metropolis would pour out – a frightful population, whose multitudes, when gathered together, might almost exceed belief! The streets of London would appear to teem with them, like the land of Egypt with its plagues of frogs: and the lava floods from a volcano would be less destructive than the hordes whom your great cities and manufacturing districts would vomit forth![7]

Twenty years later, the ideal of Carlyle's *Latter-day Pamphlets* (1850) is not the containing of misery and poverty within 'the lanes and alleys and cellars', but its channelling away:

The general well and cesspool once baled clean out today will begin before night to fill itself anew. The universal Stygian quagmire is still there; opulent in women ready to be ruined, and in men ready. Towards the same sad cesspool will these waste currents of human ruin ooze and gravitate as heretofore; except in draining the universal quagmire itself there is no remedy.[8]

For Southey, the fear is of an infective discharge of the inside into the outside; Carlyle warns against a collapse inwards, into the dark and seething corruption of the body. In inheriting and extending the sense of the city as a corporeal volume, Dickens reflects this new complexity of conceptions of the idea of the body of the city in the middle years of the nineteenth century. For these were the years in which scientific attention began to be directed toward the dynamic processes which relate individual bodies one to another; whether in the transmission of disease, or in the movements of wealth, or in the new sciences of thermodynamics, there was a growing emphasis on exchange, interchange and transformation, rather than stable relations of equivalence. This shift may be observed in the passages from Southey and Carlyle just quoted. For Southey, the city is in a quiescent state until torn apart by the eruption of riot; for Carlyle, the city is always already in metabolic process. For Southey, therefore, the city must be protected from its hidden, demonic energies; while Carlyle sees urban reform as a cooperative regulation of a physiology which is itself naturally and irrepressibly in motion. By mid-century, the city came to be imagined as a dynamic, rather than a merely emblematic body; an organism rather than an anatomy. But this enlargement of the body-city association also produced instabilities. Imagining the city as a kind of body had always been a way of inhabiting it more fully, as a differentiated, but bounded whole. When the body dissolves into a more general series of physical processes, this may bring about a weakening or confusion of the sense of propriocentric belonging which the corporeal metaphor had previously allowed. In *Barnaby Rudge*, this conflict between different kinds of metaphor is focused in particular upon political questions; in this novel, the conflict is not between the body of the city and what assaults it from within or without, as between two different kinds of body, the well-governed urban physiology and the body of riot.

Barnaby Rudge begins, however, with an apparent confirmation of the stability of place and space:

> In the year 1775, there stood upon the borders of Epping Forest, at a distance of about twelve miles from London – measuring from the Standard in Cornhill, or rather from the spot on or near to which the Standard used to be in days of yore – a house of public entertainment called the Maypole.
>
> (1:43)

The Standard, which used to be at the corner of Gracechurch Street and Leadenhall Street in the City, is here offered as a stable centre, an abstract mathematical or cartographic point, by which to measure what lies inside and outside the city. This is appropriate for a novel which will alternate its scenes almost exclusively between London (though not the City) and Chigwell on its outskirts. The novel therefore begins with the same act of joining and distinction which characterises Turner's panorama of London, and establishes the simultaneous connection and dissociation between the city and the country. One of the most important effects of the riots represented in the novel will be that destruction extends out of the city and into the country, with the burning of the Warren and vandalising of the Maypole.

The opening of the narrative continues this evocation of the fixity of place and definitions, with its account of the mounting-block before the door of the Maypole which is reputed to have been used by Queen Elizabeth. John Willet disposes in Johnsonian manner of the doubts of some of the local inhabitants about the genuineness of the story: 'whenever the landlord of that ancient hostelry appealed to the mounting-block itself as evidence, and triumphantly pointed out that it stood in the same place to that very day, the doubters never failed to be put down by a large majority, and all true believers exulted as in a victory' (1:43). Of course there is something worryingly specious about this appeal to fixity of place. The Maypole itself comes gradually to be seen as a place of stagnation and oppressive stasis rather than of blissful rural retreat, and it may be that its denial of change and progression comes about by a contraction of time into space, a concentration of history into rigid, motionless repetition.

Against the fixation represented by John Willet and the Maypole, *Barnaby Rudge* seems to suggest the desirability of discriminated spatial difference. This is expressed principally through the prominence of locks in the novel. Locks mark two very different alternatives with regard to place. First of all, they signify confinement, the forcible partition of space into inside and outside. The novel is ambivalent about this kind of privative distinction. The significance of Gabriel Varden's trade becomes apparent in the scene where he refuses to tamper with the lock at Newgate Gaol, for the novel seems to stake a great deal on the necessity for locks that keep distinct the regions of crime and respectability, violence and sanity, order and disorder. However, locks and keys are also responsible for the many instances of illegitimate and dangerous constriction in *Barnaby Rudge*, for example in Joe Willet's and Barnaby Rudge's confinement, and the caged canaries who are thrown alive on to the flames by the rioters – this prefiguring, of course, the burning of Newgate and the danger it poses to the prisoners in their cells of being burned alive – not to mention the various shut-up houses through the novel, such as the Warren and Mrs Rudge's house, in which Haredale keeps his relentless nightly vigil.

There is also a comic modulation of this theme of the restriction of access in Miggs's ruse to keep Sim Tappertit from getting back into the house after his midnight expedition by filling the lock with coaldust (9:121). Dust is like oil, slime and fog in Dickens's writing in being an undifferentiated substance which is capable of spilling or slipping easily across boundaries. The blocking of the lock here seems oddly equivalent to the blurring of divisions, for in both cases the transition between defined and separated regions is prevented. The preoccupation with locks also allows Dickens to suggest the imminent and violent breakdown of spatial distinctions: when Haredale and the vintner retreat into the vintner's cellars, they hear 'the voices of the foremost in the crowd so close to every chink and keyhole, that they seemed to be hoarsely whispering their threats into their very ears' (67:610). Here the potential breaching of the partition between the mob and the fugitives is reduplicated in nightmarishly intensified form in the sensation that their voices are about to force entrance into the body through the ear. In Dickens's writing about the city, sound often has this power to undermine the spatial command of the eye. Like the other non-visual senses to which I have already alluded, smell, taste and, to a lesser degree, touch, sound works not so much through the establishment of distance and discrimination, as through the principle of transmission. To see an object, you must stand back from it; to hear a sound, is to be physically penetrated by and to participate in it. The clamorous city of riot becomes a disintegrated, yet frighteningly intimate body of flows and influences, rather than a visualised anatomy of sectors and regulated transitions.

But keys and locks can turn in two directions, can release as well as confine. Locks seem also to express an ideal of *regulated interchange* in *Barnaby Rudge*, an ideal which attempts to coordinate the emblematic body with the body-in-process. This ideal is gestured towards in the scene in which Gabriel Varden is seen at work in his Volunteers' uniform, in which even the locks and keys that surround him are affected by his good humour:

> The very locks that hung around had something jovial in their rust, and seemed like gouty gentlemen of hearty natures, disposed to joke on their infirmities. There was nothing surly or severe in the whole scene. It seemed impossible that any one of the innumerable keys could fit a churlish strong-box or a prison-door. Cellars of beer and wine, rooms where there were fires, books, gossip, and cheering laughter – these were their proper sphere of action. Places of distrust and cruelty, and restraint, they would have left quadruple-locked for ever.
>
> (41:382)

There is an interesting uncertainty in this passage, which reflects Dickens's own political uncertainty regarding the question of restraint and liberty. The keys ought to fit the locks of cellars of beer and wine (ought to enable the regulated flow of cheering spirits), rather than strong-boxes or prisons. But to say that one of the things that the keys would have left quadruple-locked is *restraint itself* is a metaphorical conundrum indeed (it resembles Sir John Chester's paradoxical desire to lock away Tappertit's lock that we noticed earlier) and implies a deep irresolution about the question of liberty and restraint. If restraint is to be quadruple-locked, is this to say that it will give way to release, or that it will itself be subjected to further restraint?[9]

This irresolution seems actually to be present from the beginning of the novel. The ideal of regulated interchange between distinctive spaces and places is always liable to be contradicted by two extreme conditions: by unjust and oppressive constriction of place on the one hand, and by the extremity of flow, or dissolution of all spatial boundaries, on the other. We might identify these two alternatives with those forms in which David Trotter has argued that Dickens's novels embody the thwarting of his physio-economic ideal of free circulation: blockage and uncontrolled overflow.[10] This irresolution is expressed in the contrast between Haredale's brooding, immobile incarceration within Mrs Rudge's house, as he waits for Rudge's return, and his subsequent anxiety that the riots will allow Rudge to escape. The novel here condemns the excesses both of position and of process, of constriction and of freedom.

This anxiety expresses itself particularly with regard to the spaces of interiority in *Barnaby Rudge*. Interiority often represents safety, comfort and civilisation, as, for example, in the description of the snug interior of the Maypole during a storm at the beginning of chapter 33. The Maypole stands as the type of all 'private dwellings' with their 'happy indoor people' who 'forgot to be political', braving the politically suggestive gales and blasts that howl outside their windows (33:314–15):

> The profusion, too, the rich and lavish bounty, of that goodly tavern! It was not enough that one fire roared and sparkled on its spacious hearth; in the tiles which paved and compassed it, five hundred flickering fires burnt brightly also. It was not enough that one red curtain shut the wild night out, and shed its cheerful influence on the room. In every saucepan lid, and candlestick, and vessel of copper, brass, or tin that hung upon the walls, were countless ruddy hangings, flashing and gleaming with every motion of the blaze, and offering, let the eye wander where it might, interminable vistas of the same rich colour. The old oak wainscoting, the beams, the chairs, the seats, reflected it in a deep, dull glimmer. There were fires and red curtains in the very eyes of the drinkers, in their buttons, in their liquor, in the pipes they smoked.
>
> (33:315)

But if there is profusion and richness here, there is also oppressiveness, in the ominous self-echoing of the scene, with its 'interminable vistas of the same rich colour' and the 'deep, dull glimmer' of the ubiquitous and proliferating redness, that at once keeps the premonitory storm outside at bay, and seems to predict the breaking in of the political storm upon the Maypole which occurs later in the novel. Like the fog at the beginning of *Bleak House*, the

reflective and multiplying fire connects everything by sinisterly
dissolving distinctions, this being particularly evident in the detail of
the 'five hundred fires' which have been kindled in the tiles of the
hearth whose purpose is to 'pave and compass' the fire. Thus
the metaphorical enactment of interiority dissolves the very
spatialisations which are required to maintain interiority.

Later on in the novel, the Maypole is indeed to be rudely penetrated
by the forces of riot that are here so insecurely kept at bay, in a scene
which itself anticipates the two other notable break-ins in the novel,
into Newgate jail and the vintner's cellar. The storming of the
Maypole is described as a quasi-religious transgression, a profaning
of boundaries and, when the maypole itself is left crudely thrust
through the shattered window, a sexual violation. The description of
the scene is a spectacular evocation of the collapse of boundaries
between inner and outer, and the repeated references to religious
spaces (the 'hallowed ground', the 'infernal temple', the 'sacred
grove') suggests the anthropological dimension of this 'sacrilege in
the sanctuary' as the running title to this chapter has it. But the
description involves more than transgression, since the incursion of
the rioters seems to hurl the very structure and relations of space
themselves into doubt. The sheer swarming activity of the invaders
('men everywhere – above, below, overhead, in the bedrooms, in
the kitchen, in the yard, in the stables', 54:497) seems to dissolve the
clear distribution of spaces of which the Maypole is constituted.
Without even having to tear down the walls which divide the inner
from the outer, the rioters are able grotesquely to reconstitute its spaces
and the media of access between them: 'men everywhere . . .
clambering in at windows when there were doors wide open; dropping
out of windows when the stairs were handy; leaping over the
banisters into chasms of passages' (ibid.). Space is not only
reconstituted in this description, it is also *saturated*: 'Yes, Here was
the bar – the bar that the boldest never entered without special
invitation – the sanctuary, the mystery, the hallowed ground; here it
was, crammed with men, clubs, sticks, screams, hootings' (54:497).
This physical and acoustic congestion, with its suggestion of an
imminent collapse under its pressure of the enclosing walls, recurs
in the description of the storming of Newgate, when the rioters swarm
through a tiny hole in the wall into Rudge senior's cell, in a process
which seems to suggest some fearful inverted parturition: 'they
enlarged the breach until it was large enough to admit the body of
a man, and then came dropping down upon the floor, until the cell
was full' (65:587). Saturation of space is equivalent to the liquidation
of boundaries; here it portends a reversibility of inner and outer, a
collapse of the structure that will cause the men who have swarmed

221

from the outside into the inside to be expelled into the outside again. Such ambivalence of space, which holds us at a point of catastrophic extremity where the structure of space is just about to give way, is more disturbing than the relatively simple dissolution of spatial distinctions represented by the tearing down of walls.

In fact, the novel's opening description of the Maypole has prepared us for this crossing of borderlines and the unregulated convulsion of interior and exterior. The house is thronged by birds, and especially by swallows, who have built their nests 'in the chimneys of the disused rooms'. This suggestion of an exterior life thronging an interior is complemented by the description of the house itself, which suggests an interior that is about to collapse into the exterior: 'With its overhanging stories, drowsy little panes of glass, and front bulging out and projecting over the pathway, the old house looked as if it were nodding in its sleep' (1:44). It is not easy to decide whether this represents a benign system of interchange between inner and outer, civilisation and nature, or a prefiguration of the agitation of distinctions which is so conspicuous an effect of the riots later in the novel. The description of the Maypole here connects it with a number of other descriptions in Dickens's work which evidence the fascination with buildings on the point of collapse, the most notable example in *Barnaby Rudge* being the burnt-out turret of the Warren in which Rudge betrays his presence by the slipping and crumbling of the ash under his climbing feet (56:514–15). (The sound of the slipping ash connects the Warren with the whispering premonitions of the collapse of Mrs Clennam's house in *Little Dorrit*.) Imminent collapse of this kind is close in its function and effect to the saturated space of the Maypole or the prison cell crammed to bursting, for it holds together in one moment the fixity and the dissolution of spatial distinctions.

The Warren, too, is a paradoxical space within the novel. The descriptions of the house emphasise its oppressive fixity, as in the scene in which Mrs Rudge and her son come to speak with Haredale and his niece. The deathly enclosure of the room where the murder has been committed 'deadened and shut in by faded hangings' seems to effect an absolute, unnatural identification between the place and its inhabitants: 'Nor were the group assembled there, unfitting tenants of the spot . . . [They] were all in keeping with the place, and actors in the legend' (25:254). Like the Maypole, the house is turned in upon itself, in an engrossing of time by space. And yet, the house is also spectrally insubstantial, so locked into the past that it does not have secure tenure on the place that it occupies in the present: 'It seemed a place where [gaiety and revelry] . . . had been, but could be no more – the very ghost of a house, haunting the old spot in its old outward form, and that was all' (13:154). The very name of the house expresses a spatial ambivalence. A 'warren' originally meant a piece of land enclosed for breeding game, especially, by the nineteenth century, rabbits. It is this particular use of the enclosure which suggests the increasingly more common meaning from the nineteenth century onwards of a space penetrated and hollowed out by labyrinthine interiority.

The Golden Key, the locksmith's house, also possesses the qualities of strange or paradoxical space. Like a number of other interior locations in Dickens's novels, and perhaps, in particular, Bleak House, in the novel which bears its name, the Golden Key possesses a principle of spatial connectedness which is enigmatically, and not a little sinisterly, concealed. Visitors to the house are perplexed by the problem of how the back parlour connects with the upper rooms of the house:

> Any stranger would have supposed that this wainscoted parlour, saving for the door of communication by which he had entered, was cut off and detached from all the world; and indeed most strangers on their first entrance were observed to grow extremely thoughtful, as weighing and pondering in their minds whether the upper rooms were only approachable by ladders from without; never suspecting that two of the most unassuming and unlikely doors in existence, which the most ingenious mechanician on earth must of necessity have supposed to be the doors of closets, opened out of this room – each without the smallest preparation, or so much as a quarter of an inch of passage – upon two dark winding flights of stairs, the one upward, the other downward, which were the sole means of communication between that chamber and the other portions of the house.
>
> (4:77)

Although in the cases both of Bleak House and the Golden Key, this spatial complexity is a mark of comfortable quirkiness, there are also more sinister associations; for, just as the topographic irregularity of Bleak House connects it with the mazy complexity of the law, the ominous interiority of the Golden Key connects it with the uncanny and lawless underworld of riot and dissipation in *Barnaby Rudge*. This underworld is evidenced, for example, in Stagg's pit, where Simon Tappertit goes to meet the 'Prentice Knights:

> It was not a very choice spot for midnight expeditions, being in truth one of more than questionable character, and of an appearance by no means inviting. From the main street he had entered, itself

little better than an alley, a low-browed doorway led into a blind court or yard, profoundly dark, unpaved, and reeking with stagnant odours. Into this ill-favoured pit, the locksmith's vagrant 'prentice groped his way; and stopping at a house from whose defaced and rotten front the rude effigy of a bottle swung to and fro like some gibbetted malefactor, struck thrice upon an iron grating with his foot. After listening in vain for some response to his signal, Mr Tappertit became impatient, and struck the grating thrice again.

A further delay ensued, but it was not of long duration. The ground seemed to open at his feet and a ragged head appeared.

(108–9)

Stagg's pit is an involuted or redoubled interior, a hollowness within the enclosure represented by the 'blind court'. These spaces of unexpected involution recur throughout the novel. As we have seen, the most frightening characteristic of the invasion of the Maypole is that it is not smashed open, but somehow burrowed into, the rioters preferring to clamber in at windows 'when there are doors wide open' (54:497). Underground or excavated space is associated throughout the novel with the traversal of limits and the collapse of spatial opposites. The sense that London is connected by some alternative geography, which is interior and subterranean at once, leads to the suspicion that the rationalised and recognisable disposition of places and spaces above ground and in the light of day can be bypassed or dissolved, and that this threatens the disposition of spaces as such – including the very structure of ideas which quarantines otherness within the defined spaces of the inner and the underneath. The underworld is both visibly underfoot and invisibly omnipresent, both contained within spatial imagination and unrepresentably transgressive of the limits of space. The most emphatic enactment of this is once again in the storming of Newgate, where the collision and paradoxical exchange of inner and outer is embodied in the agony of Rudge in his cell, unable to wish either to be left alone in his confinement, or to be released (65:586). This is matched by the grotesque retreat of Dennis into the condemned prisoners' portion of the gaol, where he sits as comfortably as the occupants of the Maypole bar, while the storm rages around him. It is an image of interiority within exteriority which expresses perfectly the political ambivalence of this novel, in which the principle of justice is at once separated from and at the spatial heart of riot. The inner world of Newgate becomes a seething exteriority, once it is inhabited by the crowd, which 'dispersed themselves about it, and swarmed into every chink and crevice, as if they had a perfect acquaintance with its innermost parts, and bore in their minds an exact plan of the whole'

(65:589). The crowd can fill up Newgate, we are to assume, because in a sense they are already replete with it.

There is no more powerful image of paradoxical spatiality in this novel than the position that Gashford takes up on his rooftop to watch the progress of the riots. It might seem as though this commanding aerial point of view belonged much more to the official and public world of sight and distance than to the interior or subterranean world of the riots. But, as with the crammed and thwarted perspective offered to the viewer from the roof of Todgers's in *Martin Chuzzlewit*, there is no distance obtainable even from this height, as Gashford sits in the deepening darkness surrounded by 'the piles of roofs and chimneys on which he looked [and] . . . the smoke and rising mist he vainly tried to pierce' (53:490). Hablôt Browne's illustration, which shows that Gashford has emerged on to the roof through the narrowest of hatches, though this is not mentioned in the text, suggests the chiasmic association between height and burrowing constriction.

Even this limited panorama is denied to most of the characters in the novel. However, there are two characters who seem capable of transcending the limitations of place altogether. The first is the elder Rudge, with his uncanny capacity for multilocation: 'He was seen in such distant and remote places, at times so nearly tallying with each other, that some doubted whether there were not two of them, or more – some, whether he had not unearthly means of travelling from spot to spot' (16:181). Rudge's restless mobility is combined oddly with his inability to keep away from one particular location, the house where he has committed his murder. Rudge's counterpart in uncanny pervasiveness is Hugh, who seems to express the spatial convulsiveness which is the very essence of the riots: 'in every part of the riot, he was seen . . . was here, there, and everywhere – always foremost – always active . . . Turn him at one place, and he made a new struggle in another; force him to retreat at this point, and he advanced on that, directly' (67:607). Hugh, like Rudge, combines fixity and dreamlike rapidity of movement, alternating between motionless sleep and an energy of movement that surpasses the eye, as, for example, in the episode where he is roused by John Willet to place his wig on top of the pole (29:283).

The threat to relationships of distance which such weirdly pervasive characters pose is made clear with the arrival of Stagg in the village where Barnaby and his mother have taken refuge. This represents a decomposition of those distinctions of difference and distance between the town and country which we saw the novel establishing so emphatically in its opening paragraph. Stagg's arrival in the village where the two have taken refuge has the uncanniness of

Oliver's vision of Fagin breaking into his dream of rest and
contentment in the country in chapter 34 of *Oliver Twist*. In both cases,
it is as if the interloper from the city streets moved in some
alternative geography, and as though distance and space had been
nightmarishly compressed or pleated upon themselves. The very
fact of Stagg's blindness contributes to this uncanny effect; Stagg
belongs to a literal and figurative underworld and seems, like some
subterranean or deep sea creature, to have no need of light to see by.
Furthermore, his very denial of the normal constraints of space and
distance seems to mark some antagonism between the world of sight
and the murky visceral world in which he moves.

The climax of the riots represents a bursting out of that very visceral
region, the interior of the body, which is so feared through the novel.
Not the least of the reasons why the storming of a vintner's
(67:617–18) seems so appropriate in *Barnaby Rudge* is because of the
violent contrast it offers to the self-enclosed world of the Maypole
bar. The breaching of the casks is represented as a terrible cloacal
overflow, the effluence of an interior liquid which Dickens is careful
to associate with the contents of the sewers. This overflow bursts
out of all the channels, running, not only along the gutters, but
through 'every crack and fissure in the stones', and gathers, like the
human ordure of Carlyle's vision in *Latter-day Pamphlets* quoted
earlier, in 'a great pool, into which the people dropped down dead
by dozens' (67:618). But if the spirit is a kind of excremental superflux,
it is also the source of greedy consumption. The flow of spirits 'laps
in' all it meets with, even as it is itself furiously lapped up, by the
crowd which is itself said to have 'poured out of the city in two great
streams' (67:607). It is as though the process of the body had dissolved
its own bodily form, as its borders are violently traversed, and
ingestion and expulsion collapse into each other. This merging of
opposites is emphasised by the fact that the spirit is also on fire,
and eventually literally consumes those who consume it, so that they
'became themselves the dust and ashes of the flames they had
kindled, and strewed the public streets of London' (67:618).

The problem of representing such riotous space is a real one for
Dickens. For one thing, he is taking care to represent events that
have taken place in the very London with which his readers were so
familiar, a London which was apprehensible in terms of the
increasingly complex forms of visibility and distinction that grew up
in the nineteenth century. The particular force of Dickens's
enactment of a riot which seems to have struck at the spatiality of
space itself and all of the political distinctions that it embodied, is that
it responds so closely to the complex forms in which space itself was
being remodelled in the nineteenth-century city. Dickens is, in a sense,

the first modernist in his representation of the city as a psychological space, organised according to psychopolitical investments and projections rather than according to the reliable Euclidean dispositions and equivalences of an earlier period. As we have seen already, the orderings of space were already beginning to become highly complex in mid-nineteenth-century London. Undoubtedly, there are particular political anxieties involved in this, not least among them the threatened incursions of Chartist crowds into the city during the 1830s. And perhaps we ought to add to these a more general political determinant, in the steadily increasing momentum of capital and capitalist exchange themselves, the very engine for the prodigious expansion of London. By 1858, it had become apparent to Marx in his *Grundrisse* that 'capital by its very nature drives beyond every spatial barrier. Thus the creation of the physical conditions of exchange – of the means of communication and transport – the annihilation of space by time – becomes an extraordinary necessity for it.'[11] The capital city had become the spatialised embodiment of these capitalist energies; it was the place where determinate space was swept away.

Barnaby Rudge mimics both sides of this topical and spatial reorganisation: the dissolution of space and its construction. This relates closely to the question of narration itself. What position are we to occupy, what perspectival authority are we to possess as readers of *Barnaby Rudge*? At one point, Dickens advertises his freedom from spatial restrictions of all kinds, declaring that 'chroniclers are privileged to enter where they list, to come and go through keyholes, to ride upon the wind, to overcome, in their soarings up and down, all obstacles of distance, time, and place' (9:119). But, as the novel progresses, this position of authority is steadily compromised, as Dickens struggles with the question of what position he must occupy in order to represent the dissolution of the possibility of position. Dickens described his difficulties in a letter to John Landseer of 5 November 1841:

> In this kind of work the object is, – not to tell everything, but to select the striking points and beat them into the page with a sledge-hammer. And herein lies the difficulty. No man in the crowd who was pressed and trodden here and there, saw Wilkes. No looker-on from a window at the struggle in the street, beheld an Individual, or anything but a great mass of magistrates, rioters, and soldiery, all mixed up together. Being always in one or other of these positions, my object has been to convey an idea of multitudes, violence, and fury; and even to lose my own dramatis personae in the throng, or only see them dimly, through the fire and smoke.[12]

The discomfort that some readers have felt with *Barnaby Rudge* comes from this sense of the loss of clear point of view, the sense that it is not clear what political position Dickens himself occupies with regard to the riots he depicts with such fascinated horror. There may also be a close relation between this perspectival difficulty and the desire for imaginative occupation of the body of the city. Jean-Paul Sartre has suggested that there is a fundamental conflict between corporeal being and visual command, since, if one sees with and through the bodily sense of sight, one can never see that act of seeing: '[The body] is the instrument which I cannot use in the way I use any other instrument, the point of view on which I can no longer take a point of view.'[13] In a similar way, for Dickens to see with and through the body of the city is to surrender the possibility of determinate perspective. The mobile energy of this novel is expended equally in attempting to fix a point of view to grasp and display the embodied totality of the events and in dissipating the point of view in the intensely inhabited body of riot.

Notes

1. See IDA DARLINGTON and JAMES HOWGEGO, *Printed Maps of London Circa 1553–1850* (London: George Philip and Son, 1964), p. 37.
2. CAROLINE ARSCOTT and GRISELDA POLLOCK, 'The Partial View: The Visual Representation of the Early Nineteenth-Century City', in *The Culture of Capital: Art, Power and the Nineteenth-Century Middle Class*, ed. JANET WOLFF and JOHN SEED (Manchester: Manchester University Press, 1988), pp. 195–6.
3. I examine the relationships between contagion and categoriality in *Bleak House* in my *Charles Dickens* (Oxford: Basil Blackwell, 1985), pp. 61–6.
4. *Barnaby Rudge* (Harmondsworth: Penguin, 1987), ch. 75, p. 673. All references, by chapter and page, will be to this edition, and will be incorporated in the text.
5. See the chapter entitled 'The City, the Sewer, the Gaze and the Contaminating Touch', in PETER STALLYBRASS and ALLON WHITE, *The Politics and Poetics of Transgression* (London: Methuen, 1986), esp. pp. 139–45.
6. MARY DOUGLAS, *Purity and Danger: An Analysis of the Concepts of Pollution and Taboo* (New York: Praeger, 1966), p. 115.
7. *Sir Thomas More: or, Colloquies on the Progress and Prospects of Society* (1829), repr. in *The Idea of the City in Nineteenth-Century Britain*, ed. B. I. COLEMAN (London: Routledge and Kegan Paul, 1973), pp. 59, 61.
8. *Latter-day Pamphlets* (1850), no. 1, 'The Present Time', reprinted ibid., p. 96.
9. MYRON MAGNET has an illuminating discussion of the political ambivalence of locks in *Barnaby Rudge* in his *Dickens and the Social Order* (Philadelphia: University of Pennsylvania Press, 1985), pp. 148–55.
10. DAVID TROTTER, *Circulation: Defoe, Dickens and the Economies of the Novel* (Basingstoke: Macmillan, 1988), p. 89.

11. KARL MARX, *Grundrisse: Foundations of the Critique of Political Economy*, trans. Martin Nicolaus (Harmondsworth: Penguin, 1973), p. 524.
12. Pilgrim Edition of *The Letters of Charles Dickens*, Vol. 2, ed. MADELINE HOUSE and GRAHAM STOREY (Oxford: Clarendon Press, 1969), p. 418.
13. JEAN-PAUL SARTRE, *Being and Nothingness: An Essay on Phenomenological Ontology*, trans. HAZEL E. BARNES (London: Methuen, 1958), p. 329.

Further Reading

The volume of criticism on Dickens, and the variety of approaches taken in are so huge that a listing of titles alone would require several volumes. The following highly selective listing concentrates on important work produced in the last twenty years or so and attempts to represent the most important styles of critical approach to Dickens within that period.

Biography

ACKROYD, PETER, *Dickens*. (London: Sinclair-Stevenson, 1990.)
ALLEN, MICHAEL, *Charles Dickens' Childhood*. (Basingstoke: Macmillan, 1988.)
KAPLAN, FRED, *Dickens: a Biography*. (London: Hodder and Stoughton, 1988.)

Letters

HOUSE, MADELINE, STOREY, GRAHAM, TILLOTSON, KATHLEEN, et al. (eds.), *The Pilgrim Edition of the Letters of Charles Dickens*. (Oxford: Clarendon Press, 1965–.)

Reference and Background Material

BOLTON, PHILIP H., *Dickens Dramatized*. (London: Mansell, 1987.)
CHITTICK, KATHRYN, *The Critical Reception of Charles Dickens, 1833–1841*. (New York: Garland, 1989.)
CHITTICK, KATHRYN, *Dickens and the 1830s*. (Cambridge: Cambridge University Press, 1990.)
COHEN, JANE R., *Charles Dickens and His Original Illustrators*. (Columbus: Ohio State University Press, 1980.)
PAGE, NORMAN, *A Dickens Companion*. (London: Macmillan, 1984.)
STONE, HARRY (ed.), *Dickens's Working Notes for His Novels*. (Chicago: University of Chicago Press, 1987.)

Periodicals

The Dickensian. London, 1905–.

Dickens Studies. Boston, MA: Emerson College, 1965–1969. Continued as *Dickens Studies Annual.* (Carbondale, IL: Southern Illinois University Press, 1970–.)

Dickens Studies Newsletter. Louisville, KY, 1970–1983. Continued as *Dickens Quarterly.* (Louisville, KY, 1984–.)

Social, Historical and Political Themes

ANDREWS, MALCOLM, *Dickens on England and the English.* (Hassocks: Harvester Press, 1979.)

ARAC, JONATHAN, *Commissioned Spirits: The Shaping of Social Motion in Dickens, Carlyle, Melville, and Hawthorne.* (New Brunswick, NJ: Rutgers University Press, 1979.)

BROWN, JAMES M., *Dickens: Novelist in the Market-Place.* (London: Macmillan, 1982.)

CLARK, ROBERT, 'Riddling the Family Firm: The Sexual Economy in *Dombey and Son*', *ELH*, 51 (1984): 69–84.

EIGNER, EDWIN M., *The Dickens Pantomime.* (Berkeley, CA: University of California Press, 1989.)

FELTES, N. N., 'The Moment of *Pickwick*, or the Production of a Commodity Text', *Literature and History,* 10 (1985): 203–17.

FELTES, N. N., 'Realism, Consensus and "Exclusion Itself": Interpellating the Victorian Bourgeoisie', *Textual Practice,* 1 (1987): 297–308.

MILLER, D. A., 'Secret Subjects, Open Secrets', *Dickens Studies Annual,* 14 (1985): 17–38.

NUNOKAWA, JEFF, 'For Your Eyes Only: Private Property and the Oriental Body in *Dombey and Son*', in JONATHAN ARAC and HARRIET RITVO (eds), *Macropolitics of Nineteenth-Century Literature: Nationalism, Exoticism, Imperialism.* (Philadelphia, PA: University of Pennsylvania Press, 1991) pp. 138–58.

PATTEN, ROBERT L., *Dickens and His Publishers.* (Oxford: Clarendon, 1978.)

PERERA, SUVENDRINI, 'Wholesale, Retail and for Exportation: Empire and the Family Business in *Dombey and Son*', *Victorian Studies,* 33 (1990): 603–20.

POOVEY, MARY, 'Reading History in Literature: Speculation and Virtue in *Our Mutual Friend*', in JANET LEVARIE SMARR (ed.), *Historical Criticism and the Challenge of Theory.* (Urbana, IL.: University of Illinois Press, 1993) pp. 42–80.

SANDERS, ANDREW, *Charles Dickens: Resurrectionist.* (London: Macmillan, 1982.)

SCHLICKE, PAUL, *Dickens and Popular Entertainment.* (London: Allen and Unwin, 1985.)

SCHWARZBACH, F. S., *Dickens and the City.* (London: Athlone Press, 1979.)

SELL, ROGER, 'Dickens and the New Historians: The Polyvocal Audience and Discourse of *Dombey and Son*', in JEREMY HAWTHORN (ed), *The Nineteenth-Century British Novel.* (London: Arnold, 1986) pp. 63–80.

TAMBLING, JEREMY, 'Death and Modernity in *Dombey and Son*', *Essays in Criticism,* 43 (1993): 308–29.

TROTTER, DAVID, *Circulation: Defoe, Dickens and the Economies of the Novel.* (Basingstoke: Macmillan, 1988.)

WALSH, SUSAN, 'Bodies of Capital: *Great Expectations* and the Climacteric Economy', *Victorian Studies,* 37 (1993): 73–98.

WICKE, JENNIFER, *Advertising Fiction: Literature, Advertisement and Social Reading*. (New York: Columbia University Press, 1988.)

Dickens, Women and Gender

BROWN, CAROLYN, '*Great Expectations*: Masculinity and Modernity', *Essays and Studies*, 40 (1987): 60–74.

HOLBROOK, DAVID, *Charles Dickens and the Image of Woman*. (New York: New York University Press, 1993.)

INGHAM, PATRICIA, *Dickens, Women and Language*. (Hemel Hempstead: Harvester Wheatsheaf, 1992.)

MARSH, JOSS LUTZ, 'Good Mrs Brown's Connections: Sexuality and Story-Telling in *Dealings with the Firm of Dombey and Son*', *ELH*, 58 (1991): 405–26.

SLATER, MICHAEL, *Dickens and Women*. (London: J. M. Dent, 1983.)

Language and Narrative Theory

BAUMGARTEN, M., 'Calligraphy and Code: Writing in *Great Expectations*', *Dickens Studies Annual*, 11 (1983): 61–72.

BAUMGARTEN, M., 'Writing and *David Copperfield*', *Dickens Studies Annual*, 14 (1985): 39–59.

COLUMBUS, CLAUDETTE KEMPER, 'The (un)Lettered Ensemble: What Charley Does Not Learn About Writing in *Bleak House*', *Studies in English Literature*, 28 (1988): 609–23.

CONNOR, STEVEN, 'They're All in One Story': Public and Private Narratives in *Oliver Twist*', *The Dickensian*, 85 (1989): 3–16.

COTTOM, DANIEL, *Text and Culture: The Politics of Interpretation*. (Minneapolis: University of Minnesota Press, 1989.)

DALDRY, GRAHAM, *Charles Dickens and the Form of the Novel: Fiction and Narrative in Dickens' Work*. (London: Croom Helm, 1987.)

GOLDING, ROBERT, *Idiolects in Dickens: The Major Techniques and Chronological Development*. (London: Macmillan, 1985.)

HOLLINGTON, MICHAEL, 'Adorno, Benjamin and *The Old Curiosity Shop*', *Dickens Quarterly*, 6 (1989): 87–95.

JAFFE, AUDREY, *Vanishing Points: Dickens, Narrative, and the Subject of Omniscience*. (Berkeley: University of California Press, 1991.)

JORDAN, JOHN O., 'The Purloined Handkerchief' [on *Oliver Twist*], *Dickens Studies Annual*, 18 (1989): 1–17.

LAMBERT, MARK, *Dickens and the Suspended Quotation*. (New Haven: Yale University Press, 1981.)

LOESBERG, JONATHAN, 'Deconstruction, Historicism, and Overdetermination: Dislocations of the Marriage Plots in *Robert Elsmere* and *Dombey and Son*', *Victorian Studies*, 33 (1990): 441–64.

MARLOW, JAMES E., 'Pickwick's Writing: Propriety and Language', *ELH*, 52 (1985): 939–63.

METZ, NANCY ADCOCK, 'The Blighted Tree and the Book of Fate: Female Models of Storytelling in *Little Dorrit*', *Dickens Studies Annual*, 18 (1989): 221–41.

Further Reading

Miller, J. Hillis, *Charles Dickens: The World of His Novels* (Cambridge: Harvard University Press, 1958.)

Miller, J. Hillis, 'The Genres of *A Christmas Carol*', *The Dickensian*, 89 (1993): 193–206.

Moglen, Helene, 'Theorizing Fiction/Fictionalizing Theory: The Case of *Dombey and Son*', *Victorian Studies*, 35 (1992): 159–84.

Tick, Stanley, 'Dickens, Dickens, Micawber ... and Bakhtin', *Victorian Newsletter*, 79 (1991): 34–7.

Psychoanalytic Readings

Brooks-Davies, Douglas, *Fielding, Dickens, Gosse, Iris Murdoch and Oedipal Hamlet.* (Basingstoke: Macmillan, 1989.)

Carmichael, Virginia, 'In Search of Beein': *Nom/Non du Père* in *Great Expectations*', *ELH*, 54 (1987): 653–67.

Kucich, John, *Repression in Victorian Fiction: Charlotte Brontë, George Eliot, and Charles Dickens.* (Berkeley: University of California Press, 1987.)

Lloyd-Smith, Allan, 'The Phantoms of Drood and Rebecca: The Uncanny Reencountered through Abraham and Torok's "Cryptonymy" ', *Poetics Today*, 13 (1992): 285–308.

Sadoff, Dianne F., *Monsters of Affection: Dickens, Eliot and Brontë on Fatherhood.* (Baltimore, NJ: Johns Hopkins University Press, 1982.)

Simpson, David, *Fetishism and Imagination: Dickens, Melville, Conrad.* (Baltimore, NJ: Johns Hopkins University Press, 1982.)

Reader-Centred Theory

Horton, Susan R., *Interpreting Interpreting: Interpreting Dickens's 'Dombey'.* (Baltimore, NJ: Johns Hopkins University Press, 1979.)

Horton, Susan R., *The Reader in the Dickens World: Style and Response.* (London: Macmillan, 1981.)

Morgan, Nicholas H., *Secret Journeys: Theory and Practice in Reading Dickens.* (Rutherford: Fairleigh Dickinson University Press, 1992.)

Schad, S. J., *The Reader in the Dickensian Mirrors: Some New Language.* (London: Macmillan, 1992.)

Studies of Specific Themes

Andrews, Malcolm, *Dickens and the Grown-Up Child.* (Basingstoke and London: Macmillan, 1994.)

Frank, Laurence, *Charles Dickens and the Romantic Self.* (Lincoln, NB.: University of Nebraska Press, 1984.)

Hollington, Michael, *Dickens and the Grotesque.* (London: Croom Helm, 1984.)

JAFFE, AUDREY, 'Spectacular Sympathy: Visuality and Ideology in Dickens's *A Christmas Carol'*, *PMLA*, 109 (1994): 254–65.

LARSON, JANET L., *Dickens and the Broken Scripture*. (Athens, GA.: University of Georgia Press, 1985.)

McMASTER, JULIET, *Dickens the Designer*. (Totowa, NJ: Barnes & Noble, 1987.)

MARLOW, JAMES E., *Charles Dickens: The Uses of Time*. (Selinsgrove: Susquehanna University Press, 1993.)

MEIER, STEFANIE, *Animation and Mechanization in the Novels of Charles Dickens*. (Bern: Francke Verlag, 1982.)

NEWMAN, S. J., *Dickens at Play*. (London: Macmillan, 1981.)

SADRIN, ANNY, *Parentage and Inheritance in the Novels of Charles Dickens*. (Cambridge: Cambridge University Press, 1994.)

STONE, HARRY, *Dickens and the Invisible World: Fairy Tales, Fantasy, and Novel-Making*. (London: Macmillan, 1980.)

STONE, HARRY, *The Night Side of Dickens: Cannibalism, Passion, Necessity*. (Columbus: Ohio State University Press, 1994.)

WALDER, DENNIS, *Dickens and Religion*. (London: Allen and Unwin, 1981.)

Index

Index